Without a Net

Without a Net

Librarians Bridging
the Digital Divide

Jessamyn C. West

LIBRARIES UNLIMITED

AN IMPRINT OF ABC-CLIO, LLC
Santa Barbara, California • Denver, Colorado • Oxford, England

Library of Congress Cataloging-in-Publication Data

West, Jessamyn, 1968–
  Without a net : librarians bridging the digital divide / Jessamyn C. West.
    p. cm.
  Includes bibliographical references and index.
  ISBN 978-1-59884-453-5 (pbk.) — ISBN 978-1-59884-454-2 (e-book)
1. Libraries and the Internet—United States. 2. Libraries—Information technology—United States. 3. Internet access for library users—United States. 4. Public access computers in libraries—United States. 5. Library employees—Effect of technological innovations on—United States. 6. Library orientation—Technological innovations—United States. 7. Information technology—Study and teaching—United States. 8. Libraries and community—United States. 9. Digital divide—United States. I. Title.
Z674.75.I58W47   2011
020.285'4678—dc22   2011000993

ISBN: 978-1-59884-453-5
EISBN: 978-1-59884-454-2

15 14 13 12 11   1 2 3 4 5

This book is also available on the World Wide Web as an eBook.
Visit www.abc-clio.com for details.

Libraries Unlimited
An Imprint of ABC-CLIO, LLC

ABC-CLIO, LLC
130 Cremona Drive, P.O. Box 1911
Santa Barbara, California 93116-1911

This book is printed on acid-free paper ∞

Manufactured in the United States of America

In memory of
Steve Cisler

Contents

Preface

We are stuck with technology when what we really want is just stuff that works.

—Douglas Adams, *The Salmon of Doubt*

Why I Am Writing This Book

I'm writing this book because it doesn't already exist. The digital divide is real; the need to engage it is pressing. Libraries are one of the few institutions with national presence and digital infrastructure that are taking on this large project. And they could use help.

I have been doing basic technology instruction since I began library school in 1993, and rural technology instruction since 2002. If you want to get nitpicky about it, I've done technology instruction since I showed my mom how to get the VCR to stop blinking 12:00. This would have been in about 1979. And the classic struggle is exactly the same. My mom knows how to push a button, how to tell time, and how to follow instructions. But somewhere along the line, the combination of steps required to do simple tasks—tasks with a technological aspect—started to seem impossible to her.

There's a whole body of work surrounding the idea of *techno-stress* and how it affects us and why, for example, people don't set their VCR clocks when they'll set every other clock in the house. Why inserting a computer into the steps involved in performing a task can sometimes cause people to not do the task at all. Until six months ago, I was driving around in a car with a clock that was an hour and seventeen minutes off because I couldn't figure out how it worked. I am no stranger to either side of this issue.

However, this isn't a psychology text, for the most part. This book gives you practical data for both technology instruction and general education. That said, part of technology instruction is not just being able to tell someone how to get their email or run a virus scan, it's how to make technology exploration and learning something that people are motivated to do. At least part of this motivation comes from within, ideally. For most people, part of this motivation is also external. People have to get online to apply for jobs, to interact with their government, to receive social services. And they might want to get online to interact with friends and family, read the news, watch current or vintage television shows, or just look at photos of puppies. Being online is not merely an available option, for most people in the United States it's now part of their daily lives.

Finding the right combination of personal motivators is key to helping people learn, more so than individual intelligence or technical background. The library setting is integral to this: a public setting, available to everyone, with computers and internet access and at least the occasional staff member to help out. While many people regularly use computers at work, school, and home, some people lack this access for a variety of reasons. Some studies claim the number of "offline" people in America is as high as one-fifth of all adults. When those people need to use technology, they're often at the public library. We need to be responding to these people appropriately and effectively. We are one of the integral bridges across the digital divide.

Where I Came From

I'm one of those people who grew up with computers, even though I'm slightly older than most people in this category. My father was an early technologist and worked with computers starting in the late seventies. While he didn't bring his work home with him, I did grow up in a culture where computers were part of the normal environment and they were something manageable and masterable. We had the normal video games at home (Atari 2600!) and when I was in high school we had a VAX computer in our school's lab, a lucky side benefit to being up the road from Digital Equipment Corporation. My informal high school yearbook photo shows me in the computer lab.

That said, I'm not a programmer. I can write HTML and CSS and even edit a little bit of javascript and PHP, but I can't write my own computer programs. I think this is important to state at the outset. All of the work I've done and the examples I am giving in this book come from a sophisticated end-user perspective. I went to library school at the University of Washington beginning in 1993, before the graphical web. I took a year off between my first and second year of school and went to Romania with my partner who had gotten a one-year professorship there. I got a job working with the Freedom Forum Library in Bucharest Romania, helping them set up their library. Since the library was run pretty much by the Gannett Company, this mostly involved taking books about journalism and *USA Today* founder Al Neuharth out of boxes and putting them on shelves. However, they also had an internet connection.

In 1994, an internet connection in Romania was something that you paid Sprint dollars-per-minute for. And the internet didn't have any pictures. With my high school VAX background and UW experience using the Pine email client, I was the de facto technology expert. I began teaching classes for journalists in how to use Gopher for research and how to use Pine for email. My students didn't know anyone else with email addresses, so we practiced sending email to other people in the same classroom. I like to think of those students now impressing their friends "I was sending email in the mid-nineties!" And yet, I still sign people up for their first email accounts even now.

I came back to Seattle and finished library school and found myself in a crazy wonderland where having any tech skills at all meant that you could get a high paid job doing pretty much anything. I was a VISTA volunteer at Seattle Public Library where I started the Wired for Learning program. I worked with the City of Seattle's family centers to get them set up with computers and donated internet connections. I took a tech support job with Speakeasy where I learned the ins and outs and nitty-gritty details of the DSL business. I did freelance computer support on the side—realistically anyone who is at all good with computers does this, either for free or for pay—and plotted a return to smalltown New England where I'd come from.

Where I Am

I currently live in rural Vermont in a town about the size of the one where I grew up (3,500 people). I've lived here or nearby for about ten years. I've done a variety of jobs here, both library-related and non-. I've been an outreach librarian at a large public library; I've worked on several automation projects. I'm active in the Vermont Library Association and help run their website. While my jobs are varied and interesting, at some level most of them come down to helping novice technology users make sense of their systems.

I started my current job as an AmeriCorps volunteer at the local vocational high school. My library contract had run its course and I was looking forward to taking some time off. I told people I would not be taking another job that summer unless I opened the paper and saw a job involving "teaching email to old people," which was and is my favorite thing to do. Amusingly, that's exactly what happened. The local school was looking for an AmeriCorps volunteer to start an outreach program enabling them to share their technology offerings with people in the community. The Randolph Technical Career Center is a regional school, serving students in seven towns in Central Vermont. When the kids go home at 2:30, there's an empty building filled with computers and high-speed internet in the middle of a very tech-poor section of the state. RTCC saw that as an opportunity.

The Adult Education coordinator and I worked to design a combination of adult education classes, drop-in time, and public library visits to serve the tech education needs of the community. The original idea was that the school served seven small towns and yet was mostly a presence in Randolph, the town where the school was located. We wanted to reach further into the communities and offer more for people who were not high school age. I became a roving librarian, giving computer assistance and instruction at many of the libraries belonging to what we called the "sending towns." Many of these libraries did not yet have broadband and were struggling with aging Gates Foundation computers and local populations clamoring for access. I showed up once or twice a month and ran virus scans and software updates and occasionally taught librarians or library patrons about their systems. I did some local internet safety classes and mostly helped people check their email, make flyers, and surf the web.

I also taught evening classes a few times a week with titles like "Getting Started with Email" or "What Is a Web Page?" And, because we found that some potential students didn't even have the skills to begin taking a class, we started drop-in time which is just what it sounds like. After school lets out, I hang around one of the classrooms for a few hours. People can drop-in and I'll help them with their computer questions. I've been doing this for over five years now. My experience forms the basis of much of the practical advice in this book.

The job has evolved somewhat over the time that I've been there. I'm on staff and no longer an AmeriCorps volunteer, though I still work part-time. I no longer do library visits. Most of the libraries in the region now have broadband and wireless. Drop-in time shrank to one day per week and has recently expanded back to two days. I have some students who have been coming in for the full five years, but most are local folks who saw the ad in the paper—we've found it's our best recruitment tool—and stop by with a question or two. I work a few hours per week doing computer fix-it work for the teachers and staff at the school in addition to my community technology work.

What We Have

The computers in the classroom serve the students mainly, though I've been able to get a few software programs installed for the general public. There is an IT company that does the high-level maintenance of the school's network and administers the mandatory web and content filters that we must have. Most web browsing is okay. All chat is blocked and Skype is unavailable. We had to lobby hard to get access to YouTube and other video sites. There are mostly PCs in the classrooms, although people can bring in their own laptops and get on our wireless network which is an ad-hoc network created by me sharing the internet connection from my own laptop. The computers are desktop machines running Windows XP with flatscreen monitors which are a few years old. They have a small assortment of software on them including both new and old versions of MS Office, a typing tutor, some career chooser software, Internet Explorer and Firefox, and Photoshop Elements. Ninety-five percent of the time people are just there to use the web, unless they're working on their résumé or messing with mailing labels for holiday cards.

Working out of a student computer lab is not ideal. I do not have the level of control over the system that I would prefer. However, while it may not be ideal, it is certainly realistic. In many technology situations, novice users will not be able to have complete control over their computers. They'll either share with a family member, use a work computer, use a public PC at the library, or otherwise gain temporary access to a computer and/or the internet. At least, our internet access is consistent. We have a regular broadband connection to the internet that, aside from the filtering, works well and consistently. And for many people in my region, this is what they are lacking. They may have dial-up at home or know someone who does, but what you can access on the internet in 2010 is quite limited if you're still using dial-up.

Most importantly, we have a can-do attitude. The school believes that it is their responsibility to help the people in our region across the digital divide. This helps our neighbors find jobs, interact with their government, save money, and generally do more with less. As the person leading this initiative, I can say that I would not be able to do it without the full support and backing of the institution where I work. While I still think that there are a lot of things that can be done with limited support, either financial or professional, this is often the key to turning a regular job like mine into something with the potential for more influence. I don't work as much in public libraries lately, but I spend a lot of time sharing my technology knowledge and instruction tactics with librarians.

Where We're Going

One of the more poignant parts of my job is the extent to which I've been teaching "basic computer classes" for upwards of fifteen years now. I'm not sure how I thought this was going to go, maybe I thought everyone would at some point (how?) learn the basics and we could move on to more complex topics like usability and design. But there are always people who need to learn the basics. I'll get into some of the reasons why this is the case in Chapter One.

This is what the digital divide is all about—some people lacking the skills that other people consider basic, starter, or remedial, and not having a peer group or an educational system that can teach you. It's also about people assuming "Oh, everyone knows that." and moving right on by. The digital divide isn't about not having a computer, though that can be part of it. The digital divide isn't really about not knowing how to use a computer, though many people I work with can't. The digital divide is about not knowing anyone who knows how to use a computer well enough to teach you. It's about not being part of a tech-literate culture and not knowing a way out of that setting.

Slowly, this is changing—both the ability to access technology as well as the populations who are trying to access it. I have seen broadband access come to many of the local communities in the time that I have lived here. I have seen the phone companies put up hand-painted signs saying "DSL IS HERE" because it was the best way to let people know it was available. I've seen students at my drop-in times start coming less frequently when they finally could get broadband at home (now they email me). I've seen more public places than just the library start offering free wireless, and I've seen people using it.

The amount of tech literacy one can pick up through osmosis—from television, newspapers, other print media, seeing people use it in public, talking to people—is increasing. This is a difference between the rural and urban digital divides as I see it. In rural America, people who didn't or don't have jobs with computers may have missed a learning opportunity, but anyone with children or family that includes younger people will be interacting with people with steady access to technology. As our rural populations age, they are replaced by a tech-savvier younger population. The same is not as true for urban underserved populations where immigrant populations come from other countries as adults and may or may not settle into an area with tech-literate people. Often they settle into urban areas with other immigrants, areas that are traditionally tech-poor. As they acquire skills and cultural literacy and fluency, they often move out of these areas, to be replaced by other new immigrants. This means that there's a geographical area where the tech literacy rate stays very low over time, even as the general tech literacy rate of the nation as a whole is increasing. This is a different sort of problem. At the same time, areas of urban poverty often have tech infrastructure—available internet access, strong cell phone signal, availability of free or low cost wireless—that are not available in rural areas. Both rural and urban tech literacy are pervasive and pernicious, but are addressed using different tactics and strategies.

Part of my skill in this area is both being able to use a computer fairly well and also being able to explain what I know to people who are just getting started. I have basic metaphors and simple explanations at the ready. I use them all the time. People know I am quite familiar with technology, but they also know I can remember being unfamiliar, or fake it well. I'm unusually "plugged in" for someone in my community, a community where people are just starting to use Facebook, where my neighbors are more likely to make a phone call than email, and where Twitter is something you read about in the newspaper. For those of us who grew up with technology, it can be difficult to remember what it was like before you knew what a URL was, or the first time you used a search engine. I am fortunate enough usually to get to show someone the miracle that is Google almost every single month. I'd be lying if I said that the light-bulb moment, the hyperspace consciousness jump when people suddenly realize that the internet world is vast and available to them, wasn't a bit of a kick for me as well. I hope to share what I know here so that you too can help other people solve their own problems with technology. Join me.

Caveats

This is not a manual. If there were a recipe for how to solve the digital divide, we would not have a digital divide. Addressing the problem head-on involves a combination of skills, knowledge, and personality, optimally among many different motivated people in a community. This book addresses itself towards public librarians and the things they can do. However, saying "Teach classes like *this*." or "Install *this* software." is actually only a small part of addressing the overall systemic problems occurring with technology and novice patrons. Accordingly, I try to address some of the root causes of the digital divide, and the environment it has created at the same time as I try to offer concrete "do this" types of suggestions.

I have strong opinions. They are not reflective of any of my employers; they are mine and mine alone. While I've gotten better at not saying that things *suck* over the past few years (preferring the term "sub-optimal"), I think we do ourselves no favors by pretending there are no qualitative differences between types of hardware, software programs, and the ways we use them to help information have-nots. We need to look at outcomes. We also need to look at who is studying what, and why. We are librarians. We are hired to make judgments about information to assist our communities in solving their own problems. We should be bringing these skills to the world of technology in the same way that we have brought it to the world of books for centuries.

This book is also very American-centric. Even though digital literacy and technology access are issues that are even more pressing and dire in other parts of the world, our particular technological situation and public library institutions in the United States are the focus of my attention and research. I strongly encourage librarians and educators in other parts of the world who are reading this to use what they can, and give feedback to the library community where other approaches would be useful.

And finally, a word about nomenclature. I specifically asked my editor before I began this project, if I could use the words that people in the tech world actually *use* when they talk about technology, if I could apply my own style guide. This meant using words like *email* and *website* which are often copyedited—wrongly, in my opinion—to *e-mail* and *Web site*. She said that was okay. I'd like to assure everyone that any errors in spelling or style are also mine and mine alone. I've tried to avoid jargon, but I will be stopping short of providing a glossary or spelling out every acronym that I use. As people interested in information, libraries, and technology, I trust you can seek definitions if you require them. Unless I am referring specifically to myself, all example URLs are intended to be fictional. If you want to use a domain name for the purposes of instruction that is not a real domain name, please use *www.example.com* which was created specifically for this purpose.[1] All brand names should be presumed to be trademarks or service marks of the companies that own them. Thank you for reading.

Acknowledgments

Many people have given me support, encouragement and various pieces of crucial advice over the years. In addition to local and distant friends, family, my boyfriend and all the Boxboro librarians, I'd like to extend special thanks to a few people from my library past who were influential to me.

David Remington was the earliest advocate for rural libraries who I knew, he helped set me on the right path. Randy Hensley taught me how to talk so that other people would listen. Peter Hiatt and Ed Mignon gave me great advice and sincere encouragement. Phil Agre's examples of how to write plainly and intelligently about technology have been models for my own writing. The folks at the Randolph Technical Career Center, including my boss Ruth Durkee and the principal Bill Sugarman, believed in my work and found a way to make it happen. My five years there have been transformative.

The community at MetaFilter gave me a great place to try out ideas; having a job there meant that I didn't have to go broke while writing a book. Sharyn November gave me mature and sensible advice. The crew at Computers in Libraries gave me a forum to try out some of my ideas for a librarian audience. Amy Ranger made me a blanket out of rabbit fur that I sat on while I was writing this.

All my students, all my teachers, all my audience members and all my readers have helped make this book what it is. Thank you each and every one.

Introduction

Information. What's wrong with dope and women? Is it any wonder the world's gone insane, with information come to be the only real medium of exchange?

—Thomas Pynchon, *Gravity's Rainbow*

Why Our Work Is Important— Defining the Digital Divide

The digital divide is unsexy. It doesn't make good television. It can't be fixed with a grant-funded website. It may not be able to be fixed, period. However, it can be mitigated, and its effects can be lessened. People can learn, and they can share what they know. For every person who has that "Aha!" moment when sending their first email, there are ten more people who don't know what questions to ask, or who lack some fundamental skill that is keeping them from interacting with the online world. We see many of these people at the public library.

In order to move beyond simply giving beginner's email classes forever, it's my opinion that we need to understand the forces that keep people from getting comfortable with technology, from learning, and from being able to solve their own problems. Some of these forces are societal, some are political, some are personal, some are situational and some are of course, technological. I feel that the technology is the least difficult to address of all of these solutions, so I'll be talking quite a lot about the other forces that have gone into creating the digital underclass that we see in the United States. Those of you wanting to get straight to the "how to do it" stuff can jump ahead to Chapter One. Those of you who are looking for a background in digital divide issues, keep reading.

The digital divide is a simplistic phrase used to explain the gap between people who can easily use and access technology, and those who cannot. The term digital divide has been in common use to refer to this sense of technological haves and have-nots for over a decade. It's not a term that anyone owns and it's not a term that, to the best of my knowledge, any one person has taken credit for coining.

Carrie Bickner, who was at the time a librarian at New York Public Library, wrote a cautionary tale about the Children's Internet Protection Act for the website A List Apart[1] in 2001. She explains that the phrase digital divide:

> ... *initially referred to PC ownership. It was a term used to point out the fact that while computer ownership was generally increasing, this increase was limited to certain ethnic groups with particular economic means in limited geographic areas. As the use of the term evolves, a better definition begins to include those who are more generally cut off from information. A more up-to-date definition would include the idea that lack of access and lack of training are barriers to information wealth.*

Bickner was being polite, but what she was describing was the fact that computer ownership *was* on the rise, but mostly among middle- and upper-class urban white people. This is different from the more generalized statement "Hey, more people are getting computers!" which was how it was often represented. Nowadays, when we read the news stories that say "Hey, more people are getting online!" we should remember that these increases do not happen proportionally among all segments of society, and we can point out and predict where people are getting online in greater numbers, and where they are hardly getting online at all.

At the beginning of this century, the digital divide was more about access to computers and less about access to the internet. A computer cost a few thousand dollars in 2001; many people couldn't afford one. The Bill & Melinda Gates Foundation was a major player in a national campaign to assist libraries in obtaining and maintaining public access computers with internet access, office software, and games for kids. Many of the libraries in my area still use the computers they purchased with Gates Foundation grant money. People now have free access to computers with internet access via public libraries in most places in the United States. So, why is there still a digital divide?

It turns out the problem is more complicated than simply having computers available. People who can physically sit down in front of a computer still don't necessarily know how to use one. In fact, many times they don't even know how to turn one on. And who is responsible for teaching them? Even as more businesses and government agencies are interacting with customers and constituents online, there is still no national program for helping people with basic technology skills, no safety net to ensure that people can access the services and programs that have been provided for them digitally. That job has become the task, some say the unfunded mandate, of America's public libraries.

Computers, We Have Them

I'm happy to be writing this at a time when we no longer have to argue *if* computers have a place in the public library. For the first half-decade of my career in librarianship, this was still an open question. Some libraries had computers available for the public, some didn't. Some offered OPACs but not internet browsing. Or you could use the internet, but not type up a résumé on a word processor. On the other hand, some libraries still offered coin-operated typewriters. It was a mixed-up time to be a public library. Living in a large city on the west coast meant that access to technology was practically a given, but the form it would take was still up in the air. When I first started working at Seattle Public Library, the DYNIX terminals did double-duty as web surfing machines via the miracle of Hytelnet, if I recall correctly.

And you know, I probably don't remember correctly. While we all like to swap tales about our early tech experiences, they're more of a secret handshake sort of thing among people who *do* understand technology and not at all interesting to people who don't. In fact, telling people who have never used email that you've had an account since 1985 does nothing to assuage their concerns of being dreadfully behind the times. It just makes things worse.

I'm assuming since you've read this far, you're someone who is interested in technology, and/or pedagogy, and/or the intersection of these two things in and around the public library. You may or may not be "good with computers" and you may or may not be in a position to do anything about it. My hope is that you're curious enough to want to do *something*. What I'm hoping to do is give you a combination of some good data about the general digital divide, an explanation of why we (still) have it, and some techniques and skills for helping people manage it, both from a library perspective as well as an educator perspective.

People Are Offline for a Reason

When we think about people in difficult situations, it's often a knee-jerk but human reaction to try to examine what they may have done to get themselves there. While this is a problematic approach in many respects, it's important to understand what aspects of people's situations are within their control and which are not, and work on fixing the things that can be addressed and remedied or fixed. I live in a rural part of Vermont, by choice. When I assess the good parts and bad parts of living where I live, I am aware of what choices I've made to get here. I know that if I decided that I no longer enjoyed living someplace without a nightlife, for example, I could move. Many people live in Vermont for various reasons of their own choosing. Many other people live in Vermont because they were born here and lack the resources to make a location change even if they wanted or needed one.

My experience has led me to believe the same is true for people who are offline. People are offline for a reason. It may be by choice or it may not be, but uncovering people's reasons for being offline is part of the journey towards solving people's individual problems with getting online.

This seems somewhat counterintuitive. You have to have a *reason* to be offline? To not participate? Isn't it the other way around? While this may not have been true a decade ago, in 2010 being at least somewhat online is the norm in America. This is a fact. In fact, being online *with broadband* is now the norm in America according to the numbers. This creates a set of situations larger than just people's access to online tools. Here's how I see the progression occurring:

1. Businesses start to provide goods and services online to reach additional markets.

2. Governments and other institutions use online methods to provide goods and services to people to take advantage of economies of scale and save money and time.
3. Business and governments start to make decisions about these multiple delivery methods over time, which ones to keep and which ones to discontinue.
4. Costly methods may get discontinued or not optimized for. This could mean no longer offering phone-based tech support, or it could mean no longer designing websites for people with dial-up in the same way that we no longer design websites for people using Netscape. As a recent example, Seattle Public Library is no longer sending overdue notices by mail.[2] This is great news for them, saves money. Patrons' choices for now are email or automated phone message. How long until the TeleCirc gets discontinued?
5. People who are not online, therefore, lack access to online goods, services, and communication. If offline delivery methods are discontinued, their only options are to find a way to get online or lose access to these things.

So, getting people online becomes, for non-profit do-gooders like ourselves, a bit of a race against time. It would be nice to get people online more at their speed and comfort level and less because they had to get online to perform a necessary task or interact with their government. More and more places every year are requiring people to apply for jobs online—even places that do not require computer skills in order to perform the job tasks, such as Home Depot or McDonald's—either via the web or in-store kiosks that are only sort of computer-like. Lately, I've been seeing people come to my drop-in time needing to fill out their weekly unemployment claim online. The Vermont Department of Labor is mandating that all people filing unemployment do so online. If you don't fill out the forms, you don't get paid. This is a real struggle for some people.

When Katrina slammed the Gulf Coast leaving people without shelter and in dire need of financial assistance, most were presented with two options: call the Federal Emergency Management Agency (FEMA) via a telephone number that was perpetually busy or use an online form to apply for disaster relief funds. Not a great time to learn to use a computer. Not a great time to teach someone to use a computer. When I explain the work I do, it is this sort of thing that I give presentations about.

Moral Imperatives and Technological Definitions

Before we continue, I'd like to say that generally speaking, I don't believe that getting online is a moral issue. I am not a technology booster. I enjoy using technology and it works for me in my life. If you decide that you don't want to spend the majority of your time interacting with a computer, that's a fine choice. However, like other choices to keep up with the Joneses (or not), there is a cost to taking a different path. I think of the gentleman in my town who never learned to drive. This is a valid choice. It worked well for him in New York City, but now he's at the mercy of other people to drive him places. He doesn't mind and they don't mind, but it limits his options for doing many things and reduces his independence somewhat. Similarly, being unable to swim is fine right up until the time your boat capsizes. And, of course, you don't have to swim anywhere to pay your taxes.

I believe that having a basic understanding of how to operate a computer and interact with a web page is a skill that is required in American society. Whether you decide to go on beyond that is up to you. I'd prefer that people who were not using technology were doing so because they had made an affirmative decision not to, not because they were lacking information or resources to understand their technology options.

You'll see me using some terms interchangeably here. While the terms *broadband* and *high speed* have different nuances of meaning, they're both used here to mean access to the internet that is always on and faster than dial-up. The FCC on their Broadband.gov website defines broadband as "high-speed internet access that is always on and faster than the traditional dial-up access."

Similarly, while my general focus here will be discussing public library computing and I'll use the shorthand PC, I intend to refer to a sort of brand-neutral computer or computing device unless otherwise specified. One of the things that working in rural technology has taught me is that you can't really be too much of a brand partisan. While I think it's important to be able to make qualitative assessments about different flavors of operating systems or computer hardware, I often don't have the luxury of only troubleshooting my operating system of choice.

Assisting people with their technology—if you're doing it well—doesn't involve telling people that the choices they've made up to this point have been bad ones. Unfortunately, that is the stereotype of the techie or IT person. When you have a problem, you're concerned that they'll tell you that you brought it all on yourself. I felt this way when I'd go in to get a haircut after I'd trimmed my own bangs; my stylist flipped out. I dreaded haircuts for a while afterwards. Remembering that feeling, I can bring some of it to my technology instruction in order to try not to make people feel that way. If a good deal of people's reasoning for remaining off-line is in some capacity emotional, it's important that we learn to respond to their concerns and questions while understanding this component of their decision-making process.

Who Is Offline, and Why?

Getting online is often an affirmative decision adults must make. While younger people are often online by default at work or school, or through owning smart phones, people who live in a home without technology have to decide to seek out technology access and technology instruction. A computer will not magically install itself in their home or if it does—the gift of a well-meaning friend or relative—it will not be self-instructing. I was initially sur-prised, when talking to my adult education students, how many of them had computers at home that they never used. In some cases they were even paying for internet service, but "something hap-pened" and the computer was not functioning properly and they were stuck waiting for a friend or relative to return and take a look at it. I had decided early in my tech support career that the one thing I would not do was take care of people's computers in their homes, too much risk of owning a bad problem, and these stories always tugged at my heartstrings. And yet, who were these people that didn't know a single person who could help them with techni-cal problems? And what motivated them?

The year 2007 was the year that broadband saturation reached 50%, where over half of Americans had broadband at home. This was nine years from the time broadband became widely available. Can you remember when you first used broadband? Can you remember when you first got it at home? Citing a short report from the Pew Internet & American Life Project, "[T]o put this in context, it took 10 years for the compact disc player to reach 50% of consum-ers, 15 years for cell phones, and 18 years for color TV."[3] As new technology adoption goes, the adoption of broadband has been speedy.

People's main impediments to getting online are social and also financial. There are many people living without home broadband in the United States. Thirty-five percent of adults have no broadband at home; twenty-two percent do not use the internet at all. And yet, like adults who are unable to read, their lack of computer skills is largely invisible to those around them. The good news is that people recently have been concerned about underserved populations in America. This is for a few reasons—more on these reasons in Chapter Three of this book—but generally speaking, similar to the rural electrification program, getting people with the program means you can sell them things. And getting Americans up to some basic level standards means that you can use technology to create economies of scale saving money and time in the process. And when the government saves time and makes fewer errors with, say, processing people's income tax forms online, we all save money.

So, people have been studying offline populations in a variety of ways. There have been many surveys undertaken in the past half decade to try to figure out who is offline, why they're offline, and what role the library plays in helping these people do the things they want to do with technology. I'll summarize a few major reports here and others are mentioned in Chapter Three. These are primarily people looking at the digital divide in general, not the overlap of the digital divide and library services. There are certainly more than these reports. Please feel free to read them yourself; the links are in the Bibliography at the end of this book.

The Pew Research Center

The Pew Research Center is a nonpartisan group that frequently produces reports and surveys about Americans and internet use. In the Center's own words, the topics they cover are "the issues, attitudes and trends shaping America and the world." One of the interesting things about their reports is how they trace trends over time, with very similar surveys being given over several years with results that are then comparable. Lee Rainie, the director of the Pew Research Center's Internet & American Life Project, frequently does presentations at library conferences. The Center also doesn't have much of a dog in this particular fight. Unlike other reports that are partially funded by organizations that I would consider closely tied to library vendors, the Center maintains a non-partisan stance that makes their numbers, to me, more authoritative.

The Pew Research Center has a digital divide section on their website which specifically addresses populations who are not online. According to them, 2005 was the year in which broadband overtook dial-up as the most popular form of home internet access. Since then, the numbers of people using dial-up has been on a precipitous decline. In their report on home broadband usage in 2008, they gave us some data about who, specifically, is offline and online among adult Americans. They report that 55% of adult Americans had broadband internet connections at home, up from 47% in March 2007. This number drops modestly to half when they look at the 50 to 64 age group and then drops-off sharply to only 19% of those 65 and older.

They show similar trend lines related to home income level with households at most income levels showing an increase in home broadband adoption between 2007 and 2008. In fact the only income level showing a negative trend, where people are actually losing broadband, are households with incomes under 20K.

Pew reports that only 25% of people in households at this income level have broadband access at home. While this stands to

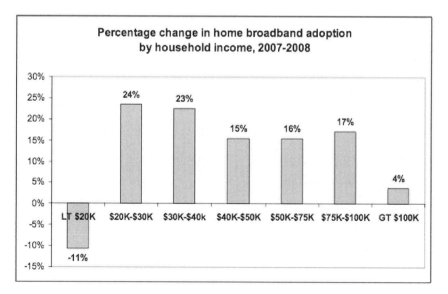

Chart from page 13 of Pew's *Broadband 2008* report

reason, if money's tight high speed access may be a luxury, it's also distressing since it results in people who are historically under-served continuing to have less access. We also see a racial divide in people's broadband adoption rates. African Americans had home broadband at lower overall percentages (43% in 2008) from the national average and also a slower adoption rate.

What's most interesting about these Pew Research Center sur-veys is that they ask people their reasons for not adopting broad-band technology. This can be one of those loaded-sounding "Why DON'T you keep up with the trends?" but it's clear from their results that people are not responding from a position of defensiveness. The Center seems to be able to ask questions that elicit truthful-seeming answers.

The FCC

The FCC recently came out with their National Broadband Plan with its big outline for how to get all of America connected. That plan was preceded by an in-depth phone survey looking at the reasons that people were not online. The FCC has a real problem to solve. They can't just start doing business online and decide that if they lose the 10% to 20% of people who don't interact online, they'll just lose their business. They actually have to solve the problem of getting the rest of the people online. They're the government, for everyone and it's a huge task. So in order to do that, the FCC has to figure out what their reasons are to begin with. I'll summarize a few of their major points, but I strongly suggest reading the entire study. It's fifty pages long, but full of useful data and very easy to read. A chart on the next page summarizes this information graphically.

The FCC separates offline people into four categories; percent-ages are out of the overall U.S. population. I've noted who is in the groups that they delineate:

1. Digitally distant (10%)—people who see no point in being online
   Who is in this group? older and retired people
2. Digital hopefuls (8%)—people who like the idea of being online but lack the resources, often financial, for getting online
   Who is in this group? low income folks, heavily Hispanic and African-American

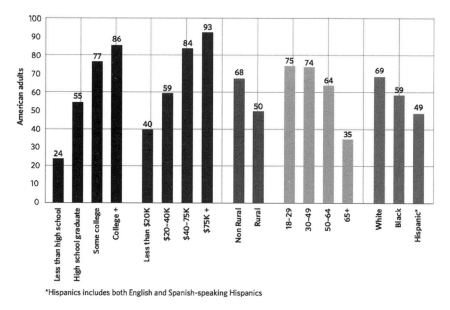

*Hispanics includes both English and Spanish-speaking Hispanics

Chart from page 13 of *Broadband Adoption and Use in America*.

---

3. Digitally uncomfortable (7%)—people who have resources but lack interest
   Who is in this group? no specific demographic
4. Near converts (10%)—people who often use broadband internet elsewhere but haven't yet paid to have it at home
   Who is in this group? younger folks, who often have internet access at work

People who are especially offline, according to the FCC study, include

- Seniors—only 65% have broadband at home
- Disabled people (self-reported)—are online two-thirds less than non-disabled, also do less online even if they do have broadband, fewer different activities, less activity online overall
- Less educated people—there is an extra multiplier if they are disabled or poor or Hispanic

At the very bottom of the list, you find Spanish-speaking Hispanic communities where less than 20% of the population has broadband at home. This is a huge gap from the national average of 65%. When we start asking who is offline, we should be looking at these numbers.

The IRS (and Other Government Agencies)

Government agencies that serve the entire U.S. population have an obligation to provide services in a way that all citizens can access. This means that if they want to move to online tools they have to figure out a way to either make people use services online, or find alternatives for people who can't or won't get online. I was surprised to find that the Internal Revenue Service has been studying the digital divide problem from their own perspective of "How can we get people to see paying their taxes online as a solution to a problem?" This section has a little more narrative to it because I have a bit of a personal librarian perspective with this issue as well.

When the IRS sent my rural library a letter saying they were discontinuing their delivery of paper tax forms to our library, it created a problem for us. This was a few years ago, when the library had a dial-up internet connection shared among four computers, and downloading and printing tax forms was time-consuming and costly to the patron. Making photocopies from the big IRS binder was additionally costly to the patron or to the library depending on who was paying for paper. The librarian was not very good at finding tax forms on the IRS's website, though she tried. People without a computer at home were disproportionately affected by the IRS's decision to discontinue paper forms. If you didn't get a form mailed to you, what were your options? I was peeved because I felt that the IRS wasn't paying attention to users who lacked technology skills.

The "What should the IRS be doing?" question is a great exercise in untangling the tricky lines between social problems and technology problems especially among people who are new to technology. The IRS is, at some level, the American government. When they save money and do a better job, it benefits the American people (ignoring sociopolitical tax arguments). The IRS is also an organization that almost every American needs to interact with in the course of a given year, as opposed to social services that are primarily directed towards people who are poor, sick, or in trouble. So, decisions the IRS makes concerning how to implement technology or design their web content affect every American and need to be tailored towards everyone. People who have difficulties with their use and understanding of technology wind up at a societal disadvantage when the IRS makes bad choices. That said, I was very surprised at how much research went into the IRS's decisions about paper versus online filing options.

Until the late nineties, the IRS was processing most tax forms using sixties-era mainframe computers. Currently, most paper tax form processing happens automatically with only the problematic forms being touched by humans. In 1990, the IRS decided to try to get people to file their taxes online, at a time when less than 1% of people in the United States had internet access. As of this year, twenty years later, 66% of all tax forms are filed electronically. The Cleveland Plain Dealer[4] wrote an article on the IRS's shift to e-filing, explaining both the pros and cons of the plan, and the sticky issues of making online tax preparation a genuine option for Americans. The article states: "It costs nearly $3 to process a paper return, but processing an electronic return costs only about 35 cents. The error rate on paper returns is 20 percent, which consumers must compute and workers must enter into IRS computers, compared with 1 percent for e-filed returns." To put it another way: the United States saves money when taxpayers file online, up to several dollars per taxpayer.

And why do people still fill out paper returns? And how can we get them to stop? The IRS did a study in 2008, the *Advancing E-file Study Phase 1 Report*, in which they compiled all the information they had been gathering. They call the report "a major effort to collect, synthesize, and analyze all substantial data in one document on the IRS e-file program . . . to help the IRS validate and launch future studies, research, and other activities to meet the congressionally-set goal of an 80% e-file rate." It's 248-pages-long and gives a close look at technology adoption trends and what to do about non-adopters. The IRS found that the trendline for e-filing mirrored the trendline for online bill-pay and technology adoption generally. This consisted of some early adopters, a lot of people getting on board in the middle, and a group that one of their cited sources refers to as "laggards," people who will not adopt a new method until other methods become unavailable. The IRS places roughly 32% of taxpayers into this last category for e-filing.

Non-adopters for a similar technology, bill-pay, were split into named groups according to their responses to questions about whether they used online bill paying in a survey done by Forrester Research.

> Holdouts—71% agreed with the statement "No, and I do not intend to pay bills online in the future."
> Fence-sitters—23% agreed with the statement "No, but I plan to in the future."
> Quitters—6% agreed with the statement "No, but I used to."

It's the IRS's job to figure out how to manage, nudge, and cajole all the different sorts of people they call "laggards" into being e-file adopters. They're in a somewhat different position from banks because as they state "The IRS by law is precluded from directing or mandating e-filing behavior of taxpayers." If your bank moves to online banking and you refuse to use it, you can find another bank. If the IRS does it (and they're not going to), you're stuck. So, they have to find ways to encourage people to e-file without having the ability to legally mandate them to do so, at least under current laws. The IRS split non-e-filers into three categories of their own:

- people with no access to a computer or ability to use a computer
- people who don't want to spend the money to file online
- people who don't want to put their personal information "in cyberspace"

The IRS is trying to manage the latter two categories through incentive plans like free online tax filing and public awareness campaigns about the security of e-filed returns stating that they've "never had a security breach affecting e-filed returns." They engage in PR campaigns about online safety generally. However, people in the first category who have lack of access or lack of skills training fall solely into our ballpark.

Offline Populations

Here's a little summary at this point. The stereotype of an offline user is someone who is elderly and isn't "getting with the times," and who is resisting upgrading from dial-up to broadband, but this is somewhat misleading. Older adults, especially wealthier, educated, white adults, are online more than middle-aged adults without a high school education. I bring a little bit of personal bias to this since I've been working with offline populations for a decade and I can outline the people whom I see who don't have, for example, enough technology experience to fill out a job application online. Here are some people I see:

- Anyone over the age of about 30, who didn't go to high school with computers and then didn't go into the white-collar work force where they needed to use a computer. I know many people younger than me in similar situations, in rural areas especially.

- People who lived with someone who was "the computer person" who then died or moved on or out. The FCC survey is notable in that it shows a 2% difference between percentage of households with broadband (67%) and percentage of people with broadband (65%). They explain it this way: "Some survey respondents are non-broadband users but live with someone who, at home, is." That person, who may be a spouse, a child, or a roommate, is the one who does the computer work. If that person is no longer there, the person remaining may not opt to get a computer.

- People with mild or severe disabilities. I had a student at my drop-in time for a while who had severe epilepsy and very little long-term memory ability. Learning things on the computer was very difficult for him because he needed a list of steps to follow in most situations. Moving from the library's computers to the computer lab's computers threw him off. People who are managing mental illnesses also may have extremely high levels of anxiety, risk-aversion, or self-esteem issues that make them feel that they are poor candidates for learning technology.

- People with strong emotional aversions to change or a stubborn perspective that I can only call "not letting people tell me what to do." I see a large number of people who have trouble with technology who seem to feel that they have been betrayed by technological promises, in the media, or by educators or relatives, that were made and not kept. I do not lump this in with people with disabilities, but I do feel that it's a certain type of personality that I see co-presenting frequently with the people who have no technological experience in 2010.

So, the situation is not as clear-cut as it might seem if we were only looking at the numbers. Offline populations can be urban or rural, young or old. They tend to be less educated and less wealthy than their online counterparts. They may have reasons for being offline, or they may have simply never found a reason to affirmatively be online. In some cases, they may have the desire to be online but lack either the technology itself, or someone to teach it to them in a way that is relevant to them and their learning style. Historically, technology educators were more concerned that people did not have physical access to computers and the internet.

Nowadays, we're more concerned that this access exists and is fairly quickly propagating through areas where it does not exist. We're now dealing with both the technology and the people that provide the most formidable challenges: places and people that are difficult to get online.

What Libraries Can Do

With the exception of schools and possibly post offices, libraries are uniquely positioned to reach most of the U.S. population. They have public space, computers, internet access, and they have staff. People already go to libraries with their questions and information needs. According to the Institute for Museum and Library Services (IMLS) most recent Public Libraries Survey for fiscal year 2007, there were 9214 public libraries, serving 97% of the population of the United States. From that same survey, "Internet terminals available for public use in public libraries nationwide numbered 208,000, or 3.6 per 5,000 people." This is 12,000 more internet terminals than IMLS reported in the same report a year earlier. I like knowing just exactly how many publicly accessible computers there are where the public can gain internet access. I like to think, in fact a lot of us like to think, that the library is just one of many places where people can use a free internet-connected computer. We are finding that this is not the case.

In New York City, for example, the city did a survey of public access internet facilities in 2008 as part of their Broadband Landscape and Recommendations report and identified 310 public access points, i.e. places where someone could go to get free internet access. Of these, 212 were library locations. Not only is this the largest provider of internet access in one of the largest cities in the United States, but ninety of these are run by one organization: New York Public Library. So if NYPL makes a policy decision about public internet access, it affects 30% of the public internet in

New York City. When NYPL surveyed their public access comput-ing users, 67% of the those without broadband at home reported that they were using the services at the library "...because they cannot access the internet anywhere else."

In fact, according to the American Library Association, 71% of libraries report that they are the only source of free access to com-puters and the internet in their communities. In my region (Ver-mont), this is definitely the case. In New York City, this number drops to the 33% range according to this same broadband report. That said, this is in a city where cable service is available to 98% of all addresses and DSL is available to 87% of addresses. And yet this same survey reports that no New York City borough reported more than a 58% broadband adoption rate in a phone survey given in 2006–2007. Most importantly, only one quarter of New York City Housing Authority (NYCHA) households had broadband and this drops to 5% of NYCHA residents over 65 years of age. This is pub-lic housing that is run by the city, meaning that broadband could be made available there if it was deemed to be a necessary service, the same way I'm sure all people in NYCHA have electricity, even if they possibly can't pay for it. To be fair, while many NYCHA resi-dents reported wanting to acquire skills in internet and office soft-ware, few took advantage of NYCHA training programs. While one of the recommendations of the NYC Broadband Landscape report was to "encourage provision of broadband service in afford-able housing" in order to make sure that New York City becomes a "leading edge Digital City," these steps have still not been taken at this time.

People still go to the library to use computers. And they go there because it's often the only place they *can* go. Knowing what is motivating people to go to the library and being realistic about what they're likely to find when they get there, can help us opti-mize and tailor our offerings to have the most effective and longest-lasting impact.

About This Book

As I've traveled and spoken to librarians in the United States and around the world, I've found that my personal combination of tech savviness and extensive experience with offline populations is somewhat unusual. That is, there are many people in the library profession who teach people to use computers. There are also many people in the library profession with extensive technology backgrounds. However, I haven't seen as much overlap in these groups as I thought I would. Add the third category "people with enough time to write all this stuff down" and you have a rare combination.

I wanted to centralize a place for analysis of the technology and library statistics I carry around with me, the course materials, and "how to do it" information I've collected, as well as the observations that come from nearly twenty years of technology instruction with primarily novice users.

I don't intend to be fatalistic or doomsaying when I predict that some form of the digital divide may always be with us. There will always be a bottom 10% of users in whatever setting we look at. Since we work in libraries, we have an obligation to provide service to all of our patrons and provide them with tools that they can use, or at least learn to use. For some librarians who may not be tech-savvy themselves, this can be challenging. Even tech-savvy librarians may find it difficult to get traction within their institutions, or may understand the *how* but not the *why* of the technology.

It is my hope that this book spurs real conversations about how we provide and improve technology instruction for all of our staff and patrons. Thank you for joining me.

1

People in the Library

I love the internet. I love that libraries are one of the few places in the world that provide free internet access. But when we talk about electronic resources and the wonders of the web and putting the world at people's fingertips, I think it's good to remember that for a significant number of people, we're giving them an hour of that world at a time, quite probably on Internet Explorer 6.

—Laura Crossett, Adult Services Coordinator
at the Coralville Public Library

There are many stakeholders in the process of making people aware of technology, getting them online, and enabling them to solve their own problems using the computer as one of many available tools. Each individual set of people has a different role to play in this process and should be aware of the roles, motivations, and experiences of the people in the other groups. It's easy to be dismissive of people whose actions and approaches seem to be antithetical to helping people bridge the digital divide. However, it's important to understand the motivations of all the differing stakeholders so that we can best learn how to work together.

Here is a collection of groups who all affect the systems we have in place for assisting novice users in learning technology. Each section ends with a tl;dr (too long, didn't read) summary for people who want to skip ahead to the actual techniques sections.

Library Staff—You Are Here

While this book is written primarily as a how to guide for all of the people who work in libraries, these people are also sometimes the target user demographic. In any location where there is a large percentage of digitally divided folks, some of the people negatively affected by the divide will be working at the library.

In rural areas this can be a bit of a coin flip; the librarian you get may be tech savvy or a tech novice and that can determine the entire tech vibe of the institution for years to come. In larger areas, you often wind up with tech novices on the job in ratios somewhat proportionally to the general population. This doesn't seem to make sense; libraries should be hiring people who are comfortable with and excited about technology, right? Shouldn't the average librarian have more tech knowledge than the average local patron? Not necessarily. In populations where there isn't a lot of tech saturation, two things happen. First, people with tech skills often move to places where their skills are worth more money in the job marketplace, and don't stay around to have low-paying jobs in non-tech fields. Second, even ascertaining who does and does not have tech skills is a muddled process. People without tech skills frequently do not know how to hire people who have tech skills or even ascertain if people have those skills in the first place.

I'm of the opinion that librarianship is a profession that requires people to have a higher-than-average amount of computer literacy. That said, my opinions are not fact. There are many public library jobs that seemingly don't require advanced computer skills. This can go two ways. First, in a larger library system, you may find a lot of job specialization. This means that library staff hired into jobs that are not directly computer-related, such as tech services positions, may not get as much of a chance to work on their skills or use the skills they do have on the job. Second, in rural libraries, there may not be a call for technological know-how as much other tasks a librarian must perform in the limited amount of time they have to work on the job. If a public library has to choose between fundraising and computer skills for their part-time library director, the choice is fairly obvious.

What We Ask For

Here are some excerpts from recent job descriptions from the Vermont Library Association's job list. I'm sure the follow-up interviews fill in a lot of the blanks here, but these seem to be fairly open-ended requirements.

- For a Vermont college circulation position: "[Must] be proficient with common office computer applications."
- For a tech services position at a Vermont college: "Proficiency in basic office software and database software such as Microsoft Access."
- For a librarian position at a Vermont college: "Experience teaching groups using a variety of instructional technologies."
- For an "embedded librarian" position at a Vermont college: "Ability to produce instructional and outreach materials, both in print and digital formats."
- For a children's librarian position in a large public library: "Demonstrated ability to use computers and library-related software and applications."

Now, I may be incorrect in my assumptions, but I suspect that many of these jobs require quite a lot of computer interaction. And that the job descriptions don't seem to make technology experience or ability a necessary part of the job description. Or perhaps this sort of experience is just a foregone conclusion in most workplaces nowadays.

What Do *We Expect?*

These assumptions bring me to a larger question of expectations, another meta-topic. The expectations we have or should have about a person's technological skills for library work can be a contentious issue. If a job, such as a delivery person, requires frequent driving, that requirement is in the job description. However, if a job requires occasional travel to remote sites, access to a car or even having a driver's license may not be a specific job requirement. Lacking driving skills might make someone problematic for the job even though they might get hired for it. It might even be discriminatory to not hire someone who was unable to drive. On the other end of the spectrum, we don't require basic reading and writing skills for most jobs because there's an unstated expectation (sometimes incorrect) that people applying for jobs in the United States will have these skills. Figuring out what is a generally expected job requirement versus what needs to be specifically outlined as a skill necessary for a particular job is something which many libraries still seem to have difficulty with.

And yet, it's difficult to explain a job requirement that is essentially "Must not be on the other end of the digital divide." In the adult education program where I work in my town, we teach a lot of starter classes such as "Getting Started with Excel" or "My First Email Account." (You'll find more on these classes in Chapter Three, the Techniques section of this book.) We see people coming into these classes without even the basic skills necessary to take a computer class, mostly tech vocabulary and mouse skills. More importantly, while vocabulary and mouse techniques can be easily taught, the larger problem is that people in these classes often arrive with an attitude that the classes are going to be difficult, if not impossible, and that they are going to be unable to learn the topics that are taught. In fact, the attitude is more difficult to circumvent than the lack of actual hands-on skills. And yet, for classes on basic technology topics to be effective, the attitude as well as the "point here, click here" aspect needs to be addressed.

Although I see this with both staff and with patron populations, I bring this up in the staff section because visible attitudes towards technology are important for creating an environment conducive to learning or at least to understanding. I don't want to seem too pollyanna-ish about this, but having an institutional "You can do it!" attitude is one of the best usability tools out there for public technology. The institution should be not only encouraging this with affirmative hiring practices and opportunities for on-the-job training and continuing education, but it must also take this to all parts of the organization, from the board to the vendors we work with to the patrons we interact with daily. While technology isn't always going to be a ray of sunshine that beams into every day on the job, it can at least be seen to be a tool that helps us do our jobs more effectively, a tool that ultimately we have some measure of control over.

A Word about Technostress

Technostress is a somewhat hand-wavey term that people use to describe a particular reaction to technological change and expectations. John Kupersmith, whose work I discuss more in Chapter Five, has done research into technostress and has created this definition:

(computer-related stress), a common problem for reference librarians in the 1990s, a combination of performance anxiety, information overload, role conflicts, and organizational factors.[1]

This is a clearly identified problem among library staff who are balancing expectations of both patrons and management in their work lives. Staffers often feel "stuck in the middle" of technology policies set by management and services desired by patrons, with the ability to change neither. They receive the frustration from both sides and can't often make the necessary changes in order to make the system work more smoothly. Library staff feel that people have expectations about their technological abilities that are unreasonable or unrealistic which makes it difficult for them to do their jobs. This causes them on-the-job stress, job dissatisfaction, and general anxiety. It's bad to have an employee who is stressed out. If you're a patron, it's bad to try to interact with a stressed-out librarian.

What takes this sort of thing out of the realm of normal "computers are difficult" complaints and into technostress is the combination of computers plus people. It is the combination of the technology itself (which may be vexing for any number of obvious and less-obvious reasons) with the other people applying pressure either directly or indirectly to doing something with the computer that seems difficult or impossible given the system constraints. In short, it's a mismatch of expectations and abilities with the added weight of this being a necessary job skill tossed into the mix. I've written a chapter on technostress for Rachel Singer Gordon's book *Information Tomorrow* where I've reviewed the available literature. Kupersmith lists what he feels are contributory factors to a technostressful environment. I have added two of my items to the end of this list:

> *Performance anxiety*—Being concerned that you are being judged by your ability to use technology, especially when trying to demonstrate it to someone else. As Kupersmith says "It is hard—and stressful—to suppress one's anger at clumsy design when teaching a user how to get around in a frustrating system, yet we know that we must do this and project a positive attitude for the user's sake."
>
> *Information overload*—This involves not just learning about an ever-expanding set of new resources and tools, but also quickly achieving a level of competency enough so that you can explain them to new, or experienced users.

Role conflicts—Librarians feel that they are shifting from highly skilled reference work to doing more general tech support for everyone, which seems like a "deprofessionalization" of their position as well as a demotion of sorts.

Organizational factors—The larger organization makes choices about how many people are needed to address a certain task, or how much technology is needed to assist a certain number of patrons. When these numbers are off, or the perception is that they are off, people feel overworked, or that they are not being supplied with technology they feel that they need.

Burnout—When day-to-day stresses build up, staff and sometimes patrons can become exhausted. A technological hurdle can be the last straw.

Money—In today's lean budgetary times, technology is still expensive. Trying to determine how to budget for technology in the present and future when there are already budget shortages is a real challenge, and the proper balance of tech to non-tech expenditures is often contested by patrons and staff alike.

Middleman syndrome and powerlessness—Vendors and their products make up a larger part of the library budget than they did ten years ago. Many technology products come in barely-customizable forms with uncertain pricing structures and pricey support agreements. More libraries are members of consortia that make technology decisions in a one-size-fits-all fashion. The librarians work with technology not of their choosing and not customizable by them.

These are all formidable challenges to address in a work environment, but they do provide a framework for topics to examine. It might be worth noting that Kupersmith did his initial work in this area in 1992, back when library technology was an entirely different animal. I'm sometimes surprised at how timeless this list seems.

On Boosterism

Along these same lines, we must be careful to not make staff or patrons feel that they're playing a game of perpetual technology catch-up that they will never win. There has been a trend in library technology discourse lately, and I think in technology reporting more generally, where new technology is presented as not just useful and possibly enjoyable, but as literally essential. Older technologies are explained away as "dead technology" and newer technologies are embraced before our usual methodical evaluations. Of course, if some people weren't using the technology we would never get to the point of our careful evaluations. In the talks I've given, I've discussed the difference between communities in which the library's job seems to be to follow the tech trends rippling both through a community, and communities in which the library is actually the tech leader in the community, the place where patrons go to learn about new technology. The differing role of the library in these situations leads to very different approaches to technology, neither of which is better or worse than the other, merely community appropriate.

As an example, when our libraries in Central Vermont started offering downloadable audiobooks via OverDrive, many people in town took that as an incentive to consider an MP3 player purchase, a gadget they would not have gotten themselves without some sort of good reason. And yet, in libraries serving more wired populations, patrons can search their catalogs via mobile devices and even get shelf status of items via SMS.

In my communities, I know there is some level of anxiety about being able to keep up with technology that seems to grow and change at a rapidly expanding pace. And at the same time, if their communities are happy, who cares that the library doesn't have a blog? Again, this is a situation where setting decent expectations and having a good level of transparency about how the library makes decisions is integral to helping an entire community understand what the library's position is regarding technology.

On Planning

Part of creating a library with staff who are prepared to patiently and capably assist patrons involves having staff themselves feel comfortable and supported in their own personal technological explorations and experiences. Staff must not only feel valued for the skills and abilities that they have, but also that they will be supported with professional training and development opportunities for the things that they do not yet know. Of course, this is a two-way street. As much as many of the things that are part of the library's technology environment were not things that were available to learn in library school—my program started before the graphical web existed, as an example, and I'm solidly in Generation X—the reality is that staff are expected to learn new things, whether it's the new Windows operating system or the new patron address validation scheme. There are better and worse ways to get this information across to staff.

At the same time, changes in a technology environment need to be made with the understanding that many people, both staff and patrons, need time to adjust to new technology environments. Upgrading the public computing operating systems? Make sure you give staff time to learn the basics of navigating and interacting with the new environment. Changing the patron PC sign-up process? Give staff useful documentation that explains not just how to use the software, but how to troubleshoot it and who to contact if something doesn't go as planned. Too frequently we see "documentation" that is nothing more than marketing materials telling you how easy and intuitive a piece of software is. This is worse than no documentation if the software isn't working as you would expect it to work. Make sure staff have not just access to vendor documents, but also clear troubleshooting steps—including when to give up and call in the pros—so that they can approach problems with confidence and some level of authority. Novice users assume, rightly or wrongly, that library staff are the ones who know how the computers work. If solving a technological problem is impossible, or portrayed as impossible by library staff, patrons will assume it must also be impossible for them.

At one library I worked at, we had a systems librarian who was not very capable with computers. Often tech problems would be referred to her, she would try some things, and if she couldn't fix the problem she'd refer it to the library's IT consultant. She would also tell the patrons, "Oh, this computer has issues, sometimes computers just don't work." which was, to my mind, exactly the wrong message to be sending about technology. While it's possible that problems with computers are complex, and sometimes more complex than we may be able to untangle in the time we have available, it is incredibly rare that they behave in a random fashion. The occasional hardware failure may occasionally produce erratic results, but for the most part if a computer is doing something hinky, *there is a reason*. If you don't know what it is, that's fine. If you can't solve a problem, that's fine. Telling patrons that the computer is behaving in a random emotional fashion is doing a disservice to the patron's understanding of technology.

The best response to the computer mysteries in a work environment is not to pretend that you have any idea what is happening (if you don't), but that it's possible for people to figure these things out. There's a huge difference between flatly saying "I don't know." and saying "I don't know, but I can find out." Optimally then, go to find out and report back to whomever needs a report. The information storage and retrieval concept that I learned about in graduate school has been surprisingly useful to me in a 2.0 world where being transparent and providing feedback is considered an essential part of managing expectations and providing good service. Problem-solving doesn't stop once the problem has been resolved, the solution becomes part of a larger system where the answers to the problem are rolled into the problem-solving system for next time.

tl;dr

Staff should be deputized to increase their technological knowledge, troubleshoot to the best of their abilities, and interact with patrons and technology in an environment that is conducive to learning and exploring for both them and the patrons. Whatever is getting in the way of this needs to be addressed from a systemic standpoint and, with any luck at all, rectified. My secret hope is that librarians will read this book trying to assist their patrons and wind up learning a thing or two themselves.

Library Patrons—What They Need, What They Receive

The patrons, the people who come into our library, are why we do our jobs. The easiest thing to do is to cater instruction directly to the individuals with whom we work with every day—sort of a triage mentality, "Take the people who walk in the door, get them what they need." In a tiny library with few patrons, this may work. However, we also have to look at who we're *not* currently serving, and how to reach them. This is the library's outreach challenge. Specifically with digital divide issues, people have come this far without understanding technology and there's likely a reason for that. If the reason is one that we can address, maybe by making our technology offerings more accessible, palatable, usable, etc., we should be moving in that direction.

The technostress discussion from the previous section applies here as well. Instead of being trapped between a work obligation and a perceived lack of knowledge, patrons often feel pushed into interacting with technology by someone or something else outside of their comfort zone. Many of them are frustrated and anxious. They may have not made much use of the library before. To many of them, their emotions about technology become their set of feelings about the library generally. We have some control over this, so we should tread carefully. In our dream world, or in my dream world, we could do a technological intake interview or something, where we could assess what skills the patron had and did not have, to try to figure out if they needed a class, a PC to use, or maybe a referral to a workplace readiness office or something similar. Of course, we rarely have the time that something like this requires.

You don't have to play armchair psychologist for patrons every time you lean over their computer monitor, but it can help to put yourself in their shoes to determine the best way to frame your approach to them and their technological challenges.

Assessment and Intake

The other thing to remember is that patrons often misreport their own technological abilities either because they really don't understand what their abilities are, or because they don't understand the overall technology environment. In my experience, there are as many people reporting that they are **less** skilled than they actually appear to be as there are people over-reporting their own abilities. Being able to make this assessment, of course, requires its own level of tech skill. I usually ask patrons a quick set of questions as a way of seeing what they know:

- "Can you use a mouse?" While patrons may not understand the nuances of right-clicking, if they're reporting that they don't know how to use a mouse, my advice is always "Go straight to Mousercise, do not pass go."
- "Do you have a computer at home or work that you use?" This can open the door to "Mac/PC?" questions and also give you an opener for additional open-ended questions.
- "What do you do with the computer?" General open-ended questions will give you an idea about patron vocabulary and how they talk about their technology.

- "Do you have an email address? What is it?" You can know a lot about a person by what their email address is such as who they use for their ISP, whether they have webmail and maybe, how knowledgeable they are with email.
- "Do you have a website?" I've found that sometimes people can have small websites set up for them by other people and no idea how to access or change them. This is not as unusual a situation as you might think.

The answers to these questions are important, but so is the way in which patrons talk about technology, and what it reveals about their own tech perspectives. Similar to any reference-type interview, knowing what a patron *thinks* they want is important, as is knowing what they really want.

Tech Planning for People in Your Community

I've found that it's helpful to model "sample patrons" when thinking about planning technology delivery. I think about grouping patrons into four main types like this:

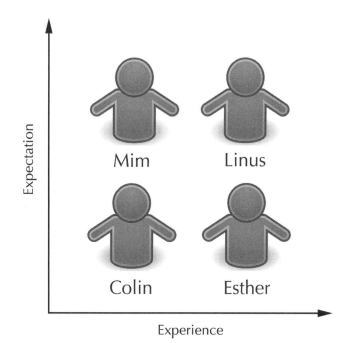

Viewing generic types of patrons on a grid.

Libraries in any location will have patrons with a wide range of previous computer experience. They will also have patrons with varying degrees of expectations. In a perfect world, people would be able to accurately assess their own abilities and set their own expectations, but ours is not a perfect world. Accordingly, librarians need to be able to determine these things and make suggestions, recommendations, and assessments. A patron with low technical abilities who wants to take an advanced technology class may have to be gently directed towards a more basic class. A patron who wants to use library computers to manage the donor database for her non-profit may need to be told that staff can't assist her with advanced formatting questions. So in this situation, when considering a new technology environment, or new handouts, or thinking about service delivery, you can ask "How would this new system work for Colin?" or "Would Esther be able to understand this signage?" For management teams, this same sort of approach can be useful for staff.

You can personalize this sort of image by creating sample patrons instead of generic images and populate the user groups somewhat. Jesse James Garrett discusses this approach in his book *The Elements of User Experience* (Peachpit Press, 2002). Have a few index cards that model general types of patrons you have (not individual patrons that you know in real life), so that you can use them in discussions about technology offerings. These are intended to be more like real people and less like generic "types."

Give these sample patrons names and personalities and keep them in mind when you are creating library technology services. This is a better idea than having one or two actual real-life patrons monopolize your decision-making just because they may be very vocal in their likes and dislikes. Individual patrons' opinions are, of course, important, but they need to be folded into the desires of the library community as a whole. It is often simpler to design and respond to the most vocal users and this, not to put too fine a point on it, is one of the ways that underserved patrons become underserved. They don't make a fuss and you stop noticing that they're there.

You can even go a step further and have a tech advisory panel. This idea, which we see implemented quite a lot in teen services divisions, involves getting stakeholders together to discuss not just what the library is offering, but the manner in which they are offering it

Kevin - 16

- no computer at home

- does homework at library

- uses ipod & dig. audiobooks

- social at the library

Use sample patrons for your tech planning.

and assisting the library in planning for future offerings and directions. Having a combination of tech-savvy and tech-novice patrons on such an advisory panel can be helpful. This is not just so those groups may get to know people in other groups, but also so that staff who may lean towards one side or the other get to understand the breadth of technological understanding that may be present in their patron base. This is especially useful if you have a staff that is not very sophisticated technologically, yet are also used to being the "experts" on library topics relative to the patron base.

Setting expectations is one of the meta-lessons here. Your library certainly can't be everything to everyone. Being a good public servant does sometimes entail saying "no" to people, but finding a way to have that conversation sound like "No, but I'll find out how you can do that some other way" not "No, get lost." Rightly or wrongly, many people who have technological issues and come to the library feel that we are saying "No, get lost." to them when they may just have unrealistic expectations about what they can receive from the library or from technology generally. They may have gone to another library in the past that offered different services. Or they may have been told by a social service worker that they could come to the library to apply for a job or put a résumé online and were dismayed to find that it wasn't quite that simple. While their misunderstandings may not be our *fault*, they can be our responsibility to help solve the problem and also do a little outreach.

Who May Need Help? Tech as a Genuine Option

In many cases, we see people at the library who have a tech problem that needs solving. William James gave a talk that he later published around the turn of the last century called *The Will to Believe*.[2] He discussed how people make decisions and how they approach their own personal philosophies. He outlined what he called the "genuine option" where people making decisions see a path as one that will possibly help them out. For an option that is being considered to be seen as genuine, the option needs to be three things:

1. Living, as opposed to dead; meaning that both choices are real and valid options personally,
2. Forced, as opposed to avoidable; where not choosing is not possible,
3. Momentous, as opposed to trivial; where the result matters.

For people who are in the position of trying to convince others to do things—take public transportation, recycle, go vegan—the trick is often figuring out what makes the option that you are pushing into a *genuine* option for the person you're trying to convince. So, while I'm not saying you need to necessarily delve into the rest of James' oeuvre, it's a good idea to understand how people get encouraged into actually making a decision as opposed to just mulling one over. In this case, the decision to show up at the library and say "I need help using a computer."

Often it's difficult to tell just who is being underserved at our libraries. I know there are many people in my profession who expect a tech novice to be an older person or a person with low income or an obvious disability; and they don't quite get it when they get asked by a thirty-year-old man if they can help him set up an email account for the first time. My definition of a novice user in most of these cases is *anyone who does not have the technological toolkit to solve their own tech problems*, whatever those problems are. As I mentioned in the introduction, there are many groups of people who are offline and they may need different approaches or assistance. I'm going to outline a few use cases to get the ball rolling. Some examples from my particular work life include:

- A 50-something woman who was recently told she needed to apply for unemployment benefits online, not with paper forms
- A 30-something man who was using online dating for the first time
- A 50-something man who wanted to apply for a job at Home Depot
- A 60-something woman, recently widowed, whose children got her a laptop for a gift
- A 50-something woman who was looking for a new job and needed a word-processed résumé and customized cover letters
- A 50-something man who was in vocational rehabilitation after an injury forced him out of his job
- An 80-something woman who wanted to buy a book she'd heard about on the radio

Each of these people have different motivations for getting online, different skills, different needs, and different long-range goals. For someone who needs to get online just to fill out a form, they're going to approach their tasks differently than someone who is looking for a tech solution to a personal problem, or someone who sees a tech angle to an offline hobby they may have, for example.

Special Needs Patrons

The FCC National Broadband Report highlighted the different major groups who are offline and looked at ways to reach them from a policy level. One note they made was that broadband adoption is 23% lower than the national average for people with disabilities, 41% lower for people who lack a high school degree, and 30% lower for people 65 years or older. In a general sense, these are all people who have barriers to access that may be more straightforward than some other patrons' barriers. They may have physical barriers such as mobility or fine motor skills limitations; they may have intellectual barriers such as low vocabularies or difficulty reading; or they likely have combinations of these which have a multiplier effect and make learning new skills extra difficult. It's important to keep these groups in mind as you think of your technology offerings. This is both because these patron groups can be invisible if they're not coming into the library and also because it's easy to casually address these issues in the standard ways—have lots of older patrons, use larger type!—without reality-testing to see if these usability improvement attempts actually do improve usability. Do people understand your handouts? Can they adapt the technology to their circumstances? Do they know who to ask if they need help?

This sort of situation is sometimes the showcase for our inability to think outside the box. We assume people will tell us what they need when, in fact, they may not know what is available to them. Patrons who have trouble using a mouse because they can't stabilize the mouse while they double-click (a very common problem) would have this problem vanish if they could use a trackball. How would a novice patron know what a trackball is when they've never used a mouse? Patrons with poor fine motor skill co-ordination could use a large trackball such as a BIGTrack and have a much easier time navigating through a windows environment. Patrons with visual disabilities could have accessibility features enabled which would allow menus to be read aloud to them.

Many larger libraries have accessibility programs for people who need adaptive technologies; Seattle Public Library offers the LEAP (Library Equal Access Program), for example. However, smaller libraries that can't fund or staff a new department can still increase the usability of their technology in small ways in order to be the most accommodating to patrons who are least likely to have experience with the technology in the first place. As another example, any library with a Gates Foundation PC has a 'big print' login option available in addition to the standard child and adult logins. These patrons often will not know what accessibility features are available to them, so it's up to us to make their availability known. I'll be discussing this topic more in Chapter Four, the Accessibility section, but I wanted to stress that it's the library's job to proactively reach these patrons in the interests of bridging the digital divide.

Non-Tech Interactions

One of the things that is difficult for library staff or frequent library users to understand is how mystifying the library can seem to a non-user. While many people can adapt easily to new situations and suss out the implicit and explicit rules and roles in a new setting, others can't. Since one of the things we know about people who are offline is that they are often afraid of technological risks or uninterested in trying new things, we can extrapolate that if they are non-library users, they may encounter some of the same challenges in just getting in the door. Accordingly, sometimes we need to shift our approach from simply being available to being actually welcoming to our patrons.

I spend a lot of time telling patrons at my library jobs "These are YOUR computers, I'm just here to help you use them. You can't really use them wrong." and other pleasantries that make it clear that I'm not trying to be some sort of information gatekeeper, standing between them and the resources that they want to access. Librarianship has a bit of a PR problem in my opinion. I love most of the librarians I live near and work with, but I know that when I go to a new library location it's often hit or miss whether I have a decent user experience in a library. Often, I can't figure out how to use the system, and find that my only way to get more information is to talk to someone. Not a problem necessarily, but I've found staff in libraries to sometimes be terse, confusing, or downright rude. I roll with this as everyone has a bad day sometimes, because I know how library systems work overall, and I'm not easily dissuaded.

For someone unclear on the "We are here to help YOU" concept, it may be more difficult to get over this hurdle. Chelmsford, Massachusetts public librarian Brian Herzog came up with the idea of Work Like a Patron Day, an annual one-day exercise where librarians took themselves out from behind the desk and tried to see their workplaces through the eyes of the people who used the library services. So, you use the public restrooms, follow all library policies, and use only the public computers to do your work. It's harder than you might think, using patron restrooms and waiting in line to look up a book in a pokey online catalog.

While the library often excels at personalized service for the people who always come into the library, we can forget that even in the smallest communities, there will be people coming into the library for the first time. When I moved to Central Vermont and first went to the public library in my town, the librarian there said "Welcome to town, we're glad you're here." when I filled out a form to get a library card. That may be setting the bar somewhat high for all new patron interactions, but I know that I never forgot this welcome. So, making the rules of the library clear can help make the place seem more explicable for people who might not otherwise be willing to try something new. Clear signs using straightforward language and no confusing colors, along with available brochures and printed (not just online) policies can go a long way towards making a system that is commonplace to *you* be understandable to everyone.

tl;dr

Adults who have never used a computer often have circumstances in their lives that helped create this situation. Effectively assisting them in technology usage involves understanding these circumstances. Anxiety and frustration are real hurdles for some people and can't be addressed simply through better handouts and websites. Breaking through this frustration often means starting before a patron even approaches a computer.

2

The Bigger Picture—Who Makes the Tools We Use

The problem is that the divide is not digital alone—it is profoundly embedded in society in the U.S. and in many other countries globally. Those who are comfortable do not want to think about what it means to be uncomfortable or discomfitted never mind have an awareness of what it would mean to change this societally.

—Kat Deiss, Content Strategist for the Association of College & Research Libraries

One of the awkward parts of being a librarian working with technology is that in many cases, really almost all of them, we don't make our own stuff. We don't build our own furniture, we don't design our own buildings, we didn't even write most of the books in the buildings. We mostly don't code our own software and we don't build the different delivery mechanisms for a lot of the digital content that we offer. We mostly operate other people's programs and devices. We rely on third parties to provide these "solutions" and we pay them for that. This is fine as this is true for most people in most jobs. However, the blurry line between the content we provide and the way it's provided has become problematic as devices and delivery mechanisms get more complicated and sophisticated. We need to keep up. Keeping up becomes an additional part of our job.

We are also in the sometimes awkward position of explaining and apologizing for these systems even though we didn't create them. I sometimes liken this to a patron complaining that a book had a terrible ending and me telling them "Well, I didn't *write* the book." While I feel that this particular fact is clear, the extent to which we can and do determine the features and functions of the various hardware and software that we use in our library is less clear to everyone, patrons and librarians alike.

There are many different companies which provide the services that we use in the public library world. I'll discuss a few of them and break them down into a few categories that are linked thematically to the companies in some way. Please keep in mind that these are my subjective opinions based on almost two decades of experience, but I am not an expert in most of these topics. While I've tried to be factual, I also have strong opinions about many of these companies and their approaches to novice users and digital divide issues. I'll try to be clear when I'm stating facts and when I'm opining.

Of all the subsections of this chapter, this one is the most important specifically because it doesn't seem like it has much to do with novice technology users. What does the telephone company or a PC manufacturer have to do with teaching email to older adults? Lots, especially in the case of software. Every item that is mass-produced from chairs to software to coffee is designed to a set of standards. (See the book *The Measure of Man & Woman* in the bibliography if this is your special interest area.) Chairs must be this high. Coffee must be this hot. Software must ... must have certain features turned on by default, others adjustable by the user and others not adjustable at all. Who makes these decisions?

What Is a Default and Who Decides?

The concept of defaults is often a tricky one for novice users to grasp, and the application of defaults is not at all clear. Part of helping novice users eventually master technology is helping them to be able to examine an interactive environment and to be able to ask these questions and think about their possible answers.

- What elements make up this environment? (colors, buttons, menus, functions)
- Which elements are fixed and which are changeable?
- Which elements are changeable by me and do I want to change them?

- Which elements are changeable by an administrator and do I want to change them?
- Which elements are not changeable that I might want changed anyway?

Many users have difficulty with software and just think that computers are supposed to be hard. They don't know they can change things, especially things that might make the software easier to use. Put another way, it's one thing to keep the little Clippy character (remember Clippy?) popping up on your desktop because you find the feature helpful. It's entirely another thing to have it continually pop up because you can't turn it off or don't even know that it can be turned off. Many people suffer through the default settings in software programs because they literally do not know that there are options. When Microsoft Word introduced Clippy in 1997, it was likely trying to help users solve a problem, not introduce an annoying character that bothered people. And yet, some people were bothered. Sometimes with a large user base, you can't make design choices that make everyone happy. At the same time, sometimes you make a design choice that more people dislike than like.

Undoing a design choice in a later software version is tricky because people have already learned to adjust to it. A more cynical approach to design is that, similar to the new car models, a lot of design is simply brand differentiation and making the consumer believe they need to upgrade when their existing product works just fine. I don't think it's conspiracy-minded to say that businesses want to sell us things, retain our business, and stay in business themselves. This is a good thing to remember as you ask yourself why companies make the decisions that they do and try to explain these things to patrons. Understanding the concept of default settings is the first step to technological mastery after learning the basics.

Microsoft (and The Gates Foundation)

Microsoft may be the tech company that libraries are most familiar with. The Windows operating system has over 90% market share worldwide. Thanks to the Gates Foundation (now the Bill & Melinda Gates Foundation, hereafter TGF), many libraries in the United States have computers with basic productivity software and children's games and staff have received training in how to use these things. The legacy of TGF lives on in many small libraries that are still using their Gates computers from several years ago. I often say that TGF is both the best and the worst thing that has happened to Vermont's public libraries. Best because many of these libraries might not have otherwise decided to get technology without the nudging of TGF or might have made do with donated only-sort-of-working machines. Worst because while these grants were technically for money-for-technology, the reality of the granting program meant that you'd only get supported hardware and software if you purchased PCs as opposed to Macs or some combination of hardware and operating systems. The "support" end of this agreement lives on in the WebJunction community, now partly funded through the Online Computer Library Center (OCLC).

Certainly, some libraries bought Macs with their Gates grants. However, most libraries bought PCs, with Microsoft operating systems and software and did this without making much of a conscious choice or needs-based assessment as to whether this was the best solution for their communities. Again, I think many of these libraries might not have bought this technology at all if left to their own devices and budgets. That said, this made a technology choice moving forward for these libraries that became a decision made externally, not internally. So while any operating system is likely to have its ups and downs, high points and low points, the fact that the TGF machines were granted by an external agency can give people a convenient scapegoat to point to when things go wrong, instead of taking on personal responsibility for fixing problems. Folks at TGF with whom I've spoken to over the years are always surprised that there are some libraries even still using these machines. Most of the small libraries in my region still have their TGF machines actively working as public access computers.

Some of the TGF machines had features that were suboptimal. They required updates that took half a day on dial-up lines; they had complicated security procedures. Internet Explorer was not the best browser for some situations and occasionally led to security exploits in improperly secured systems when operated by novice users. That said, there's the basic adage that life's all about choices and if something isn't working for you, it's worthwhile to figure out if you can change things. Obviously, some things are difficult to change and require a lot of money, time, or effort that people might not have. People who want a longer look at the operating systems wars can examine Neal Stephenson's book *In the Beginning Was the Command Line.* It's a fascinating read.

The Bill & Melinda Gates Foundation still runs library grant programs, but as a much smaller subset of its overall activities which include global development and health projects. They've partnered with WebJunction to provide the "learning and training" aspects of their granting program. WebJunction.org is, according to their website, "an online learning and training portal that provides assistance to library staff in all states—especially small and rural libraries who lack training resources." It's full of useful resources but requires a somewhat sophisticated understanding of technology to navigate and get the most out of. WebJunction also sells "branded portals" to states who then have a customized version of the WJ content to offer to their libraries. Vermont did this for a few years and found that it did not solve a technology problem for us, and took money away from local programs and projects.

The most important thing, from my perspective, about Microsoft's operating systems and their popular applications is that the use case they're designed for is much more geared towards a business environment. That is, their operating systems work better when they're regularly maintained and administered by people who have a fairly complex and nuanced understanding of all the aspects of managing a computer network. When managed properly, a Windows network can be secure, functional, and devoid of viruses and other "malware," software that causes problems. However, there are many ways to run a Windows network insecurely so that it's vulnerable to malware, and gets filled with lots of what we call *cruft*, obsolete or unneeded bits of code or software.

To put it another way, the operating system environment is so customizable it can be customized into being almost unusable. Microsoft has attempted to address this in almost every operating system update they've done, inserting additional "Are you SURE?" warnings and "Your computer might be at risk!" alerts and adding a user-customized firewall and virus-checking software. Internet Explorer also went through several versions where their default settings would allow various exploits to a user's operating systems if a user visited certain nefarious websites. If configured correctly, the browser functioned just fine. If configured incorrectly, it could be the doorway to Trojans and viruses. People who did not even know that they were using a browser learned to be afraid of cookies and Javascript without even knowing what these tools did.

Microsoft's operating systems are still quite difficult for novice users who are timid and somewhat hesitant and alarmed by the preponderance of alert messages and inscrutable dialog boxes. I have a Windows machine at home and I like it just fine. However, I am an expert user. Many expert users I know love the power and flexibility of Microsoft's operating systems. I think we do ourselves a disservice when we deliver confusing operating systems to our users without explaining both that they are customizable to be less confusing, but also that some of this stuff is vexing even to an experienced user. It's a subtle line between "Windows sucks!" and "Yes, they made some design choices that do make this process a bit complicated . . . ," but I feel that the latter explanation is a) closer to the truth and b) a better way to get users to accept something that they don't have too many choices about in the first place. It's possible to go through your technological life in constant battle with your operating system, but this is neither optimal nor necessary.

Apple (and DRM)

Apple is known as the expensive more "design-y" brand of operating system. Apple and Microsoft produce the two major operating systems that are in use in the United States with various flavors of Linux coming in third. Apple is different from Microsoft because they not only build the operating systems, they also manufacture the hardware for those operating systems. So when you're using a machine that is running the Apple operating system, OSX, you are also using a machine that was built by the company that made the operating system. This means they have more knowledge of and control over the way the software and hardware interact and many people argue this leads to a better user experience. They also are fairly rigid in terms of design specifications[1] for software that will run on their hardware so there is a more consistent "look and feel" to the Mac universe than there is to the Windows universe.

Most people, however, know Apple as being the company that created the most popular MP3 player in the world: the iPod. They also created the most popular smart phone: the iPhone. As of this writing (2010), it was still unclear what the iPad would turn into. Apple also pioneered selling music in such a way that the use of this music could be restricted using Digital Rights Management. If you buy a song from the iTunes music store you have two choices. You can buy a song that is in AAC format for $.99 which will only allow you to copy it to a certain number of approved devices, and burn it in playlists a certain number of times. Or you can pay a little bit more ($1.29 last time I checked) and get an MP3 file with no usage restrictions. Many people still opt for the cheaper file with the restrictions.

This brings up another larger topic in technology work: dealing with *Digital Rights Management*. It's hard to talk about this topic from a purely objective viewpoint because even the term itself is somewhat loaded, it's like saying "peace officer" instead of "police officer." However, DRM is the term I use and you can read more about it on Wikipedia if you'd like. Apple created DRM that people could live with, for better or worse.

The reason I even bring it up at all is because, in my opinion, DRM is actually at the root of a lot of the tech problems we have in the public library world once we're beyond the "how do I use a mouse" stage. Many things that you can't do with a computer are things you can't do because there's a limitation built into the software. Often this limitation is built in because being able to do the thing you want to do—usually some variants of making a copy of a file—will eat into the revenue stream of whoever created the content in the first place. How you feel about this often depends on how you feel about the marketplace in general, but you'll see it as a recurring theme in the technology world, while you very rarely see it as an up-front topic in technology instruction. I'm usually fairly value neutral about it, to the extent that I can be, but I also try to be honest: "The reason that you can't make a copy of a DVD easily with your computer is because the people who created the DVD technology do not want you to be able to do this, so they built non-copying technology into the DVD itself. There are also legal reasons why you might not want to copy a DVD." This is usually enough explanation for most people. We do our patrons a disservice when we do not explain the *why* behind technology's failure to do certain things.

Back to Apple . . . Unlike Microsoft and the Gates Foundation, Apple doesn't really position itself towards the library market. They made inroads in the educational market a decade or two ago, and now they're more or less selling personal computers and portable devices to individuals and some businesses. If you spend a lot of time on the internet, you'll probably hear people saying "Get a Mac!" when people complain about viruses and malware. One of the upsides to owning a more boutique-y computer is that it's seldom a target for viruses. There are almost no viruses created for Macs and owning a Mac means never having to run antivirus software, at least at the current time.

From the internet you may also know that Apple has sort of pioneered what people call the "walled garden" approach to hardware devices. They make things that are attractive and fun and not too difficult to use; and in exchange they have an exclusive right to sell applications for this device. This started with the iTunes music store and has continued via the app store with the iPhone and the iPad. Again, this is generally not a basic technology topic, but we are seeing people getting iPhones and iPads who don't even really use computers yet, and the paradigm shift between a computer where you can buy and install software built by many companies and a mobile device where you can only buy applications vetted by one company, are somewhat different environments. That said, the average American will know about Apple because they have, or know someone who has, an iPod. This leads me to one of my favorite vendor topics, digital audiobooks.

OverDrive and Ebooks
(and Whether the Customer Is Always Right)

Most libraries that I know of that provide digital audiobooks to their patrons do so via a company named OverDrive, though there are other companies who offer this service as well. OverDrive provides downloadable audiobooks in a variety of formats using a "checkout" mechanism that is similar to how books get checked out from a library. While this checkout mechanism is simple to implement in a library with physical materials, it's much more complex when applying it to digital materials. People who have experience working with digital files know that when you have a digital file you can, with almost no additional effort, make an exact copy of that file. Now you have two copies. This is good news for people who like to share files and bad news for people who would like to make money selling you access to digital files, which is what OverDrive and audiobook publishers would like to be able to do.

So, instead of just sending people to a website where they can download audiobook files, OverDrive has created this checkout mechanism. If you ask them, and I have, they say that they do this to both serve the needs of publishers who are concerned about their revenue stream and librarians who are concerned about having digital content with "checkoutability." So, instead of clicking a link and downloading a file, patrons need to log in to the system, install additional software on their machine or upgrade the software that they have already, and download the audiobook, which comes as multiple separate files. Then, the files can be listened to on a laptop or moved to a variety of audio players. This system is so complicated and fraught with pitfalls that it has become something of a running joke in library circles.[2]

However, this service has also been evolving. When it was first created, the audiobooks were only available in WMA (Windows Media Audio) format that was only playable on non-iPods. Depending on who you asked, this was either the fault of Apple or OverDrive, but the result was the same: libraries were offering digital content that was only available to people using some brands of computers. OverDrive responded by saying that the only way to get digital media files that "expired," which allowed for the check-outability feature that librarians were clamoring for, was to offer digital files in this format. And publishers would not allow them to offer files in a more open format because they didn't want them to be copied and shared.

Over time, and after lots of patron and librarian input, Over-Drive has made more of their digital content available in MP3 format and created ways for people using iPods and Macs, as well as smartphones to listen to digital audiobooks. Libraries still have the WMA files that they had already purchased, however; and in order to offer these titles in MP3 format, they need to purchase the title a *second* time in the second format. This leads to a confusing situation in the catalog where different files are marked with a complicated series of icons indicating which titles can be accessed via which operating system and music player. And some titles can be officially burned to CD and others can not. Going to the online help files nets this not-very-useful pair of FAQ answers.

What Is an OverDrive WMA Audiobook?

An OverDrive WMA Audiobook title is a digitally-protected audiobook that has been optimized for download. OverDrive WMA Audiobook titles are built using the Microsoft Windows Media Audio format, which greatly enhances the sound quality for desktop listening, play of CD copies (where permitted by the publisher), and portable device use.

What Is an OverDrive MP3 Audiobook?

An OverDrive MP3 Audiobook title is an audiobook that has been optimized for download. OverDrive MP3 Audiobook titles are compatible with many different devices including most cell phones, PDAs, and MP3 players.[3]

How much of that do you think makes sense to a novice technology user? How much is marketing disguised as help? To be fair, most patrons, once they've learned how to use this system, are fine with it and go on their merry way listening to downloaded books and are happy for the service. However, for novice patrons, teaching them this complicated hokey-pokey system involves crash courses in

- digital files and digital rights management
- downloading and installing software
- selecting and using an MP3 player
- upgrading software on their computer
- explaining the difference between how OverDrive files behave and how most digital files behave

In my experience, there is really no way to explain this complicated system, and I say this as someone who actually understands how and why it all works, without advancing a "computers are hard" perspective. In fact, patrons can actually take our books on CD home and rip them to their computer's hard drive (and/or move them to the music player of their choosing) much more easily. I explain that this action may be considered illegal. So this is a genuine conundrum. If we want to solve the patron's problem, it's easier done by not using the solution that we as libraries are offering up generally. And while I believe that software generally is getting easier to use and a "rising tide lifts all boats" and I have been happy to see OverDrive responding to critique, I am still left wondering why, in 2010, we are paying money for systems like this?

OCLC/WebJunction
(and the Idea of a Worldwide Library)

OCLC is the acronym for the Online Computer Library Center. They are one of the few places that libraries get their MARC records nowadays. They work with many regional consortia who contract with them to provide records to participating libraries. Aside from having a nice set of websites and a very strong digital presence, they are well known for both their massive OPAC called WorldCat, thought to be "the world's largest online public access catalog," and their large-scale research projects and white papers which they publish frequently. They have a somewhat entangled relationship with the Bill & Melinda Gates Foundation and WebJunction, which is a little complicated to go into here.

The short version of the story is that after the Bill & Melinda Gates Foundation's library program had put computers into most U.S. public libraries, there was still a strong need for support and learning opportunities among public librarians. OCLC led a partnership with a few other organizations to create WebJunction, which bills itself as "online community for public libraries." WebJunction supports itself with grants and partnerships with states (who receive a branded version of WebJunction and an online location for their own content) and selling low-cost continuing education materials. OCLC, nominally a non-profit organization, primarily supports itself through memberships by organizations, receiving grants and the sale of reports and continuing education materials. If you are online and moderately tech savvy, they have many attractive options for you.

However, OCLC is also a business which means that if you are not online, or not tech savvy, it's not really their place to get you there. While their WorldCat catalog is amazingly full-featured, easy on the eyes, and really the closest thing to a union catalog out there, it also only has records for member libraries while using language that implies otherwise "Find items in libraries near you" which is a very different statement than "Find items in MEMBER libraries near you."

In OCLC's dream world, this would be every library. And at the same time they don't have a plan for bringing smaller and poorer libraries into the fold. And again, I point back to the lack of national/international library organizations that could take this role. The Library of Congress isn't really a national library, it's the library for Congress and the American people, but it's not the national coordinator of library services. ALA is an advocacy organization. And OCLC has the best tools out there, but despite their non-profit status they have a business-based approach as to how they offer products and services. This makes sense and at the same time, we wind up seeing this approach reinforcing the digital divide, not assuaging it. Their business model works better in a world where everyone is already at least decently competent online.

That's not quite the world we live in yet.

Google/Yahoo (and "Hey, Use It, It's Free!")

I had yet another student come to drop-in time this week because she'd read an ad in the paper for a job she wanted to apply for. The ad had a URL and a job number and she wanted to figure out how to apply for that job. She knew how to use a mouse, but not how to go to a URL. We found the website and started clicking through the steps to figure out how to apply for the job. The steps went like this:

1. Type job number into search box and search
2. Get job up on web page, scroll down to read it
3. Click "apply for this job" link
4. Get sent to job application website which involves creating a profile before you can apply for the job
5. Start to set-up profile, realize it requires an email address

At this point the student looks at me and says "I don't have an email address." and I look back at her and say "Well, it looks like you're going to have to get one to apply for this job." I give her a 50/50 chance that she'll decide to do this and I think about how much has changed. I just changed health insurance companies and went to the website of my new company to get some information about my benefits. In order to access the website, which is not strictly 100% necessary in order for me to be insured, but fairly important, I needed to have an email address and agree to have documents sent to it. And this requires not just having an email address, but also checking it. The sign-up form is shown on the next page.

Notice how the "I'd like to get marketing information" box is pre-checked. Who is this convenient for? This is a recurring theme in the world of free tools online. People get something they want in exchange for giving up some of their personal information or agreeing to be marketed to. Savvy technology users can make these decisions from an educated perspective, but unsavvy users don't necessarily know enough to uncheck the box, or possibly even how to do it.

Fifteen years ago, you were unlikely to see jobs that required email addresses because email addresses weren't free. Ten years ago you weren't likely to see email addresses required because getting online to access email wasn't free. Five years ago, almost anyone in the United States could get online and get a free email address. Nowadays, they're telling us that email is only for old people and the kids today are texting, facebooking, or SMSing.

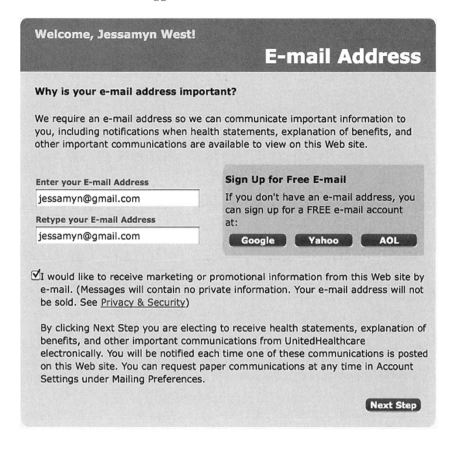

While there's a sense in which this is true—I use email much less for "Hey, how's it going?" communicating than I used to—email or a phone is still necessary for most interactions involving the workplace. In some workplaces, sending you your work schedule via email is considered a courtesy, which keeps you from having to come in on your off-days. And yet, for people without email or ready internet access, this isn't very convenient at all.

The first free large-scale web-based email program was arguably Hotmail, which launched in mid-1996. At the moment, the three major web-based email services in the United States are Hotmail, Gmail, and Yahoo Mail. All of them offer free web-based email that is accessible from any computer with an internet connection and a web browser. "Free" in this case means advertiser-supported and all three email services come plastered with advertising. This is to be expected but, at the same time, it can be both distracting and sometimes confusing to novice users. You'll find more about signing up for one of these accounts in Chapter Seven, the email chapter of this book. The important things to know about free services from a novice user perspective are these:

- These services come with no warranty, no guarantee, and very little support. Most support comes in the form of user forums where users help each other with minor help issues.
- These services may change at any time, and often do. While Gmail is okay at offering experimental features via Google Labs, Yahoo is currently supporting two slightly different email versions, Yahoo Classic and whatever the current version is called. People who accidentally click "OK" to try the new version may have difficulty getting back to the interface they were familiar with.
- These services are free because of advertising, and also because the data harvesting that goes on behind the scenes is valuable to the companies who create the services. I could fill a whole book just talking about the implications of the amount of data that is able to be collected from someone who is using free web-based services, but this is the reality of how companies do business now.
- There are downsides and upsides to this sort of environment, but there may be no better alternative for novice users just getting online. Many people with broadband at home also have some sort of free email that came with their internet service. I often mention to them that while this email is technically free, it will also go away if they change internet service providers.

These three big companies have a suite of services available to users with an email login that allows people to write documents, get travel directions, share photos, recommend products and services, and keep their calendar and contact lists. This is an awful lot of personal information. And just to be clear: I also use all of the above tools. I figure people can bore themselves to death with my life, but for the people who the FCC describes as the "digitally uncomfortable," being asked for this amount of personal information isn't helping them at all. There are many free products that are available online and for download that solve various technological problems. Again, our role as librarians is to make some decent selection decisions and give people an overview of their options and then, let them choose. At the same time, we must remind people that even though something is free, that doesn't mean it's either a "must have" or a "must avoid." As always, the choices and options are more complicated.

Ebook Manufacturers (and the Walled Gardens)

There is no ebook standard; anyone who tells you differently is trying to sell you something. In fact, there's an important distinction to be understood between an ebook, a piece of digital content, and an ebook reader, which is the hardware tool that you use to access the ebook. As of now (2010), there are several competing ebook products, all of which would like to be the thing people think of when they think of "electronic books."

There is an international ebook standard, called ePub, but having a standard is different from people actually using that standard. There are a few major big brand ebook reader products out right now including the Amazon Kindle, the Sony Reader, and Barnes & Noble's NOOK. There are many other reader products available that read a variety of ebook formats. In addition, most phones with any screen area at all can run ebook reader software and can be used for book reading. As always, Wikipedia is the best go-to place for more information on this complicated and evolving topic.

The complicated part of this issue is that ebooks are different from books. In some ways ebooks offer a better user experience: you can keyword search them, leave non-damaging annotations, carry around 200 of them at once. In other ways, they're less practical: they require a power source to function, the readers are expensive, and most importantly *an ebook is legally a different thing from a paper book*. This is very important for you to understand as a librarian, and somewhat less critical for our patrons to understand.

People who sell ebooks would like you to think that ebooks are just a different delivery mechanism for content. And to an extent this is true. However, because this delivery mechanism—digital files—allows for unlimited copying in its most basic form, no-copying systems need to be built into an ebook that is designed to be sold as a consumer product. This involves Digital Rights Management, a copy-protection and/or copy-distribution scheme that sets limits on what can and can't be done with an ebook, limits that are different from those of a paper book and limits that are different from a typical digital file. Put another way, most ebook publishers use the language of licensing rather than ownership when talking about their digital content. This is legally supportable since the first-sale doctrine, allowing an item's purchaser to sell or otherwise give away a copyrighted work, is not applicable to licensed items. These limits are put in place by the content producers, and in many cases have not been legally tested. For example, there is still some debate about whether the Kindle's licensing terms allow it to be circulated in a public library. Despite this, some libraries circulate Kindles.

Most ebook distributors who sell ebooks to libraries in some form or another use this same model. NetLibrary specifically states in their marketing materials "The ownership model means that the library owns the eBook and NetLibrary provides access via a hosting fee that is either billed annually or as a one time fee charged at the time of purchase."[4] While it's fine for libraries to enter into whatever business agreements they feel will benefit their community, these licensing agreements are dramatically different from traditional library content purchasing models which are "We bought it, we own it." This agreement not only restricts what the library can do with the digital material, it restricts what the patron can do with it as well. The effect on the novice user, aside from the extra technology necessary to access the library content that I do not see as a large concern, is that the hype differs from the reality and the patrons look to us to explain the difference.

Keep in mind that for people with very little hands-on experience with technology, much of what they may know about it comes from news articles (more on that in the next section of this chapter) and advertising. Advertising's job is to make the product sound appealing and desirable; and one of the major ways to do this is by saying that a product is familiar—"It's just like reading a book, only better." or "One click to 1000 books."—and the reality of the situation may not jibe with the marketing projection. This is true for many things in the real world and I don't fault ebooks or publishers or vendors for this state of affairs. However, if we can't explain why ebooks are different, if we don't understand some of the nuances of copyright and licensing agreements and digital rights management ourselves, we may lose some of our credibility as the people who know all about content. Obviously, there are reasonable middle grounds here, but for many of us this is a time to start studying up, getting used to a playing field that is shifting, and learning to explain some of the differences between digital and non-digital content to curious patrons.

Antivirus Software (and What Is the Real Virus)

Virus threats and anti-virus responses need to be seen as part of a symbiotic system and one that does not benefit the end user as much as it claims. This area is one case where I don't have as much first-person experience as in some of the others. However, the threats of viruses, people's misunderstandings about viruses, and companies' responses to these misunderstandings have created a vicious cycle that actually winds up with more people being afraid, and likely not any safer.

The first two things I ask people who ask me about viruses are:

1. Do you connect to the internet at all, or only use dial-up? If so, you are at a very low risk for virus threats. If you never connect to the internet and don't put files from other machines on your computer, you are at zero risk of viruses. Zero.

2. Do you use a Mac? If so, you are at a very low risk from virus threats and mostly need to employ good computer hygiene like not opening email attachments from strangers.

If people are in either of these categories, I usually just explain to them how to stay safe—use Firefox, don't open mystery attachments, stay away from porn/gambling/warez sites—and tell them to maybe run a free antivirus program if it makes them feel better (see suggestions in the webliography at the end of this book). For people who are dealing with virus threats or, more likely, virus threat warnings, it's useful to explain the general system that has grown over the past decade. I try to whittle it down to its essential parts, but the basic upshot is this sort of brinksmanship situation:

- Viruses are usually malicious pieces of code that get on to your computer via infected email attachments, security exploits, or file-sharing. Some behavior leaves one more open to virus problems than others.
- There are ways to make a computer mostly secure from viruses, but most computers don't come this way "out of the box" because it can inhibit usability.
- Many companies, including operating system manufacturers, have created antivirus software to address this problem.
- Virus makers responded to improvements in antivirus software by, among other things, creating viruses that resembled virus warnings.

- Antivirus software makers got more serious about making sure that computer users could not avoid installing and updating virus software.
- At the same time, low end laptop manufacturers sold laptops with trial versions of popular antivirus software which then expired and left all sorts of dire warnings on the user's computer.

If you've read Dr. Seuss's *Butter Battle Book*, you'll know what I'm talking about.

Needless to say, novice users find this all talk about viruses to be baffling. Add to this the media attention given to "computer viruses" generally with very little in the way of specifics (that, for example, a virus they were reporting about only infects computers running the Windows operating system) and you have a large number of people who are not sure who to believe. Additionally, since the actions viruses actually take vary widely, and as such are ill-defined, people tend to blame all computer slow-downs and erratic behavior on viruses. And there are always people available to take your money to try to clear the viruses off of your computer. In many cases, the best solution to a totally intractable virus problem—reinstalling the operating system—is unavailable to people because they don't have the system software or have a laptop where the software came pre-loaded.

Honestly, someone should write an entire book on dealing with viruses for novice users, but this isn't that book. The important thing for you as a librarian to know is that while the threats are real, novice users have as much or more to worry about trying to understand the system warnings telling them that they are at risk (despite there potentially being no risk at all, for an offline computer) than dealing with viruses themselves. Fear of viruses has kept many people in the "digitally uncomfortable" zone for too long and we need to find a way to talk sensibly about the situation and offer explanations and suggestions.

Again, we are not turning the reference desk into a computer repair center. However, if one of our missions is to help people enter the information age and we've identified this issue as one of the larger impediments to computer or internet usage, we should try to meet that head-on. Some of this is just social engineering, not having staff pass on "Oh, it's probably a virus" comments when someone is having a tech support issue. More of it is leading by example with public access computers running competent and invisible anti-virus software, and showing that it is possible to use a computer, access the internet, and interact with other people online without falling prey to various hazards.

Where Open Source Fits In (and Where It Doesn't)

In recent years, Open Source has become something that is more of a genuine option for libraries. There are many good Open Source operating systems and software products that people can use for free on PCs, Macs, and GNU/Linux machines. I'll talk about FOSS (free and open source software) because it's an easy acronym. People who want to dig into the nuances between free software and open source software and GNU versus Linux should read up on these topics on Wikipedia; it's a fascinating world out there. There are many web tools that are free to use, but not FOSS-types of tools. I'll primarily be talking about the standard FOSS tools, though I have an interest in web-based FOSS tools in a general sense.

So, there is a small but growing group of advocates who recommend many FOSS solutions for libraries. This has become even more pronounced lately as two large FOSS ILS products are being implemented in many large and small library systems worldwide. From the State of Georgia who created and uses the PINES system with the underlying software called Evergreen to my local Green Mountain Library Consortium, which has grown to encompass 30 member libraries all implementing a local version of a FOSS ILS called Koha, the shift is on. And much of this is happening without a concerted marketing effort by FOSS companies. In fact, many FOSS products are still being made by a devoted team of volunteers, and there is no "FOSS company" to speak of. Sure, when you go to ALA or other big conferences, the support companies for major FOSS tools will be out in earnest, companies such as ByWater and Equinox, but generally speaking this is software made by groups of people without official corporate structures, which often means no marketing, but also no support.

In fact, one of the constant complaints about FOSS is the lack of documentation for all but the most polished software. The help files for Firefox rival those of any commercial product, but those for other products like Audacity leave a lot to be desired. The benefits of FOSS are obvious. It's low cost, has easy-to-understand licensing and if you're handy with software generally, can be tinkered with to great effect. However, for many people who do not enjoy tinkering and DO enjoy tech support, FOSS is still not quite there as a genuine option. IT departments sometimes refuse to install and maintain it. Other people spread rumors about FOSS's vulnerabilities, rumors that do not get dispelled easily since there's rarely a PR department charged with maintaining the image or the brand. And, like many life choices that come with an attached philosophy, there are a small set of "true believers" who can sometimes be aggressive about other people's choices and can't see any reason for them to continue using proprietary software. Anyone who moves within FOSS circles has met a few of these people.

I've seen libraries running nearly total-FOSS setups, with Ubuntu operating systems running Firefox and OpenOffice and other tools such as Gimp for photo editing. I've also seen libraries who are a straight Windows shop, but have an Open Source ILS running on a machine in their basement which runs Debian Linux. In my opinion, FOSS is getting to the point where the major software tools are a genuine option for people both because the tools themselves have become easier to use and install, but also because we're seeing services companies fill the support gap of concern to people contemplating an ILS or operating system migration. There are still a vanishingly small set of libraries who are using primarily FOSS tools for their public access computers. I am hoping to see more libraries attempting this sort of setup moving forward.

tl;dr

Understanding why hardware and software are created the way they are can help us understand what we need to do to make it better. While there is not necessarily a perfect hardware or software solution, there are definitely sub-optimal choices. It's okay to decide not to use software because it is difficult for patrons or staff to use. Software is sometimes hard to use by design. It is easier to work with vendors if you understand what motivates them and what they are trying to do.

The Media, the Decision Makers, and How They Interact

How many times have you been reading a newspaper or listening to the radio and you hear someone talk about the library? If this is a mainstream media outlet, you'll usually have to suffer through a few library jokes before you get to the meat of whatever they're discussing. And the stories you read about libraries in the media often take fairly predictable turns. Usually, they're in response to a library event either locally or nationally. If we're lucky, this is something nice like a librarian getting an award. If we're unlucky, this is something much less nice like an arrest at a library or a lawsuit against a library district. At a national level, a lot of library stories seem to be the result of press releases or announcements by library advocacy groups. This is fine, it's good to get publicity, but again the stories are often similar: Celebrating the freedom to read. National Library Card Week. Libraries are still important even in economic slowdowns. And then there's my favorite, paraphrased: Hey, librarians can even use computers now!

While I'm thrilled that the "cybrarian" moniker died off quickly, I'm a little dismayed that library workers using technology seems novel enough that you'd want to write a newspaper article about it. The larger point, however, is that I don't get the idea that a lot of reporters go to libraries. Or if they do, they don't find a "hook" that they can write something about. I can imagine it's difficult to find something new to say about an institution that's been around in this country for centuries. And yet, our image is important because the public still pays attention to the news and what people are saying, and also because of the close linkage between the media and the decision makers and how they influence one another.

Old Media

Say what you will about old media and/or the longevity of it, but people still listen to the radio and read the newspaper. Both types of media are ubiquitous enough that they can reach any American who can read. The same can not be considered true for online media despite how ubiquitous it may seem to us. When I was working at a large public library in Vermont, the best outreach tools we had outside of direct mailings were putting something in the newspaper and putting something in the window of a store-front downtown, which we did for Library Card Sign-Up Month. Another incredibly effective outreach tool was the local cable access channel. I did a presentation where I took a PowerPoint talk about our genealogy database along with a bunch of screenshots and narrated alongside them, explaining how to do census research using Heritage Quest. It was totally low tech, but it got people interested in the idea in a safe and familiar environment.

For better or worse, many people who are used to older media also place a large amount of faith in this media and the things they read or hear there. This is a double-edged sword for many of us, because it becomes difficult to shift this trust into the online world even though the sources may be identical, and also because reporting by old media about new media can be full of misinformation.

This is not always true, of course. However, I've personally found that newspapers seem to loathe calling a computer virus a "Windows virus" even if it's true that the virus only affects people using one operating system. As a result, people read articles about the latest virus and worry about being at risk, even if they don't even have a Windows machine at home. And reading about media trends such as Twitter or even the less-new Facebook provides such a small window into how the technology works that people with little tech knowledge often wind up more confused than enlightened. And older generations especially are used to making lifestyle decisions in part based on what they see and read in the paper, for better or worse.

When the *New York Times* technology section comes out on Thursday, I'm frequently approached by people asking for my take on whatever the topic of the week is. It's sometimes an awkward conversation because if I find fault with the reporting or say "Well, that's not exactly what's going on there..." I feel that I'm contributing to people's overall tech unease At the same time, if I agree with what I think is an incomplete explanation of something technical, I feel that I'm dumbing down technology. And at some level, the things we read in the newspaper are attempting to answer the "Why should I care?" question for people; the answer to that question is very different if you're dealing with someone who has a basic tech background as opposed to someone who has never used a computer. That said, whenever there is a news story in the paper, we can guarantee that many people will read about it and know about it, which is good for business. My drop-in time classes get advertised primarily via quarterly advertisements in the town paper and flyers I put up at the library.

And many reporters are end users, even tech reporters. They are not IT people. They are not programmers. They are not web designers. You are more likely, in my experience, to find a librarian who has created a website than a reporter who has built one. No big deal in any case, but it's important to keep this sort of thing in perspective when you are reading old media reporting on new media. It's a rapidly changing playing field with a lot of nuance. Many of these things are tough to explain in few words without hyperlinks nowadays.

The Blogerati

I was an "official blogger" at the 2004 Democratic National Convention in Boston, when blogging seemed like a new thing and no one really knew what bloggers would do at a convention, but they wanted to have them there. At the time, my blog was already five years old. I was there to hear what people had to say about libraries, and to talk about libraries to people who would listen. As you might expect, there wasn't a lot of library discussion. In fact only two speakers mentioned them: the Democratic nominee John Kerry and a state senator few people had heard of named Barack Obama.[5]

The most interesting thing about this blogger assignment was that having been chosen gave me this automatic position of authority and some sort of pundit label. Many more people started reading my blog. People asked my opinion about topics even though I was mostly just a librarian blogger who decided to go to the DNC because it was in my neighborhood. There is a sense that the blogging world has a high opinion about itself, that by benefit of deciding that what you write is worthy of putting online, you are somehow saying that people should care about you, or about your opinions. I found that early in my blogging career, I heard this a lot: "You have a blog?" people would ask "Why does someone care about what *you* think?" I would usually respond that I wasn't sure, but that people read it and even if my readers were made up of my mom and two other people, I was okay with that. The cost of having a blog is small, compared to traditional media, and the advantages can be huge. I am sure that a lot of my professional library accomplishments—being on ALA Council, getting to be the webmaster of the Vermont Library Association website, being chosen to blog at the DNC—were a result of my having a blog.

For people who don't blog or who don't have a blog, their opinions are all over the map about blogging. Blogs are more commonplace now. They're owned and run by individuals and media companies and academics. People can be professional bloggers as a job, and there are blogging media networks such at

Gawker, Gothamist, and the amusingly named Cheezburger Network. They offer some sort of participation that is a little more rich than letters to the editor, usually a comments section or sometimes a forum. They produce content round-the-clock. Bloggers may or may not be reporters, either in their own estimation or in the eyes of the law.

And yet, we still have the ongoing stereotype of the blogger as someone who tells the whole world what they had for breakfast and the world responds "Who cares?" I find this stereotype as tired as the bun and the shushing and am quick to point out the blogs of major media companies and start a conversation about whether *Time* magazine's blog is as reputable as *Time* magazine. It's an interesting exercise. The thing that we all agree about blogging, however, is that it's a heavily hyperlinked activity, i.e., part of the mechanism of blogging is the cross-linking to other online content, and it's nearly entirely occurring online. This, of course, means that it's invisible to people who are not online and who may not even conceptually understand the idea of linking, which is the main thing, to me, that differentiates old and new media. Even if someone doesn't have a television, for example, if they are in the United States, they certainly understand the idea of television. I'm not so certain the same can be said for online media.

And, from a personal perspective, I've seen this play out in my own life, occasionally in the comments section of my blog. There was a very popular post[6] I made that discussed whether then-VP candidate Sarah Palin had actually tried to ban books from her local library when she was the mayor of Wasila, Alaska. I linked to a *Time* magazine article. In the course of the comments, someone made a post saying "This is the list of books Palin tried to have banned." and it took off around the internet like wildfire. Of course, neither I nor anyone else knew the provenance of the list. I had slightly more information to go on, including the email address of the person who'd posted it and I did what I considered to be due diligence and wrote him an email. The upshot, whether I believed it or not, was that his roommate had posted the list as some sort of prank and no such list actually existed. I posted a follow-up comment to that effect and later added a note to the original blog post, but that didn't stop people from citing my blog as the "source" of this information, or reading that comment and not my follow-up comments or even my original post.

And then, like any political dispute, people started getting angry with each other and angry with me for not handling the issue in what they deemed the correct way; usually what was suggested was taking the post down. And those debating this issue were a range of tech-literate and not-so-literate people who were often talking past each other. I got a lot of angry email. The post still remains on my site, however. Sarah Palin did not get elected for other reasons. At the core of this debate, I felt, was the role of bloggers, people who can edit their posts at will and delete or edit comments. People were debating what a blogger's responsibility is to those who may not understand the difference between a blog and a newspaper, or a blog comment and the blog itself. All quite interesting to me as someone who is often looking at these websites with novice users and noting what they understand and don't understand. The difference between "I read it in *Time* magazine." and "I read it in a comment on *Time* magazine's website." is not as clear for as many people as you might think.

Biblioblogosphere

For librarians who may be just entering this field, there are a lot of concerns and considerations with putting your voice "out there." A lot depends on whether librarians are blogging for themselves, as I am, or for their institution, or for the library press. Each role comes with differing expectations of polish, professionalism, and formality. And there are people who feel like a lot of this stuff is already decided, that the etiquette rules of blogging are fixed and unyielding, and many more people who feel that it's still the Wild West in some ways with no rules at all. There is a pleasant group of library bloggers online overall and we've been quite fortunate to have a lot of collegiality among library bloggers.

We're also quite fortunate to have our own statistics junkies who compile numbers about the library blogging experience. This can be simultaneously an exercise in navel gazing, and also in giving us a view of our own professional online presence. Walt Crawford has written two books[11] about the landscape of blogging librarians, and how it has changed over time, both of which are well worth reading. The importance of the library bloggers to our profession generally is that it elevates our voice into the online realm and makes us a part of this conversation that we're always hearing about, that is happening online. I see a lot of librarians on

Facebook and Twitter and even on Foursquare, and to me it always feels like a symbiotic meshing of a traditional profession with new technologies in order to continue to provide access to information and resources.

This group of library bloggers is also around and available and discussing library issues online through community sites such as FriendFeed, LISNews, and Unshelved Answers, as well as being a presence on other social sites and in local blogs. This means that library and technology issues get discussed in the larger world and don't just become internal topics at one's own place of business. This can be good news for skill-sharing and policy discussions, but bad news when people are trying to micromanage your institutions' issues from across the internet. I think this discussion is a good thing generally, but it's taken a lot of getting used to for many people. This whole idea of the online hive mind is commonplace in some workplaces and totally mysterious in others. I assume this is a matter of time, but it's another digital divide that I see occurring in our profession: librarians who make use of social resources online to help solve problems and answer questions, and those who don't.

Political Promise Makers

Politicking is too large and volatile a topic for me to spend much time with here, but I want to mention three things about people in the political arena, in addition to what I've written above.

1. Politics is a profession of persuasion and deal-brokering, and most people who are in politics at a national level are partly there because they work well or can work well in the spotlight. They are there because they have social skills in addition to legal or economic skills. I firmly believe that some of the changes we want to see happening such as changes that will have a substantive effect on the digital divide, are going to have to come from politicians—such as mandates to provide internet connectivity or training services. We ignore this avenue at our peril. We need to approach people in positions of power with the awareness that just doing something because it's a good thing for society does not always solve a problem for someone who has a career in politics.

2. Politicians read the same newspapers as you and I, and are not necessarily any more tech-savvy than any of us. In fact, if they have been in their careers for a few decades and have employees who do most of their communicating for them, it's entirely possible that they know less about technology than the average librarian. It's almost certain that they spend less time in the library than the average person in your city or town. So, they may know more about the library from what they've read, rather than from what they've experienced. When you are trying to make a point to a politician or listen to them talking about libraries and/or technology, it's worth remembering that they may be suffering from some of the same tech misinformation as many of our patrons, with the added caveat that they're not even coming into the library for a reality check. Keeping our politicians updated in terms of what they can do about our needs is critical to the larger issue of the digital landscape in our country and our place within it.

3. Non-profits have certain restrictions about what they can say about some politicians and about politics generally. This was a huge deal when I was on the ALA Council and there were people who worked for the American Library Association who frequently reminded us that since ALA was a 501c3, using their resources, such as their mailing list, for political speech was potentially problematic and/or illegal. While it's possible that using the listserv for such discussions would be acceptable, the association felt it was a legal issue best left untested. This is why ALA has a Washington office with different funding lines and infrastructure that is not bound by the same restrictions. This restriction was exceptionally frustrating since we had, at the time, an administration that was sometimes actively hostile to libraries (such as the Environmental Protection Agency's libraries) and library associations weren't supposed to say much about it. This may or may not be true for your local library so it's essential that you understand the rules governing political speech and where the lines should be appropriately drawn.

There are many other wonderful resources online for learning about the political landscape as far as technology issues go in this country and I'd encourage people who want to explore more in this direction to get involved. We could use more librarians in the legislature generally.

Boosters and Hypesters

Also added to this list of people with influence are the people who sell us things, but who are not our vendors. I'm talking about advertisers of various stripes and even technology boosters who behave with a vested interest in making us either love technology or feel like we're abnormal if we don't. I wasn't even going to talk about this except that these voices are such a pervasive part of what I hear from people learning technology such as "I thought computers were supposed to be easy!" While we'd laugh if someone made a similar statement about their car such as "I thought this was supposed to give me sex appeal!" we hear the previous statement a lot when dealing with novice technology users. They've had their expectations set by what they've read and seen on television, much more so than people who have learned about technology from other people who were already conversant in technology.

This problem with unmet expectations can also happen with professional development in the library world, where people ask their librarian friends, "Why doesn't the library use technology in a more sensible way, like I do?" and then we shrug and say we don't know either. Or when we see a particularly motivated speaker talking about some new technology being met with crossed-arm "That will never work at my library." responses, I'm never sure where the breakdown is. I agree that we have to be sensible in our approach to technology, and that we should be able to make a good argument for making radical changes in our infrastructure, but at the same time I don't see technology adoption generally as a major step. Moving from a newsletter to a blog should not be a big step and yet with the push-pull attitude we find within our own profession, you'd think it was. So, from the inside we need to not only be reasonable ourselves but call for reason in a larger sense, and remember that whatever our personal feelings about technology are, we serve all the users, both the technophilic and the technophobic.

Novice computer users can be cynical or naive. They see someone using a computer on television and think "Huh, maybe it is that easy?" And again, this isn't all novice technology users, but it is a recurring theme. They'll ask a question about how to use a particular tool that seems to come right from the marketing brochure for that tool. And I don't just mean patrons, though obviously they're most of the people I interact with, but also librarians. I often hear from them "I thought this software was supposed to be simple to install?" Technology is a difficult field to set proper expectations for because unlike many other environments a great deal depends on the context that you bring to the table. So, software that may in fact be easy for me to install is not simple for someone to install who hasn't installed software before. The idea of "easy" in general is contrasted with the idea of "easy" for someone with a small background in doing this sort of thing. In fact, I try to never say that something is easy, preferring to say that something is straightforward, or perhaps is uncomplicated. If you say that something is easy, to me, it's subtly disrespecting people who can't figure it out. Saying that something is uncomplicated is a direct measure of the steps you need to take to do the thing or something else that's quantifiable. The combination of knowing your audience and setting their expectations, along with using compassionate and considerate language allows you to have the most useful impact assisting people in setting their own pace with technology.

There's only so much you can do about the world of advertising and boosterism that surrounds us, but you can be a hype-free oasis in the complicated world of technology and offer sensible brand-free advice that is focused on problem-solving, rather than being driven by kickbacks or affiliate relationships. You can also speak to vendors and other people who are offering these "feel-good" narratives about the world that includes their products, and give them constructive feedback and real-world examples of how their products do or do not work in your library environment. While I know that not everyone can go to national library conferences, it is a good opportunity to talk to people who work for the companies that create many of the tools that we use and give a human perspective on how their products fit into your real world. And for the people who approach technology with a bit of a sneer or approach technology within our profession as if we were blindly following trends, I generally just smile and encourage people to get used to it. If there's one thing that's constant in the technological world, it's change, and rapid change at that. It's not for everyone, but it's what we've got.

tl;dr

As Led Zeppelin says "lots of people talking—few of them know." Just because someone is in a position of power or in the media does not mean they are always correct. That said, sometimes wielding influence is the only way to solve an intractable problem and political and media influence is still a force to be reckoned with. It's worth understanding that the relationship between old media, with formal publishers and content editors, and new media with live reporting, responsiveness, editability, and interactivity are two parts to people's large personal information systems.

Synthesis—How It All Works Together

Unlike most other national American institutions, there is no centralized coordination among libraries. We have all the parts, as I've mentioned in this chapter, but there's no nationwide department of libraries boss who says, "All libraries must offer email classes and yoga DVDs." The good news is that this gives libraries the flexibility to serve their local communities in the most appropriate ways possible. The bad news is that with a few exceptions, it's difficult to coordinate things that benefit from economies of scale such as automation projects, bulk buying of database products, and any sort of standardization of what people see when they enter a library. This is good news for vendors and bad news for all but the largest libraries. It's interesting to go to other countries where they have more national-level coordination and see how the libraries differ, mostly running the same hardware and software, with more standardization of tech offerings.

There are certainly generalizations you can make about what a library offers, but even the laws about what you have to provide in order to even *be* a public library vary by state. And these sorts of guidelines change over time too, and we don't always make a big announcement "Now in the library . . . computers!". While we often hear the refrain of people missing the old days of quiet libraries and no computers, these days are not so distant for many rural libraries. Newer libraries with more progressive policies and approaches to library services—I'm thinking of teen services and programming, but it could just as easily be knitting classes and Playaway books—have to sometimes struggle to be thought of as traditional libraries.

So, there are often minimum library standards, but they're often invisible to patrons. As a result, a patron who hasn't been to the library in a while may walk into the building not knowing if the library offers internet access for the public, or wireless access, or places to plug in laptops, or digital content to supplement the print offerings. People walking into a public library for the first time, whether they're new in town or just passing through, often have to work to make sense of whatever the library has technologically. Print offerings are all out there on the shelves for everyone to see, but how do we demonstrate all of our technology offerings?

Patrons sometimes don't know what's going on at the library, and they're not even sure what goes into a library being a library. In some ways, this is great as we have a timeless institution that for many people has simply always been there. In some ways, it's not so great because people read about libraries in the newspaper or see them on television and think "Why isn't my library like that?" or, alternatively "Why isn't that library like mine?" And the answers are complicated. A lot of these people that I've mentioned in the previous sections of this chapter work together in ways that are, again, invisible to the patron. And our patrons don't read the studies that we read as librarians. In fact, many patrons don't even know that there are other rooms in the library besides the places that are available to the public such as the staff offices, or the frequently-captivating basement rooms.

A lot has been said recently in the library community about marketing and branding ourselves and while I hesitate to take on the terms of corporate America, it's important to note that the promotion and advancement of home-grown solutions that work is something available to us with the advent of technology that may have been difficult historically. I'd like to see more librarians giving each other good ideas and answering each other's questions in an effort to serve patrons better and more responsively. You'll find some of my ideas in the following chapters. Please share these ideas freely.

3

Planning—Strategies, Techniques, and Tools

Librarians should understand that what they do is create space, cognitive space in the environment. It can look like a public library, a web site . . . or whatever. Librarians need to make sure that they provide a rich space, where human beings can gather, interact, and become more than themselves. If librarians can do that, and do it well, they will be a part of the future.

—John Perry Barlow

As I stated in the Introduction of this book, this is not a manual. While you'll find links to both syllabi and handouts in this book, the goal is to further understanding of how to assist people who have little or no technological experience. There is a small set of tools that I consider indispensable for getting started with technology that technology users, present and future, should become familiar with. As I tell people in my talks and classes "You don't need to remember everything I've told you, but I hope the next time you encounter this particular technology, you will remember having heard about it and maybe a thing or two about how to use it."

Novice computer users have a particular set of learning needs and a context in which they operate. One of the more surprising things that I hear from people who come to my drop-in time is that they've often been to several classes or read manuals before, and they seem to be having a hard time making their learning "stick." I can empathize as I have a terrible time with world geography and I don't quite know my left from my right, or east from west. I can only imagine how dispirited I'd be if I had to use either of these skills on a day-to-day basis, or felt a lot of societal pressure to use these skills.

The goal here is *learning*, not mastery and possibly not even speedy competency, but being further along the path than before. Outside of the library, in my region, a lot of the funding for stuff like this comes from programs like AmeriCorps or other national service-type programs or job readiness programs. These programs do a great job working with populations affected by poverty and facing great challenges. However, my experience as a two-time VISTA / AmeriCorps volunteer is that sometimes the outcomes these projects require are unrealistic. For example, in my AmeriCorps position, we were specifically funded at one point both to train novice computer users and also to supposedly train them *up* into future tech educators in a sort of "train the trainer" style.

As much as I am a huge fan of my students and think that they were and are capable of great things, the difference between learning a technology well enough to solve your own problems with it, and learning it well enough so that you can solve *someone else's* problems is fairly vast. Believing that novice users can turn into tech educators over a few months may be unrealistic. Put another way, would you want someone who had just learned to drive teaching a Driver's Education course? Teaching Driver's Education involves a lot more than just being able to operate a motor vehicle.

While I see a lot of benefit to having tech novices learning in proximity to one another so that they are encouraged to ask each other for help, I also feel that being a technology instructor involves much more than just knowing how to be an end-user of the technology. This is especially true when working with people on the other side of the digital divide. Put another way, this is a problem that does not scale. That is, many believe that if there were a way to make a technology instruction website that was somehow self-directed, people could just teach themselves how to use a computer, and then pass on the URL and others would learn. Unfortunately, as I've stated before, many people with low technology skills are often facing a myriad of other challenges and one-size-fits-all solutions do not work for them. I've seen various things that do work well, or work better than other things, and I've compiled a lot of them together here with links, examples, testimonials, and additional reading at the end of this book.

I hope that the extensive information presented and explicated here helps to bridge some of this knowledge gap for potential educators and get this information to the people who really need it.

Library Policies

The library has a mission to offer access to information. We've moved to a world where a lot of that information is available electronically. Libraries need to be clear how providing access to the internet serves the library mission. This means not only having a clear technology mission at a library level, but making sure that staff understand the library's role in providing publicly accessible technology. Front line staff then can pass this message on to patrons. This is not to say that the library must be a static entity with regards to their public access offerings, just that the world of computer and internet access is vast and having a clear sense of the library's specific purpose can make everyone more secure that they will know when it's being done right and when the situation could use improvements.

So, the easiest way to start this process right is to have policies. If you have policies, now is the time to examine them. If you do not have policies, consider this an incentive to get them. Almost all libraries that I have been to have policies about materials, library space usage, and policies about what to do if there's trouble (ranging from natural disasters to unruly patrons) in addition to the usual personnel policies and meeting room policies. There is also usually a set of technology policies that a library should have in place to ensure that staff and patrons understand the library's technology environment. The good news about a set of technology policies is that they can be used as a positive marketing tool for the library's technology offerings, as well as a more dry "this is what we offer, this is what we don't offer" statement of facts.

If written well and enforced consistently and fairly, the library's technology policies can support a positive and engaging technology atmosphere that is welcoming to both experienced and novice users.

The Policy Gamut

It's important that you make sure that users are aware of your policies in a contextually appropriate way. While each library will have some specific circumstances that are built into their policies, generally speaking many policies are fairly cookie-cutter. Policies need to be appropriate to the library, reflective of the library's mission and above all, plainly stated and generally linguistically accessible. Let me restate, because this part is important: *if patrons agree to your policy but do not understand your policy, that's not really having a policy.* The fact that other people do this does not make it okay.

Let's be honest, for the most part you do not have policies to protect you if you are involved in a complicated legal battle. In most cases, you have policies so that patrons and library management and library staff will have a shared set of expectations about how the library technology is supposed to be managed and used. For policies that do actually involve legal situations—filtering policies if you are covered by CIPA, to name one example—I strongly suggest that you have legal counsel assist you with verbiage. For the rest, just get started, if you don't already have them. It's better to have a so-so policy than have no policy at all.

In most cases your library is not starting from scratch. You have established patterns of technology use and you may have policies in place for the systems that you have. I'll outline a short list of policies that the library should have, with some guidelines for each one. Note that not all of these policies are patron-facing. It's a good idea to have staff internet use policies and guidelines as well, if only to satisfy your board and/or human resources. I tend towards the permissive end of most usage policies so I won't tell you what your policies should say, but rather what areas they should generally cover and maybe what questions they should be asking. For a small library some of these policies may be grouped together. No matter what your library does, these policies should be part of any technology class, even if just given out as handouts.

Remember that your policy is not an end user license agreement (EULA) and it is not really supposed to substitute for a legal contract, so keep the language understandable and the tone-friendly. Also, keep track of the places your policy is located, so that if you have a printed internet use policy and a policy listed on your website, both of them are updated when changes are made. Having a revision date on an internet use policy may seem like a silly addition, but it can be very useful in figuring out if the policy you are looking at is the most recent version.

Computer Use Policy

Many libraries have this policy and the internet use policy wrapped together since nearly all libraries offer computers with internet access. However, it's possible that your library has stand-alone PCs that are available for people to word process or play games without getting online. If this is the case, it's still important to have a policy to indicate acceptable uses and the level of support and maintenance that the PCs receive. A basic computer use policy usually explains what the PCs are available for, how patrons need to save their work (On to portable media? Does the library provide it?) and what the time and space limitations are (Can people share a PC? Can people bring in their coffee?). The largest concern for non-internet PCs appears to be space. Some libraries offer laptop loaning programs in lieu of workstation-type PCs.

Internet Use Policy

Most libraries with public access to the internet have some sort of policy, but it's always a good idea to look at it with a fresh pair of eyes and make sure that the policy is keeping in line with your patrons' usage and staff's expectations and abilities to monitor and moderate PAC uses. Even in the most smoothly running technology systems, policies can use some adjustment and possibly mid-course corrections, so be sure whatever your policies are, they are revisited on a regular basis, even if this happens infrequently. A good policy contains a few sections that can be elaborated on as necessary for the library. Here's an outline in no particular order:

1. The library's mission
2. The library's policy on internet use, short form
3. Elaboration on the policy (use cases, interpretations, specifics, etc.)
4. Patrons' rights and responsibilities (what is okay, what is not okay, what happens if they break the rules)
5. The library's rights and responsibilities (what we try to offer, what we guarantee)
6. Special notes about
   - minors/parents
   - filtering/censorship
   - how and when the policy gets changed

7. Places to go or people to talk to for more information or questions or complaints or a printable/web version if one is desired
8. Other related policies as appropriate

Wireless Policy

If your library offers wireless to the public, there is a good chance that you already have a wireless policy. Is this policy made available to patrons before they log on to your wireless? Do you have what is known as a "captive portal" where users have to click-through a policy page before actually getting online? This is usually the easiest way to get users to affirmatively acknowledge your wireless policies. Larger libraries such as Boston Public Library use this method to allow patrons to choose whether they would like their internet access filtered or unfiltered. When a patron first connects to the BPL's wireless network, they arrive at a page that asks them if they want filtered access, which is available to anyone, or unfiltered access which is available to authenticated adult card holders. This sort of thing can be set up using freely available software and is worth building in to any library system that offers free wireless.

While wireless seems like it might be a bit high tech for novice users, many new laptop owners find wireless internet to be one of the first things they wind up using on their computer. Here are some questions your library should consider with your wireless policy:

- Is the wireless accessible from inside and outside the building?
- Is the wireless available 24/7?
- Is the wireless access filtered or unfiltered?
- If filtered is there a mechanism for a patron to get unfiltered access if they ask for it?
- Is the wireless access limited in any way (i.e., bandwidth caps or downloading caps)?

Social Software Policy

If the library is active in social networking sites, it may be making contacts and connections with patrons and non-patrons via other websites not owned by or controlled by the library. It's worthwhile delineating how the library will be using these tools and what constitutes appropriate use of these sites by staff members acting on the library's behalf. One of the more difficult things with libraries using social software is that often there's a blurring of the personal/professional lines; it's important to indicate the extent to which the library's other policies do or do not apply to its interactions on social media sites. For example, if your library has a Facebook page, it may be impossible to keep the names of the library's fans private. And if patrons use the library's Facebook page to ask reference questions, those questions may be much more public than patrons' questions asked at the library.

Savvy patrons will likely understand this, but for novice users who are just learning about social software, the library's use of these sites may indicate to them that there is some sort of seal of approval or extension of trust that applies to these sites. Be as clear as you can be what the level of your library's interaction is on these sites, and what level of control it has over patron data on these sites. Here are a few questions you can ask or answer:

- Which social software sites does the library use in an official capacity?
- What is the library's policy concerning interactions with patrons on these sites?
- What does the library share on these sites?
- Does the library have a policy about who they "friend" on these sites?

Privacy Policy

Your library probably already has a privacy policy that concerns the sharing of patron information, reading records and other similar information. In the digital age, this should be expanded to include information about patrons' internet usage and trackable data from the public access computers, if they use them. Generally speaking, it's good computer hygiene to make sure that personally identifying information is wiped from computers on a regular basis in any case (browsers should keep no passwords, history files, cookies, or download histories). Sometimes, people don't know all the places where patron data can hide in a large and complex system.

We're used to the idea of patron privacy when it comes to personal information and transactional information (i.e., *who* checked out *what*), but we're less clear on the line when it comes to things like behavioral data, who was on our website when, or who left a comment on our blog from what IP address. As people interact with the library digitally, they leave a digital trail that should be paid attention to and considered when thinking about patron privacy. While it may not be something that is taken into account in privacy legislation, it's definitely information about our patrons, people whose privacy we claim to uphold and protect.

Consider doing a "privacy audit" to make sure staff are aware of all the ways in which patron data is handled and retained. Michael Matis from SUNY Albany has written about privacy audits[1] and describes them this way:

> *A privacy audit is a systematic review of the data-collection practices of an organization to determine if the practices are consistent with the privacy policies of the organization. It helps to ascertain what the life-cycle of patron data should be, i.e., how data with PII about patrons is collected, how it is used, how long it is stored, and when it should be deleted.*
>
> *A privacy audit does not mandate the disposal of records. . . . It is an opportunity for librarians to discuss the role of data in the library.*

Thinking about functions like email or chat reference, or patron interactions at outreach activities, or computer sign-up lists and what happens to the patron data after it has served its purpose are worthwhile exercises for a library. In many cases, the patrons may not even know or care that their personal data exists on a sign-up list somewhere in a drawer, but if the library has policies about retaining patron data, this should apply to all data, not just patrons' reading lists. Once the library completes an audit, there should be some sort of policy-style document that comes out of it that explains the library's legal and ethical commitments to patron privacy.

Staff Internet Use Policy

Many libraries that have internet use policies for patrons do not have a similar policy for staff. While I'm personally of the opinion that it's useful for library workers to have as unfettered access to the internet as possible, limits may have to be placed in the interests of sharing a community resource. At the very least, it's good to make sure that all staff are on the same page in terms of what amounts of internet use are acceptable in the workplace and what sorts of behavior would possibly pose a problem. As I've mentioned before, I think it's worthwhile for all staff to have their own logins to shared computers and to not monitor staff internet usage, but having a policy just to outline the outer limits of acceptable behavior can be good groundwork for dealing with potential problem areas.

Policy on Technology Donations

In brief, donated technology is almost always more trouble than it is worth. If your library is in a region where people may have cast-off computers and other gadgetry, it may be appealing to try to cut some corners by reusing others' machines. Frequently, however, the library lacks the resources or staffing to accurately assess whether donated technology fits into the library's overall tech plan, or whether the material is in good working order. The library should have a policy in place for what donations they will accept and under what terms. My rule of thumb at the libraries that I work for is more or less like this:

- Monitors—Don't accept any monitor that is older than a few years. Don't accept any non-flat-screen monitors.
- Computers—Don't accept any computers that are older than the ones the library currently has. Don't accept computers without cables.
- Laptops—can sometimes be useful as additional wifi access points in the library. If a laptop is in good working order and has functional wireless, I will often take these as they're easy to store and can be used by patrons if the public access computers are full.
- Peripherals such as scanners and extra drives—rarely worth the trouble unless the library has a digitization project going that is in need of scanners.
- USB drives—always useful for patrons who may need a last-minute way to save work. Make sure patrons erase them before donating them to the library.
- Software—rarely useful though possibly okay for a library book sale.
- Computer books—treat as you would treat any other book donations.

Lastly, if your library has donated technology sitting in a storeroom somewhere, get rid of it. Take it to an approved disposal center or donate it to a local computer rehab place. Often having "backup" computers in closets or basements can give us a bad estimation of what our tech situation really is. My best advice is to clean house.

Leading versus Following—Tech Assessments

One of the larger divides that isn't mentioned much in the library literature is whether the library is dealing with a community that is generally tech savvy with some users who are not, or whether the library's community is generally not tech savvy. I see this in my work often represented as a rural/urban divide, but it isn't always. Sometimes it can be very dependent on just a few people in the community, particularly the librarian, setting the tone. So, while it may go without saying that every community will have some very savvy and some non-savvy users, having a realistic assessment of the general tech profile of the community relative to the library is important. Because if the library is an island of tech knowledge in a sea of tech ignorance, it needs to develop services and programs that position itself appropriately. The same is true for a library that may be trying to keep up with its community's tech needs.

I call this the "Tech Leader versus Tech Follower" problem. Is your library leading the community in tech adoption and interaction, or following the path the community has already set? Your library may be in a position where it needs to keep up with the tech desires of its community. We see this scenario played out over and over again by tech boosters, the "Hey, if your library isn't offering video on demand, it's going to fall behind the curve and become less relevant to its patrons!" I'd like to go on the record as saying that I personally don't feel that this is true, though I'd definitely consider non-anecdotal evidence that I am mistaken about this. I call these libraries the Tech Followers; they are providing technological services primarily in response to patron demand. This can sometimes mean letting the patrons choose what services are implemented. Frequently, we see this in terms of low-level policy issues as well as larger programming decisions. I'm thinking of examples like:

- allowing patrons to use USB drives to move documents back and forth
- allowing pop-ups or the ability to enable pop-ups so that patrons can print boarding passes
- offering Firefox as a web browser option

Alternately, we have libraries whose patron base isn't requesting tech services and the staff may not be tech-savvy themselves. They often decide to offer tech services based on a few different things:

- offering what their consortia or state offers or requires
- offering what the library staff are personally using or are comfortable with
- offering services that they perceive of as baseline-normal even if they may not be normative in the library's geographical location

In these cases, the libraries are the Tech Leaders in their communities, driving technological adoption and awareness. We see this a lot at my location in Vermont. We have databases available at a state level through the Vermont Online Library program <http://www.vtonlinelib.org/> and many libraries have signed up for the Listen Up! Vermont program <http://listenupvermont.org>, which provides digital audiobooks to libraries via OverDrive. In many cases, we're seeing patrons who are brand-new to the whole idea of digital media, purchasing MP3 players, and learning to download MP3 books simply because we've made the program available and appealing to them.

Both of these situations, the Tech Leader and the Tech Follower, are fine, but it's important to be aware of what sort of library you are. The library's relationship to its patron base is slightly different depending on whether your average patron is more tech savvy or less savvy than the library environment generally.

Community Analysis

A part of any real outreach program is doing a community analysis. You figure out what the makeup of your community is and then try to figure out how to provide services to the entire community, not just the people who are already coming to the library. This is somewhat different than just interacting with the patrons you already have, because often there are people in the community who are not coming to the library for whatever reason; effective outreach programs will often be directed towards engaging and attracting them. In many cases, these community analyses find people from different cultures or non-English language-speakers who do not see the library as having materials for them in the library. In a best-case scenario, your library can begin collection development in the languages spoken by the community, and hey, you have a bunch of new patrons!

Outreach is a little weird because it often focuses on people who we perceive as needing library services and not necessarily the people who just feel that they have no use for the library. This is important in a tech environment, because we do ourselves a disservice when we assume that people who have computers and broadband at home don't need the tech services the library has to offer. In fact, I think this is often a sign we need to step up our game and find ways to offer tech services to patrons who may already be set with broadband and computer ownership.

Having technology available that meets your patrons' needs is an essential part of providing technology to a community. However, if most of your community already has computers and broadband at home, you may need to position yourself differently. The first step is figuring out the tech make-up of your community. This can often be difficult because data such as "Who has broadband?" or "Who has a computer?" is often not available on a town-by-town basis, or it's data that is owned by the local ISPs who may be loathe to provide it. Widening the scope of the data to a level where this information might be collected, i.e., county or state, might make it worthless as an indicator of your particular community. This is not a solution with an easy answer, but it's worth trying to look into it so that you know the make-up of your entire community, not just the patrons you see in the library.

The Numbers

While I don't have the answers to these things specifically, here are some metrics below that you can look at, or try to look at, in your community. This is generally not the sort of data that you can find in the U.S. Census, but I've included some links in the webliography that give you some good places to get started.

- Computer ownership
- Computer use at home
- Computer use at work
- Laptop usage for these same locations
- Broadband use at home
- Broadband use at work
- Broadband availability in the community, i.e., What options are available?

- Dial-up use
- Cell phone use
- Cell phone availability (many rural areas have limited cell phone availability)
- Wireless access points and/or internet cafés

You can also do a separate survey to see what people are using at the library itself. This is different from a community analysis, but can net useful data. I've framed this in terms of questions below that you can ask your patrons. Usability testing and other more qualitative questions will be covered later in the chapter. Obviously, you need to make all survey responses confidential.

1. Why did you come to use a library computer today?
2. Were you able to complete the task you came here to do? Why or why not?
3. Which software programs do you use at the library? Are there other programs you feel we should offer?
4. What are your favorite things about the library's technology offerings?
5. What do you like least about the library's technology offerings?
6. Have you been to the library's website?

The Library as Tech Follower

In this scenario, the library is in a tech savvy community overall. This does not mean that you are not working with people affected by the digital divide, but it means that they may be in more of a minority position relative to their community than in a tech leading community. Your community is likely more affluent and more educated than in a tech leading community. People are more likely to have the option of broadband at home, whether or not they decide to avail themselves of it.

This was a point that was brought up when I gave my South by Southwest talk[2] with Jenny Lish from New York Public Library. She works with people who have little or no tech knowledge and yet they are living in places where they could, if they chose (and could afford it) have computers and broadband at home. Where I live, people could have computers at home, but broadband is literally not an option, or the only option is costly satellite. In the areas where broadband is available, it is often low-cost because that seems to be the only way that broadband ISPs can coax users into adopting it. People in these communities often have multiple ways of accessing the internet for free or for a low cost.

Libraries in tech savvy communities may also find that there is a disconnect between the tech savviness of their patrons and the tech savviness of their employees. This varies from place to place. However, since tech savvy communities tend to be more affluent communities and since many, if not most, library jobs pay at the low end of the scale for people who are technologically proficient, you may find yourself with a savvy community and a not-so-savvy staff. While this should be addressed with future hires, you have to play the cards that you are dealt and find ways to set expectations for staff interactions with technology and train people up to competencies they may not already have.

It also makes sense to have people from your community, people who are tech savvy, serve as some sort of an advisory group (formal or informal) to help the library determine what they should offer and support technologically. The needs of individual communities vary greatly; and knowing that the community may be technologically advanced still does not necessarily open a clear path of best practices.

Additionally, a tech-savvy patron base may mean a lot of donated labor and materials for various tech projects. If you have patrons who are upgrading their technology frequently, their cast-offs may be better than your stock equipment. As noted previously, it's important to not just blindly accept technology donations, but having a policy and procedure for what is on your tech wish list and what you do accept can give people a way to assist and possibly, help the library with bottom-line budgeting and tech planning.

Library as Tech Leader

In many locations, especially rural and remote locations, the library is the sole public provider of internet access and may be the only place that many people from the community ever go online. This means (more so than in tech following communities) that the setup of the computers and the way the internet is accessed is more likely to be perceived as "normal" because people have no other baseline from which to assess their technological landscape. This also means that the decisions that the library makes regarding technology are less likely to be challenged by the patron base, who may not know there's another way to interact with technology.

In this situation, we're in a position where we're actually "setting the tone" for people's attitudes about technology, even though we may not be aware of it. Tech novices will often look to people in positions of authority or community reputation to gauge their emotional reaction to situations that they're not sure how to take. So, if the librarian is frequently flustered and flummoxed by technology, and if she's the only person they see who is interacting with it, they'll think that this is a normative reaction. A lot rests on what the patrons perceive as attitude. Even library staff who may not be very tech experienced can set a "you can do it" tone, and present computers that are functional, clean, and properly configured.

The important thing is not to overwhelm staff or patrons with too much technology that is poorly understood, but rather to accept that technology is going to be part of the library's mission moving forward and that everyone has a lot to learn. I've seen library projects, such as small-scale digitization programs or oral history recordings, really go a long way towards easing people into interacting with various sorts of tech machinery that they might not otherwise think they were capable of. Obviously, you don't want to toss everyone into the deep end of the pool with this stuff, but you can look at small-scale projects and online ventures as a way of educating people about the things people can do online and make it seem less like something that only other people are doing. For example, in response to a patron's question, you can say "What's Twitter? Let me show you the library's Twitter account...."

What Libraries Offer

Technological offerings aren't uniform across libraries in the United States. While people have a general idea that you can get internet or wireless internet access at a library, many don't understand that the hyper-local aspect of libraries means that services frequently vary from town to town, to say nothing of state-to-state variations. This book assumes that you work in a library that has broadband access to the internet and at least one public access computer, but it's possible that even that isn't the case. I'd just like to outline a normative approach to library technology offerings and toss in a few statistics from the various studies that I've read.

Internet access at libraries is a huge deal. According to the report *Opportunity for All: How the American Public Benefits from Internet Access at U.S. Libraries,*[3] a report conducted by the University of

Washington Information School and funded by the Bill & Melinda Gates Foundation and the Institute of Museum and Library Services (IMLS), one-third of the U.S. population over the age of 14 used library computers to get online. This represents nearly half of all public library visits. The most revealing statistic in all of this is that three-quarters of these people also had internet access elsewhere.

This survey is interesting, but also needs to be properly contextualized. It contains the result of a phone survey of library users and non-users, a web based survey of only library users, and case studies at four U.S. libraries, none of which had a service population of fewer than 30,000 people despite the fact that over 75% of all public libraries have service populations of fewer than 25,000. So, I have mixed feelings about it in a general sense, but I think it's useful for some of the statistics. Likewise, the most recent as of this writing *IMLS Public Library Survey* <http://harvester.census.gov/imls/publib.asp> is a little out of date (data from 2007, published in mid-2009), but gives us a good idea of what libraries actually have.

The IMLS report outlines the average number of public-use internet computers per building and per 5,000 population (defined as living in the legal service area of the library). The state with the highest number of public access computers per capita is Vermont with 7.2 PACs for every 5,000 users. Amusingly, Vermont is also nearly at the bottom of the list of average number of computers per building with 4.7 which is not that surprising for a rural state with many small libraries and no large libraries. The thing to keep an eye on is the averages. The average number of PACs per building in the U.S. is 12.5 with the range going from a high of 24.36 in Florida to a low of 4.49 in New Hampshire. The average number of PACs per 5,000 population is 3.55 with a range from Vermont's high of 7.2 to Nevada's low of 1.92 (with Hawaii just one-hundredth of a computer higher). How does your library compare to this or to other libraries in your state?

There's a little more data on electronic offerings in this survey, but not things that *I'd* be curious about—such as what programs library computers run, or whether the library's website offers chat reference—and more of just what sort of digital offerings the libraries have. In fact, even though the average number of "Electronic Books" for all libraries nationwide is a nice big-number sounding 1,428.1, the median number of electronic books among public libraries in the United States is zero. The same is true for "Current Electronic Serial Subscriptions" where the average is 17 and the median is zero. The average number of serials subscriptions in libraries with populations of over one million in their legal service area is, however, 1512.2. So, I'm not sure what we can take away from those numbers.

ALA is the best go-to reference for this sort of information, even though their advocacy angle is obvious, and expected. Their *State of America's Libraries*[4] reports, published in 2009 and 2010 are great capsule looks at what libraries are doing, alongside the data to back up these evaluations. In terms of more normative data about what people are going to their libraries for and what they are getting, here are some more interesting statistics from that report:

- Eighty-two percent of public libraries offer wireless access
- Thirty-five percent of libraries offer technology training classes (urban: 52.5%, rural: 24%)
- Fifty-three percent provide point-of-use assistance, i.e., helping people use computers in the library one-on-one
- Two-thirds of public libraries help patrons complete online job applications
- Seventy-nine percent of public libraries helped patrons apply for or access e-government services (up 23% from last year)
- Twenty percent of libraries report partnering with other agencies to provide e-government services

This ALA report also has some of the social statistics that I'd been hoping the IMLS report would have contained, including data on what virtual reference services a library provides—62% offer email reference, 31% offer chat reference, and 19.5% offer IM reference. I'm curious about these statistics since I'm not certain what differentiates chat and IM reference, but I'm pleased to see that someone is collecting data for questions such as "Does your library have a web page?" and "Does your library filter its internet access?" More in-depth looks at these statistics are available via PLA's *Public Library Data Service* report available for purchase, but ALA has reprinted some of the statistics in their report.

It's not necessary to "keep up with the Joneses" in a general sense, but it's useful and important to know what libraries in your general region are providing as well as what libraries are providing nationwide. I expect ALA's ongoing State of America's Libraries reports to have more information on social tools in the coming years, but even now you can take a look at this report and the others I mentioned and draw some normative conclusions. Some libraries do technology training while others don't. There's a 50/50 chance that a patron in an urban public library will be able to take a technology training class, or be able to have a staff person help them when they are using a computer. This number shifts slightly (and confusingly) when people are using library computers in order to access e-government services. So, while wireless internet offerings are fairly widespread at this point, the same is not true for tech instruction. Is this an unmet need in your community?

4

Planning for Pedagogy

We need to make sure new graduates comprehend the impor-
tance of providing service and access to all populations: techno-
novices, the techno-elite, everyone in between, various age
groups, the haves, the have-nots and everyone in between. The
library should be first and foremost in the community a leveler.
There all are welcome and access is open and free. The playing
field for creativity, exploration and learning should be flat.

—Michael Stephens, Assistant Professor,
GSLIS, Dominican University

As librarians who are used to having the library's resources at our
disposal, we can sometimes forget that we have many tools to assist
patrons with technology besides the technology itself. The most
important thing on this list I think is *clout*. People look to us as
experts, rightly or wrongly, about the things within our walls. So
the things we tell people about technology are taken seriously and
given attention. This is generally true provided that the information
that we're giving out passes the "reality check" steps and people
find the information we give them to be basically credible and useful
to them.

This issue of having "cred" on tech topics is one of the main
reasons that, while I personally have very strong opinions about
certain technology topics, I try to turn off the evangelism when

I'm trying to explain things. If people want my personal opinion, and they often do, they will ask for it. Otherwise, I need to put my librarian hat on and try to give them information and access to resources that will solve their problems, not recruit another person for my sick-of-popups army.

Our Toolbox

This section is a non-tech list of some of the resources we have that may be more powerful than we think when assisting tech novices. One of the things about people who don't use technology is that you can't actually reach them effectively using technology. This may sound like common sense, but I don't think many of us totally take it to heart. If you're recruiting for a basic technology class, putting a link on your website may not be reaching the people you're looking for. Obviously a link on the website is still quite worthwhile, since people can tell other people, it's good for outreach and as a reference point; but if you want to address your offline patrons, you need to go offline to reach them.

Bibliographies and Booklists

A good booklist or bibliography can serve a useful function. Similar to a great book display, it can highlight parts of the collection that you feel could use some more attention. For every tech class that I teach, I have a short bookmark-sized booklist to hand out to people on their way out. This shows two things:

1. That the library is still committed to print-based resources on technology topics (sometimes a source of stress or concern for offline patrons).
2. That the library is a go-to place for tech information in multiple formats.

Sometimes, this is also a good professional exercise because maybe the library *doesn't* have as much information on tech topics as it could. You'll find some suggestions in the Bibliography section at the end of this book, but yes, this can be a difficult area to do collection development for. The reason this is true is because as technology becomes more ubiquitous and the cost for delivering content in print expands, many content providers turn to the web for lower-cost publishing. This, in turn, means fewer print resources available for admin   ask   meta   rct   mecha   gml   yho   libml   aba   bk   flkr   flck2   lib   fb

http://www.pbclibrary.org/mousing/m10.htm

Mousing Around: Mousercise   +

Good job! Now give this one a try. Click the 10.

5 5 5

5105

5 5 5

Page ten of the Mousercise tutorial.

people who need them the most, people who can't make good use of web-based content formats, yet.

So, in addition to the bibliography suggestion, you'll also find suggested links to a few carefully selected skill-building websites or even printouts of particularly useful tutorials that people could read along with. When someone comes into my drop-in time for the first time, and if they can't use a mouse, the first thing we do is sit them down at a computer, give them a quick "this is what the buttons do" pep talk and start them clicking away through the Mousercise tutorial created by the Palm Beach County Library.

The tutorial is a very simple series of steps each of which involves clicking somewhere on the page which reveals the next page. Students can usually proceed through it in a self-directed fashion and at the end there are some skill-building games for further practice. It's straightforward and no-nonsense, takes about twenty minutes, and seems to be fairly simple to understand for most people. It's also a decent litmus test to see how students do in a self-directed learning environment. Some people enjoy this sort of thing, other people feel like you've tossed them into the deep end of the pool without a life preserver. Gauging people's reactions will give you a good idea how to move forward.

Once people know the library website can be a go-to place for well-selected tutorials and skill-building resources, perhaps they'll click around and see that the web has other interesting things to offer?

Skills Checklists

Another print resource is the skills checklist. Patrons may often not know what they don't know. If you have a ready set of handouts that give them basic information, they may be able to, in conjunction with that, tell you what they most need to learn. I often get people in my drop-in time saying "Well, I just need to learn about computers." when in fact, what they'd like to do is look something up online, which requires certain computer skills and not others. Having checklists of skill sets can help people not just self-evaluate to see what sort of class they might fit into, but also give them an idea of what there is to learn generally.

Try giving a patron a list like the one on the next page and let them know that it's fine if they don't know things on the list, but we'd like to make sure we have as accurate an idea of their abilities as possible.

You can add to or subtract from this list based on the offerings in your classes or what you have available in your library, but the general idea is using print resources in order to gauge a good starting point for introducing a novice user to technology resources.

Partway Technology and Attitude

This could, I suppose, also be known as "gateway technology," but not everyone finds gateway drug jokes funny. As most people who use technology regularly know, the idea of "What is and is not technology?" is on a bit of a continuum. That is, most people realize that a computer is a piece of technology, but what about an iPod? A VCR? A CD? How about a microfilm reader? Letting people know, slowly and politely, that they're already using technology in small ways and that in fact the library is full of it, may ease what people perceive as the huge leap from where they are to where they're going.

I try to get this across in other ways as well. Patrons have many competencies and having competency with a computer is just one other skill to learn. It's useful for solving problems, staying in touch or maybe for entertainment, but it's not an end-all or be-all on its own. I've had students tell me frequently that they're "stupid" because they have difficulty remembering a complicated set of steps. I assure them that they're not stupid and that they have many skills that someone who is computer-smart may not have, and sometimes it's a good excuse to take a break and talk about all the things that

I Know How to

Basics
- ☐ turn a computer on
- ☐ label the individual parts of a computer
- ☐ start a program on the computer
- ☐ use a mouse to point and click
- ☐ use a mouse to drag and drop
- ☐ right click to open a context menu

Internet
- ☐ open a web browser
- ☐ go to a website of my choice
- ☐ use a search engine
- ☐ send and receive email

Files and Folders
- ☐ open a file
- ☐ save a file
- ☐ rename a file
- ☐ save a file to a USB drive

Word Processing
- ☐ start a new line
- ☐ change the font size
- ☐ print preview
- ☐ center a line of text

Spreadsheets
- ☐ type a number into a cell
- ☐ change the number formatting in the cell
- ☐ change the text formatting in the cell
- ☐ use a formula to do a calculation

Photos
- ☐ get photos off my camera
- ☐ rotate a photo
- ☐ crop a photo
- ☐ burn a photo to CD

Questions
- ☐ use a help file
- ☐ change my preferences
- ☐ contact tech support
- ☐ CTRL-ALT-DEL

they can do. Living in a rural area, I'm constantly amazed and impressed by the skills and abilities of the people who come into my classes feeling stupid. Part of being an effective instructor is about putting technology use into perspective for people and helping them find a place for it in their own lives as something other than an insurmountable obstacle.

Setting Standards

Although this is discussed in more detail in the Maintenance and Ergonomics section, it bears noting here that one of the things that we provide for novice technology users is an idea of how computers *can* work, that may be different from their experiences with computers elsewhere. Many people come to the library after their experiences at work or school or home have frustrated them, and made them skeptical about technology. Coming to the library where they can use a computer free of viruses and pop-ups and visual clutter (They can do this at your library, right?), where they can sit in a decently comfortable chair and have the keyboard and mouse be accessible and reachable by them, with a monitor that is not in the direct sunlight and not covered in cat hair can make people understand that there are ways to configure and use technology so it is not a daily maddening struggle.

Add to this description our general expectations of "Yes, this is something you can do. People do this sort of thing all the time. Let me show you how to do this." and people who might otherwise be digitally distant or digitally uncomfortable can become digital hopefuls.

The Cheeseburger in the Library

I have a generalized notion that I call the "cheeseburger in the library" problem. As libraries have expanded to fill more niches that have been created by the dwindling amount of public space in this country, there's a sense in which we've undergone mission creep. Please note that I am fully in favor of libraries doing pretty much anything that is positively supporting their missions and their communities' access to information. That said, sometimes the expanding roles don't come with clear guidelines. So when you add a café to your library, what does that do to the existing food policy? When you have gaming night at your library, do you have to adjust the children's PC filters to allow games during the daytime? And, to my original point, if people want the library to be a place where they can eat cheeseburgers and watch television, is it the library's role to meet those expectations?

As usual, I have more questions than answers and my usual response is "That depends." However, just because something is desired by the community does not mean it is the library's job to provide it. We must be mindful of our mission, our limitations, and the community context in which we operate. Public computing offerings have typically had more demand than supply. Not a bad problem to have, but it means that we need to try to be equitable about providing access to this scarce resource. Having sensible policies that you can fairly enforce is a good start and can lead to less trouble down the line when disputes enter the picture.

The Library's Computer Is My Computer

One of the more important things to keep in mind about providing public computing access for novice technology users is that while you may understand that the library computers have their own quirks and foibles, someone without access to other computers does not. If your library computers have a complicated login procedure, or if they have a restrictive firewall or filter, or if you can't plug in USB drives, a novice user will think this is how *all* computers work. Keep this in mind when deciding how to configure public access to technology at your library. Every step the library takes that makes the computers not work like a normal computer will be skewing the novice user's ideas about computing generally. And while there is no normal or average computing environment per se, we should strive for keeping people's technology experiences as hassle-free as possible (which I guess in some sense is abnormal for many of us), if we want to help people not only use the technology but fold it into their lives.

This involves, and yes this is a recurring theme, setting standards of what you think a library computer should be able to do, and letting people know this. This may also involve accepting feedback that your ideas are incorrect, outdated or confusing, and working this feedback into a new set of standards.

So think of this as a start to a conversation. I always liked how my health insurance company gave me not just a list of responsibilities when I became a customer, but also a set of rights. While I think you have to be careful with words like "rights," it was nice to know that my health insurance company felt that I had a right to a second opinion, for example. This indicated not just the legal issues involved concerning what they'd pay for, but also their general attitude towards my health care. I'll talk more about what a list of specifics might look like in the next section.

Think of these policies both in terms of responsibilities—how you require technology users to act and what your expectations are—but also rights—what offerings you expect to have and what assistance you will provide. In the "helpful but not necessary" category try to provide options for people when the library's offerings couldn't meet their needs. One library I worked at had 45-minute time limits at the computers for patrons, and these were pretty strictly enforced because we were a busy library. This was not enough for some patrons and while we'd offer some workarounds such as giving them more time if the library was less crowded, we also gave them a list of other places with public internet access where they could have more time on a public computer. This was in keeping with our other library goals of providing access to resources and it seemed to be an appreciated service.

A Cautionary Tale

I once worked at a library that had policies about email access on public access computers. They had few computers and high demand, and wanted to make sure people were using the computers for library-related tasks, mostly. So we had about twelve public access computers. Some were catalog-only, some were patron-only (i.e., you had to be a library patron with an active card to use them) and some were available to everyone who came to the library. Slightly complicated policies, but manageable.

However, the library board had decided, before I began working there, that they wanted to make email access at the library a perk for card-holding patrons. The library served a lot of tourists and seasonal workers and the board wanted to try to "convert" some of those library visitors into patrons with library cards. The idea was that people would see email access as valuable enough so they would pay a fee to obtain a card, thus raising money for the library. So, the patron PCs had email access. The non-patron PCs were divided into two categories: one quick-check computer with email access but a shorter time limit, and three PCs with internet access but no email. When I say "no email," what I mean is that our systems librarian blocked email access on those PCs by blocking the URLs of the most popular email clients. This library was near a popular vacation area and this system was complicated to explain, difficult to administer, and generated a lot of ill will not just among library users, but among the reference staff who were also in charge of granting PC access. This was in 2005 and we didn't have automated sign-ups yet.

When someone came to the reference desk to use a PC, we had to ask them a series of questions, the worst of which was "Do you want to use the internet or do you want to check email?" This was a confusing question for the tech-savvy as well as the tech novices and made me feel ridiculous asking it. We did away with the system over the next two years. I'd like to say I had something to do with it, but I'm not sure that I did. The reason that I bring it up now, five years later, is because I think sometimes the library winds up having totally reasonable positions they are trying to advance (in this case "Encourage people to get library cards by making the PC offerings for card holders more attractive than those for non-card holders"), by using technological means in ways that break technology. While we technically *could* filter all known webmail URLs, this resulted in PCs that could only access some of the internet, a de facto filtering system that wasn't really above board, and a lot of confused patrons and staff. Additionally, it meant that staff had to be on the lookout for people accessing webmail on the non-patron PCs and give the webmail URL to the systems librarian. A webmail address that might work for a patron one week would be blocked the next week.

For board members or staff who are not tech savvy themselves, this whole path is fraught with pitfalls. The board members weren't really aware that they were creating internet options that were confusing and counterintuitive, they just wanted to find creative ways to solve revenue problems. The systems librarian was tasked with solving the email "problem" without having input into the decision-making process. And the staff had to make the best of a bad situation and explain this system to patrons. Novice users felt like "internet" and "email" were separate things a computer could do and our policies seemed to confirm this. This made people's technological understanding worse, not better. So, think of policies as one way to not just regulate technology use, but also to publicize it. The more sensible your policies are, the more users can take what they learned in the library's computing environment and bring it with them into the larger world.

Setting Up the Classroom

Not everything we do is formalized instruction. It's a good idea to have delineations between the different levels of tech services we offer to patrons. Some things we need to offer to all patrons while some more specialized offerings make sense to provide in a classroom setting. My general approach is to try to have the classroom be a place where students can succeed at the things they attempt, if not the first time, then at least before they walk out the door. Here are some suggestions and tips for trying to make the classroom a place where students can have a good user experience:

1. *Have example documents for students to work on.*
   Novice users are often slow typists. If I need to teach people to format a document, waiting for them to type it is going to use up valuable class time. Have a sample document ready (I often take something from the Internet Archive that is freely available to use, Gift of the Magi for instance.) so that students can spend time actually working on a document, not creating it. Have this document already on the hard drive for them to open, edit, and save.

2. *Have a plan for saving work.*
   Lately, we've been giving students small USB drives to take work home with them because learning how to name, save, and transfer documents is useful. In any case, make sure you have a plan for students to keep their document, even if they won't need it later. Options are saving to a local My Documents folder, saving to a USB drive, burning to CD, saving to a floppy, or emailing the document to themselves. Each option has pluses and minuses. Figure out which you'd like to do before you get to the end of class.

3. *Be prepared to adjust.*
   You might have a whole class scheduled on clip art and formatting and then you figure out that a few of your students don't know how to click-drag. Make sure you have some alternative plans in case students are generally faster or slower than you were anticipating. When you're teaching a small class, a few slow students can really alter the pace you set. Along with this, feel free to set expectations and pre-requisites for the classes so that one student who can't do a basic task doesn't keep the whole class at their level.

4. *Repeat, repeat, repeat.*

   Weekly classes can be tough because adult students have lives and forget a lot in-between classes. Each class that I teach starts with a quick vocabulary lesson, which is also a good time to check how much from the last class sunk in. We talk about the words we learned last week, talk about what we're going to do in today's class, and spend a little bit of time wrapping up at the end of each class with a review. I have handouts that not only cover what we'll be doing, but also have illustrations sometimes of what exactly I'm talking about: "This is a bulleted list," "This is a numbered list," etc.

5. *Specialize.*

   MS Word and Excel have multiple ways of doing the same, or similar, things. Unlike your automobile or other physical machine where only one thing turns on the headlights, there are a lot of ways to do each thing with these programs. So, for example you can print a document by going to the file menu and selecting Print, typing Control or Option P, or clicking the Print button on the toolbar (which is more of a quick print, really). Sometimes people have taken classes before that stressed one type of action over another. So people learned the menus, but not the key commands. I usually talk about the options and then use one and stick to one. Be consistent. If you're teaching the toolbar buttons for Save and Print, also teach them the toolbar buttons for Copy and Paste. And know your audience. If students are finding mouse control challenging, then key commands may be better for them in the long run.

6. *Have a final exam.*

   I don't mean for this to be something scary, but it can be tough in a class to figure out if students on their own can actually do the work. We want them to do well and they want to do well so it's easy to see successes in areas that may not be quite so far along. For both my Word and my Excel classes, I have sort of a document-as-final that I give to students. The Excel document is a five-page worksheet and each page of the worksheet has a small set of tasks to do on it, ranging from formatting text to adding clip art to doing simple calculations. The Word document is a lot of text that gives the students problems to solve: "Make this line bold." and "Put these words in a table and put a box around it." Usually during the last class (I usually teach Word or Excel as a series of 3–4 two-hour classes), we spend the last class doing 30 minutes of review, the students work on the final for an hour, and then we do a wrap-up. It's not graded so the trick is to know if they remember how to do the different things we've learned and especially, if they have mastered some of the basic topics.

7. *This is what you know.*
   Part of the final class also involves a troubleshooting step because I firmly believe that in order to be good technology users, people must be problem-solvers, at least to a small degree. So we learn how to solve problems as we go. When I'm working on a document and showing students how to select text, I'll make the common mistake of hitting a key on the keyboard when I have several paragraphs selected. Everything is gone, replaced by a single lower-case *k*! What to do? I show students how to use the Undo Command (on the menu, on the toolbar, and especially CTRL+Z) and we learn how to rescue victory from the jaws of defeat. It's empowering and straightforward and teaches students what to look out for. Here is a list from one of my handouts about problems we can solve:

   > My document was replaced with the letter *k*!
   > Why can't I move my cursor there?
   > Why is there all this white space in my document?
   > Why is it changing the words that I type?
   > Why is it making my words capitalized?
   > I typed a whole sentence with caps lock on!
   > The picture I put in my document is too big!
   > I want to see/not see the rulers and the margins of my page.

If you don't know how to do any of these things, a quick F1 should be able to straighten it out for you.

Structure and Pacing

The big difference between teaching adults and teaching younger people in a school-like setting is that adults usually have a choice, they can be somewhere else. So while I don't totally subscribe to the "customer is always right" philosophy, I do try to understand that my students' time is valuable and that even though the class is covering basic topics, it is serious. Accordingly, we start on time, we have a break partway through, we review at the beginning and at the end, and we don't give homework. I don't see a point in giving students more work to do outside of class and, to be perfectly honest, some of the students don't have computers at home anyhow, so we have to be realistic.

I do try to explain what is different between the computers at the school and the computers they might have at home. Specifically, just because they're using office software does not mean that there are not online aspects to how Word and Excel operate in this day and age, with clip art, templates, and additional help available online. People who use a modem to access the internet might be confused when they are looking at clip art and suddenly their computer makes a phone call!

The big challenge is having tasks that are interesting enough for adults and yet simple enough for people with very low computer literacy. Especially when I was teaching Excel classes, students would get really zoned out if I started talking about random numbers, and yet they weren't sophisticated enough to start their own projects. I'd do projects that I thought might mirror small-scale projects people might try: keeping track of who had donated to an organization, keeping track of personal finances in a simple checkbook program, and keeping track of an exercise routine and tabulating results. Otherwise, the math part of the spreadsheet program would overwhelm the other very important functions and people would tune out.

Instruction Happens

I hope that by now I've made it clear that library instruction is more of a process and less of a specific "give this sort of class in this sort of way" situation. Libraries need to model sensible approaches to technology and ownership of library technology environments and issues overall. However, formal instruction is familiar to people and can be a great way to get information across that is either frequently requested—email classes, word processing classes—or very specific to your library environment—library databases, getting the most out of an OPAC. It's good practice for staff and often a good option for patrons who need a little more handholding than the average library staff person can provide them.

When I was working at a large public library in Vermont, I taught many one-off "getting started with email" classes, really just classes about email terminology more than using specific software. The classes were well-attended and we got good feedback on them. I would see some students taking this same class over and over again. At one point I asked one of the students, an older woman who was frequently in using the library computers, why she was a repeat student. She said that she didn't use email yet, but that she enjoyed the classes and said "Every time I come back I learn a little more." For her, the classes were partly an excuse to be social and get out of the house, and partly a very slow-motion doorway into interacting with technology in a way she wasn't fully ready for. When my outreach contract was over at the library, the class offerings declined in frequency until they were giving one computer class a month.

The good thing about classes is that they present a situation that involves the least "reinventing the wheel." You can create a syllabus and some teaching materials and have a class that is repeatable. With technology classes particularly, the most important part is students being able to ask questions and learning skills that they can actually apply *in the library environment*. So, while it's good to talk about "computers in general," your students will appreciate knowing how to use the computers in the library specifically. Additionally, it's good to draw a useful line between what the library is set up to help you with—computers in our library—and what is not within the scope of library services which may be people's home computers, laptop configurations, etc.

Basic Class Setup

Many libraries do not have a specific lab or area for teaching classes. This isn't optimal, but it's what we've got. We've done a few things to get creative with technology instruction in my rural library settings as shown below

1. Used the local school computer labs when we have a one-off class or set of classes. Often the schools will make their classrooms freely available once school gets out. This requires a bit of familiarization with the school's lab environment and some networking skills (the human kind, not the computer kind), but is often win/win for everyone involved.

2. Used the few public computers when the library is closed. Sometimes we'd have class in the hour before the library is technically open. This can be a little hard to finesse with the community, but it can get you some quiet time on the computers.

3. Taught without a computer. For novice users, you can often dispense with the computer altogether. I've taught email classes with handouts and had people do exercises with pen and pencil and it works fine. Sending people home with handouts that they feel that they actually understand can be better than memories of interacting on-screen that are less clear.

Some people do not enjoy learning technology topics on the actual technology itself. Many of my students bemoan the fact that their new computers do not come with an owner's manual and really prefer to have something with a print index where they can look things up. While I do have a bit of a "kick the bird out of the nest" feeling about this—I think people putting off actual computer interaction indefinitely are doing themselves no favors—it's good to also have print materials available. I've linked to some good books on basic technology topics in the Bibliography at the end of this book, but you'll need to see which ones are still current by the time you read this.

My general shorthand feeling is that the *For Dummies* guides, once you get beyond the name and help your patrons get beyond the name, are good for novice users; and the books from O'Reilly Media are good for more advanced topics. The *Visual Steps* guides are often well-liked by older students or people who prefer a more pictorial approach to learning; they have a set of companion websites that include teacher's guides for the books as well as a site called Computer Certificate for Seniors which will test information given in their guides. The guides and the certificate tests are available whether or not you've purchased the books. Note: the certificate tests will automatically sign up the test taker for the *Visual Steps* newsletter.

So, have these books nearby where you are doing the instruction, optimally available for checkout. If your library offers other regular classes, have the schedules and/or sign-up sheets available. Have other library promotional materials available in case people coming to your technology classes are not regular library users.

Giving an Overview

Even though we have limited time for instruction, it's still worthwhile to spend a little of this time getting to know students and going over the objectives of the course. Start your classes with a brief introduction of who you are and then go around the room asking people's names and what they are hoping to get out of the class. Then, ask them to tell everyone "something you like to do on the computer" or something similarly innocuous. This is not just a fact-finding mission, but also a way to gauge people's interest or disinterest in technology generally and to get a feel for people's skill and ability levels before you start talking. It is also a good time to re-set expectations, in case people were expecting something that the class wasn't going to offer. This does take up some time, so encourage people to keep it snappy, but it's worth it to have a slightly more cohesive class and some personal knowledge about the students.

You can also start classes with some brief vocabulary, again not just to make sure people know the words, but also to restate the traditional patter that if you do use a word later in the class that people don't know, to tell you so that you can make sure everyone knows it. I try to write things down as often as I can because some people just aren't auditory learners. And if I've got enough advance planning time, I try to have a handout or two that will have some of the topics I've covered in addition to contact information and hours for the library and maybe a web address or two.

The big deal with classes of novices is that you have to teach towards the middle, which is often unsatisfactory for many people. In a class with students who already have some technology skills, people will know how much they know and be okay with it; they can tell if they're a little ahead of or behind the class and can adjust. Often tech novices don't even really realize the scope of the playing field and may think that they've got a decent understanding of the topic, if only the teacher wasn't going *so danged fast*. Again, set expectations appropriately and try to leave time after class so that students who are truly struggling can get some advice after class. At the same time, make sure that after-class time is limited somewhat so that you don't get people trying to explain their tech support woes to you in the hopes that possibly you can fix them. This is really no different than most of our public interactions. Most people are normal, a few people are not, they are all our patrons and we need to find ways to most effectively serve them.

The Technology Itself

We also send out a meta-message with our technological setups and approaches. People are absorbing lessons even when we're not actively teaching them. How we create our technology learning environments and how we interact with the machines ourselves sends out signals and cues about the technology environment. So it pays to be mindful of how you structure these environments and what messages you're sending when you talk about technology.

Often computer systems are set up in the space available, with the materials that are available, without much thought being given to whether that set-up is the optimal one for how the computers are supposed to be used. Here are some things to think about when making choices about the technological context that is created at the library. Think about them when setting up systems for novice users, as well as communicating to other people who are interacting with those systems.

Maintenance and Ergonomics

If you are in a situation where you're using a computer eight hours a day and it's the primary thing you do for work, you need to be concerned with ergonomics. *Ergonomics*, as defined by the International Ergonomics Association, is "the scientific discipline concerned with the understanding of interactions among humans and other elements of a system, and the profession that applies theory, principles, data and methods to design in order to optimize human well-being and overall *system performance*."[1] In short, it's making sure that you and your tools can interact smoothly for better productivity and injury avoidance.

In practical terms, this means not just making sure you've got a workspace that is conducive to working in a non-injurious manner, but also that you establish good patterns for taking breaks, stretching, and resting your eyes. For most of our students, this is not something they necessarily have to worry about, but it's good to establish healthy patterns early. Here are a few things to keep an eye on as you're setting up computer workstations in the library and talking to patrons about how to set up their own systems.

Mice and Mousepads

Older computer mice have moving parts in them including a rubber ball that requires a certain amount of friction in order to be able to operate. Newer mice operate with LEDs and sensors and not only don't require mousepads, but can behave erratically on shiny or glossy surfaces. Often when computer systems are upgraded, a new mouse is placed on the same old mousepad without reflection on whether it is actually needed. Since mousepads do present a small limitation for novice users who can get confused when they reach the end of the mousepad and their mouse isn't all the way across the screen, they should be removed if not necessary. And students should be instructed in how to pick the mouse up and reposition it on the desktop or tabletop in order to continue the movement of the mouse in the direction it was going.

Chairs and Keyboards

In an ideal world, chairs would be adjustable so that they would fit a wide variety of patrons. If this is not the case at your library, at a bare minimum position chairs to be at an average height that allows an adult to sit at the computer with feet on the floor and legs under the desk. Children's area chairs should be appropriate to the size of the desk the computer is on. Chairs shouldn't tilt too much and they shouldn't roll too much. Having a footrest for shorter patrons is a great idea, though certainly not required.

Keyboards should be somewhere where they stay stable. If they're on a pullout tray, that tray should be able to be fixed in place. If they're on a table or desk, there should be rubber feet or something to keep the keyboard from sliding too much. If the keyboard has little feet on the bottom to angle it, flip them up!

Screens and Privacy

Different libraries have different approaches to the privacy screen idea, where a patron can see their computer screen well but others cannot. Some libraries employ privacy screens so that you have to get right up behind a patron to help them with a computer issue. Others are so dim that it makes the entire browsing experience sub-optimal. That said, if public access computers are in a public place, sometimes employing privacy screens is a better solution than having librarians or patrons constantly having to be looking at things they might prefer not to look at.

If you do employ privacy screens, make sure they are removable. If at all possible, there should be some indication that they're even being used in the first place so that patrons can know to remove them. Be sure that clean-up crews understand special considerations for cleaning privacy screens and replace them if they become uncleanable. (There are also ways to ensure that patron's *data* is cleaned after they use the computer, which is covered in Chapter Six, the Google section of this book and I think that should be a considered a part of general computer privacy considerations.)

Scunge and Schmutz

Nothing decreases user confidence than a grubby-looking work area. I'm not saying that reference librarians need to be taking the time to clean all the finger grease and lint out of the computer mouse, but someone has to at some point. Eventually the mouse will stop working well, and this is a bad first impression for patrons who don't have a clear idea of how well mice should be working in the first place. Have some sort of regular clean and tidy routine for the PC areas which includes:

- cleaning the scunge out of the mice
- getting the schmutz off of the keyboards
- cleaning the fingerprints off of the monitor
- wiping down the desktop area and removing random paper, crumbs, and stickiness

Less frequent maintenance can include making sure the keyboards are in working order and giving the monitor and/or PC a once-over with a paper towel and some cleaning fluid to keep the grunge at bay. Forward-thinking librarians may note that buying black peripherals instead of white ones will decrease the need for frequent cleaning.

Software and Upkeep

A lot of software maintenance should be relatively transparent to the end user of our PCs in a library setting. The general rule of thumb is to have some sort of process whereby your PCs upgrade themselves at an off-hour time on a regular schedule, say weekly.

This should take care of browser updates, operating system updates, Java and Flash updates, antivirus software updates, and whatever else needs updating. It may not be possible to do all of this entirely unattended, but there should be a system in place so that it doesn't happen while patrons are expecting to be using the PCs. I worked somewhere once where the system would do all crucial updates starting at 5:00 PM on a weekday which was fine if everyone went home at this time. But for someone who had to work even five or ten minutes late, they'd find the network brought entirely to its knees by all the concurrent updating. It was a suboptimal system.

Viruses and Updates

While it's somewhat outside the scope of this book, I also want to briefly discuss the issue of viruses. Thanks to bad software, malicious people (usually) in other countries, and a lot of misinformation spread through marketing channels and tech reporting, many people know how to blame computer viruses for their computer woes, but not how to address the issues that they think the viruses create. When a computer isn't behaving properly, people blame "viruses"; this somehow lessens their responsibility for getting the computer working properly again. Viruses and our protection from them comprise a large degree of the "helpful" alerts that computers give you.

It is our job as maintainers of public computers, to not only minimize or eliminate viruses on public computers, but also to minimize the *appearance* of something not working right. To a user

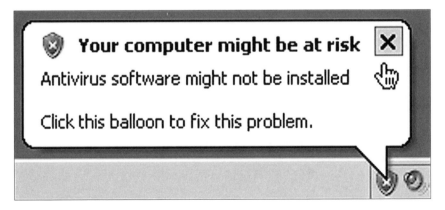

A common error message that is more scary than helpful.

who doesn't have a good understanding of a Windows environment, constant pop-ups or "helpful" reminders can interfere with their ability to use the PC in the limited time they have available. It also reduces their confidence in our systems and our ability to maintain them.

People also come into the library or computer lab with their laptops concerned about an error message they are getting. This message may be from antivirus software, from a virus masquerading as antivirus software, from the operating system warning the patron about the lack of antivirus software, or from some combination of these. While it is not our responsibility to clean up a patron's hard drive, it is nice if we can give them advice on what they might do besides "Take it to an expert." which they often interpret as "Spend a lot of money on this." Sometimes that's what needs to happen, but often there are simple ways to at least do a first pass check for problems. The usual troubleshooting steps that I might do—Googling error messages, checking software forums, and the like—are not necessarily tactics available to someone with low-tech literacy.

By the time this book appears in print, whatever is the current reigning antivirus software—I think right now people are suggesting Malwarebytes and AVG, both of which have free versions available for individual users—may have been supplanted, but it's worth knowing that antivirus software tends to work when used correctly, and is often free. Many low-cost laptops come loaded with "free" trials for subscription-based antivirus software, such as Norton or McAfee Antivirus programs. These products work, but they also toss up a ton of error messages once the free trial is over and they can be difficult to uninstall and replace with something that is actually free.

There are some basic things that can be done to troubleshoot oddly-working PCs:

- Start the PC in Safe Mode by holding down F8 when you start up the computer; use "Safe Mode with networking" if you need an internet connection
- Do Windows/Microsoft Updates first if these haven't been done
- Install antivirus software—often the easiest way to do this is have the latest version on a USB drive since viruses can sometimes interfere with internet connections

- Make sure antivirus software is updated before running it
- Run antivirus software in safe mode; this may take time
- Follow instructions given by antivirus software for removing or quarantining infected files
- Start computer normally; see if the performance problems still exist
- If the virus can't be eradicated, try other antivirus software; Google the virus name, reinstall the operating system, or take the computer to professionals
- If all else fails, back up the user data and reinstall the operating system

Obviously, these are generic steps for treating a generic problem. However, most virus eradication really is a lot of trial and error. This can be frustrating to people who see antivirus software as something that they are paying to eliminate this problem. It can also be frustrating to people trying to solve the problem, since there are a lot of dead ends and re-assessment involved, nearly impossible to do when someone is looking over your shoulder. If you have a patron who seems to have regular trouble with viruses, it may be worth making one of your early web literacy projects teaching them to Google the error messages they are getting. There are a lot of people who are smart about computer viruses and will help you for free, but they hang out online and have to be interacted with there.

One of my favorite places for this sort of assistance was the Hijack This forum where you could run a piece of software on your infected PC which would spit out a bunch of gobbledygook, to be copied and pasted into the forums so that people who were experts in reading these logs could give you advice. This forum lives on as part of the general Malwarebytes Forum <http://forums.malwarebytes.org/> and is an incredibly useful place to go for malware removal advice.

Here are some preventative steps computer users can take before they have problems. Note: this list is somewhat PC-centric, as are most viruses.

- Make sure their operating systems and antivirus software are regularly updated
- Use the Firefox web browser and be cautious when visiting adult and/or file-sharing websites
- Make sure the primary account on the computer is not an administrator; this can be a bit of a hassle for software installs, but worth it in the long run

- Run the firewall supplied by Microsoft
- Do not open email attachments from strangers

In short, if the public PC is throwing up frequent error or alert messages, see if you can either fix the problem or alter the settings to receive fewer warnings. Error or alert messages tend to rattle patrons, and as much as the best advice is often "Oh, ignore them." I don't think that it's always such a great idea to encourage people to not heed warnings. I'd rather try to ensure that they were only seeing warnings that were, indeed, important.

Touching the Patron's Computer

If a patron comes to you with their own computer and a question about it, remember that the instant you touch it, you become responsible for it—or might. This is important to know since for a lot of us the natural inclination would be to take a look, and say "What's the problem?" and then click around a try a few things to help out the patron. However, for people who don't understand the interrelatedness of all of the systems that make up a functioning (or partially functioning) laptop, they may not be too clear on the cause and effect relationships that occur with it. So, if you touch the laptop in an attempt to fix one problem ("Why can't I get the wireless working?") and try some things ("Oh, it looks like your firewall settings are too high."), you may find yourself responsible, in the patron's eyes, for whatever wacky stuff happens next ("Hey, ever since you fixed my firewall settings the sound doesn't work."). It is a good idea to use caution before touching a patron's computer.

This reaction is not necessarily a bad thing and doesn't necessarily mean that patrons are ignorant, etc. In the oversimplified understanding they often have with technology, it often seems logical that the last person to change things around on the computer, who wasn't them, might be responsible for whatever problem it is having now. I have also found this to be the case in my non-library tech support work. If you install someone's DSL, they will call you whenever it goes down. If you set up a spreadsheet for someone, they will call you with Excel questions. If you fix the sound on their laptop, they will call you when they can't figure out how to play a DVD. Unless you have unlimited free time, my best advice on the topic of touching patron computers is: don't.

Are You Accessible?

I mentioned this briefly in the Library Patrons section of Chapter One and I don't need to go over it in too much detail here, but I do want to mention accessibility. We know for a fact that people with disabilities are online less, and do less online. What we don't know for a fact is why this is true, though we can make some guesses. What we can do at the library is to make sure that our public computing facilities are as accessible as possible to the widest variety of patrons. We should also make sure we communicate with all our patrons to make sure their needs are met and test out new technology services on patrons with varying levels of abilities.

We often think of accessibility as making accommodations for disabled patrons, but I'd like to adjust that definition somewhat. While the Americans with Disabilities Act <http://www.ada.gov> does strongly encourage public institutions (under the pain of potential lawsuits from affected people) to make their products and services accessible to the letter of the law, I think we should be doing more than that. I support the idea of universal design. Universal design is mainly an architectural idea that forwards the notion that designing buildings, as well as products and other services, to be accessible and usable by *everyone* is a better goal than just trying to build in features that benefit people in wheelchairs or people with visual impairments. Of course, it goes without saying that legally-mandated access is a bare minimum, but in many cases, thoughtful design choices that offer people with disabilities access can benefit many different members of society. The common example of this is curb cuts. While they're specifically for people in wheelchairs, they also benefit parents with strollers, people who are unsteady on their feet, people riding bicycles, etc. OXO products are another good example. When I use their thick-handled can opener, I don't think "Hey, I'm using an accessible device." I think "Wow, this sure is handy to hold on to."

In many cases, we don't have a lot of control over our physical structures, or can't make changes quickly to them. However, our technology systems are often very malleable and customizable and we should be communicating this to our patrons through words and actions. Patrons without a lot of technology experience may not even know that the computers they are using are modifiable. It's our responsibility to find ways to communicate this effectively and also train our own staff and volunteers to be able to impart this information.

What Is Disabled?

When you think of people with disabilities, you might default to more traditional conceptions of disability such as someone who uses a wheelchair to get around, or someone who can't see. However, there are many different situations affecting someone's life that could benefit from some assistive technology. This is especially true for the so-called invisible disabilities such as color-blindness or cognitive impairments, such as dyslexia, in addition to the category of people who may not consider themselves disabled, but who could use some accommodation such as people with bad memories or poor hand-eye coordination.

So, building accessibility into your service and technology offerings instead of waiting for people to request them is a forward-thinking way of trying to address all kinds of people. Since the public library is for the entire public, i.e. everyone, and many studies find that about one-fifth of the population has some kind of disability at one time or another; this is a decision that makes sense.

The major categories of disability types according to WebAIM (Web Accessibility In Mind <http://www.webaim.org/>) are:

Visual—including blindness, low vision, and color-blindness
Hearing—deafness, partial deafness, or other auditory disabilities
Motor Skills—inability to use a mouse, limited fine motor control, or other mobility concerns
Cognitive—learning and reading disabilities, distractibility, inability to remember or focus on large amounts of information

I would add to this disability list some sort of emotional component. Not to say that computers making you irritable is some sort of disability akin to blindness, but that for many of the people I work with, there is a definite emotional component that seems to interfere with their ability to interact with technology. Whether this is out-of-control anxiety about putting personal information online, or irritability at not being able to make the computer do what you want it to do, we have to address users' emotional issues, or be aware of them, as we try for the "last mile" equivalent of computer and internet users. The level of accommodation we provide is dictated to a certain extent by the laws that govern us, but it should not be limited to the bare minimum.

Checklist for PC Accessibility

While acknowledging that real-world considerations occasionally get in the way of doing our best to provide access, this is a topic that requires assertive and continuous advocacy and rarely gets it. It is much easier to build accessibility in to technology systems initially than it is to retrofit. (Please see the Appendix and the Webliography at the end of this book for additional resources concerning designing for optimal accessibility.) Below is a short and incomplete list of questions your library should be asking about the accessibility of your technology. Additionally, if you are providing access to software or websites through vendor relationships, you should be seriously pressuring vendors to make their products accessible. If you are redesigning your website, accessibility should be a bare minimum of what you require from your designer.

Library PCs
- PCs are in a place where wheelchair users can access them.
- PC colors provide enough contrast to people with color blindness.
- Alternative pointing devices are available to users.
- Users can adjust volume, color contrast, and font size of PCs.
- Users know who to speak to on staff if they require adaptive technology or assistance with PCs.

The Library Online
- Website uses ALT tags for images and links are appropriately descriptive.
- Website is accessible to people with color blindness.
- Website clearly indicates linked content.
- Website uses valid HTML and CSS.
- Multimedia content on website is appropriately captioned or available in alternate formats.
- All website functions are accessible via keyboard.
- All abbreviations and jargon are defined; readability level is appropriate to users.

I also believe it's important for the library to be proactive in this regard. Let people know that you care about accessibility. Put a statement on your library's website. Have a staff member in charge of adaptive technology. Work with local disability advocates to set high standards for accessible digital and non-digital content. We're already accessible building-wise, we may as well keep moving in this direction.

Interfacing and Defaulting

Going beyond basic accessibility requires extra work. I'm assuming that you have limited control over your interfaces at the library, though you should try to simplify them to the extent that you can. My local library where I sometimes substitute recently switched over to Koha. The main catalog search page includes a search box and also a large login box which is useful if you want to place a hold on a book or do other personal tasks, but daunting if you don't understand why the box is there in the first place. New users, unfamiliar with the idea of the online catalog generally, felt vexed by the login box, even though it was over to the right-hand side and was not, in fact, necessary for searching the catalog. The librarian asked me if there was anything we could do about it. After a little Googling, it turns out that there was. We hid the login box using some straightforward CSS hack, and now the catalog has one search box. All I did was some copying and pasting.

The default search on our catalog is set to search "everything." Some catalogs default to searching just the title, which is great if someone types a title into the box, but bad if they type anything else. Remember, our novice user may not have mastered the art of the pull-down menu, so if that's where your choices are hiding, those choices are dead to them. Let's review another few user interface design tips to see if there are things you can tidy up before you start educating:

- Make sure you're not using colors as the only context clues for links.
- Try to avoid the use of technical terms whenever possible.
- Have your OPAC look as much like the rest of the website as possible and interface with the library website when needed (i.e., for help files and the like). If possible, have the search box on the main page of your website. Or have two search boxes, one for the website and one for the catalog.

- Have a special page available when a search returns no results with links to search tips and help or a search box where users can try again.
- Try to make sure that you're not just giving people the generic help files that came with your OPAC if they're not applicable to the way you have your system configured. Nothing says "I don't care about you." like help files that refer to features that don't exist.

Be responsive. If you're consistently seeing users make the same errors repeatedly, consider that the user may not be broken and that you might be getting a nudge to change something about the way people access your catalog. That said, if people are frustrated about something they're trying to do with one of your vendor's databases, something that you can't really control, you're also allowed to commiserate, "Yes, that is a little confusing. Let me give you this handout that explains the basic steps to do this." Again, I am a firm believer in using screenshots with circles and arrows as an effective way to let a novice user think that they can go forth and do a little exploration on their own, striving for improvements where you can, and acknowledging your limits when you can't.

5

Basic Instruction and Explanations

Listen and ask and then listen again. It's easy to assume you know what someone needs and go "fix" the problem. I've had people ask for help printing an email and then walked by them retyping it all into a new email—not knowing about copy/paste or forward. I now ask what they are ultimately trying to do and take the opportunity to teach.

—Kim Peine, Dorothy Alling Memorial Library,
Williston VT

Someone walks into your library and needs to use a computer. What do you do? In many cases, you point the patron to your public access PCs or possibly the PC you use for making reservations on the other PCs. What if they can't use a mouse to use the PC reservation system? Or what if they have a scrap of paper with an email address on it and they need to find a way to send a message to that person, but have never used a computer before? This is the meat and potatoes of this book, the nuts and bolts of the thing. This is not to say that the correct response is always to drop everything and chaper one the patron to an available PC and sit them down and start going through mouse exercises. It is, however, to say that you should have a plan and you should start the process of setting expectations as soon as you realize that you are dealing with someone who needs more than the standard "The computers are over there." indicators.

Obviously, the amount of time and effort that you can spend on patrons will vary dramatically not only from library to library, but from hour to hour. Here are some building blocks for not just managing your available patron-helping time more effectively, but also having materials at the ready for patrons who could get going with just a little jumpstart and some handouts. Although this information is presented in generalities since I don't know your specific setup or specific rules and regulations, remember this: anything is better than nothing. Just having some handouts with current screenshots and circles and arrows showing people how to print a document or log onto Yahoo Mail will go a long way towards providing real help for people who are too often ignored and overlooked.

Tech Terms and Meanings

At the beginning of every class I teach, I do a little segment on vocabulary. Not because I think it's always best to start with some random-seeming definitions, but to gauge what students already know, and assess what they will need to know moving forward. If I am teaching sequential classes, every class after the first class starts with a five- or ten-minute refresher on any words that seemed to be new or unusual in the last class. Every class handout has not only a small list of words in a "words we know" section, but space where students can add other words they are unsure of. It's important to try to draw distinctions for students between what is a normal vocabulary word, i.e., one they are expected to learn and know, and what is jargon.

We frequently have this problem in the library world; we expect everyone to understand and use our made-up terms, such as *OPAC*, when most people have more common words they'd rather be using, such as *library catalog*. The fact that library catalogs were not online doesn't make it any less ridiculous to be calling a catalog an *online* catalog in 2010 or beyond. Similarly, it was a huge wake-up call for me to realize that for many older adults, the word *database* is pretty unfamiliar. I'd known it since college, but I gave one of my first library outreach talks at a local senior center talking about all the great resources and databases we had. When I was done someone in the audience, fairly politely I thought, said "That's great, but can I ask one question . . . what's a database?"

John Kupersmith, a reference librarian at the University of California in Berkeley, has done some writing in two important topic areas: technostress and library design. These two topic ideas are more linked than you might expect. His personal/professional website contains a subsite called *Library Terms that Users Understand.* <http://www.jkup.net/terms.html>. It's a frequently updated collection and collation of over 50 library usability studies that examines real study data and explicates which words assist users in finding information and which words don't. Some of the studies are small or fairly localized, but it's a good reminder that words we may find totally commonplace may be inscrutable to the average library user. If you're preparing library signage, you may want to consult it.

Meaning Is Use

Along these same lines, if you expect students to know and understand words that explain technology, make sure to use them yourself in ways that are as unambiguous as possible as you explain the tools. As tempting as it is to refer to something on the screen as a *thingdoo* or a *whatzit*, you're helping your patrons when you say something straightforward like "Double-click on that icon on the desktop." and point at it.

When I teach classes, I do a little introduction at the beginning, being clear about the fact that if I am using words that my students do not understand, *I am not doing my job well.* So, if they could please help me and just raise their hand if they hear an unfamiliar word, I'll be happy to explain it for them. This is also when I point out the usefulness of websites like Wikipedia. When I teach a class in Photoshop, for example, I am often using terms that a student would be hard-pressed to look up in most conventional dictionaries. Using Google for technology terms is similarly not that helpful—though typing in the phrase "define _____" can sometimes net good results. However, Wikipedia not only includes long explanations of what each tech term mean—terms such as *jpg, open source,* and *USB*—but often interesting backstory on how that term came about, and links to references where people can read more about the term. For students who are motivated to learn more, this is a great resource and can often include a teaching moment about what is good and bad about Wikipedia while you're there.

Everyone's idea of starter technology vocabulary is a little different, but I'm including some alphabetized lists of general words in a few topic areas below to help get you started getting yourself in a novice user mindset. I'm not sure how many people saw the slightly self-serving set of person-on-the-street interviews that Google did a while back[1] where many people who regularly use the internet admitted they didn't really know what a browser was. And people viewing this video, discussing it on the web, were surprised! And at the same time, it's in Google's best interests that people are confused about the difference between the internet, a browser, a website, a search engine, and many other topics, as Google expands to create products that are hybrid versions of these things. Lots of good books on getting started with technology have lists of vocabulary. Make sure that you understand technological terms and try to use them in context when you're speaking to new users—and encourage them to ask questions if they hear a word that they don't know.

Vocabulary

Many of these technological terms do double-duty, and show up in a number of places. I've tried to mention them in the context where their introduction would be most appropriate. And again, this is just one person's opinion of words that are useful, but maybe it will help you choose words that make sense to your patrons.

Basic Vocabulary—*button, click, clipboard, default, dialog box, double click, hardware, help, key command, keyboard, menu, menu, mouse, network, options, preferences, program, right click, scroll bar, software, toolbar, trash/recycle bin, window*

Mac-specific Terms—*Apple menu, command key, dock, option key, system preferences*

Windows-specific Terms—*control panel, hibernate, start bar, start menu, system tray*

Digital Pictures—*crop, dpi, gif, jpg, layers, megapixels, pdf, pixel, png, resolution, rotate, tiff*

Email—*address book, attachment, Bcc, Cc, contact list, Fwd/forward, HTML email, mailing list, plain text, Re, To*

Internet—*back button, bookmark bar, bookmark, browser, cache, cookies, favorite, Flash, home page, HTML, Javascript, link, search engine, status bar, toolbar, URL, web page, website*

Keyboard—*arrow keys, caps lock, control key [^], delete key, enter/return key, escape key, function keys, number lock*

Memory—*backup drive, backup, byte, disk space, gigabyte, hard drive, kilo-byte, megabyte, RAM, terabyte*

Monitor/Screen—*degauss, desktop, icon, keystone, resolution, screen saver*

Other File Types—*aac, doc, docx, mov, mp3, m4p, wmv, xls*

Portable Media—*CD-ROM, CD-RW, DVD, Flash drive, floppy disk, key drive, SD card, thumb drive, USB drive, USB*

Printer—*landscape, page setup, portrait, postscript, print preview, print screen, resolution, spool*

Search Engine—*advanced search, boolean operators, flavor text, page rank, search bar, sort*

Troubleshooting—*"blue screen of death," 404, CTRL-ALT-DEL, dialog box, error message, reset button, task manager*

Word Processing—*copy, cut, font, format, margins, page setup, paste, table*

Some of these words are very context-specific and some of them are fairly mandatory knowledge for people who want to interact with computers. The trick is to use them appropriately without students or patrons feeling that they need to memorize what the word *postscript* means in order to check their email. Many people approach technology learning like schoolwork in which there is a small set of terms and actions that need to be memorized and once you know the complete set, you're done. Learning technology is not like that. It requires an ability to adapt and learn in an ongoing fashion that can be daunting to people for whom change is somewhat agitating.

Many novice users are not going to get regular exposure to these words in their day-to-day life, so it's a good idea to try to use them descriptively, a little more than you might otherwise in conversation. I've always thought it might be a good idea to make up some flash cards for people, so that they could get more repeat exposure to them and not just be surprised every time a new term comes up, which will be frequently in the initial stages of learning technology. Teaching people ways to look up words using Wikipedia or a technology book with a good index seems like it would also be a good early step in technology instruction. I often think about grade-school classrooms that have colorful illustrations on the walls with the names of things in big letters: *HORSE, CANOE, BERRY*. Perhaps, we need some illustrations with tech terms: *MOUSE, RETURN KEY, MONITOR*.

Jargon and Brands

There's also a small caveat that should be discussed here about jargon, which I mentioned above, and how it relates to brands and branding. The technology world is still the frontier in many ways and there's a lot less disambiguation between brand names and general item names than maybe there should be. So, most people are clear that Kleenex is a brand name that, over time, has come to also be a somewhat generic term for facial tissue or whatever it's really called; the same with Band-Aids and Scotch tape. Novice users don't know what's a brand name and what's a more generic term. And people who sell things have a vested interest in wanting their product's name confused for the generic name. I try to err on the side of using the correct names even when it's a little awkward.

Back when I worked at a mid-sized public library, we had a link to our catalog that required users go from our website to a page where they had to click an image that said "Click here for iBistro powered by WebCat." Now, most librarians would see that and say "Huh, that's a sort of cutesy term for an online catalog." but many patrons would see it and say "Oh, I guess library catalogs on the internet are called iBistros, and I should probably know what WebCat is. . . ."

Similarly, there are a lot of companies who make MP3 players, even though Apple makes the iPod, which is the most popular one. It's a good idea that people don't think that *iPod* is a generic term for an MP3 player. It's also maybe worth explaining that not all portable media players play the same file types. This is especially important if you're trying to help them download digital media at your library. So, I try to stick to terms like *USB drive* or *Flash drive* instead of *jump drive* or *key drive* or whatever brand name it may have. Try to not pass on brands-as-names for tech products in your library, if at all possible as it only confuses things.

What Is a Computer?

As many people know, the word *computer* used to refer to the person who was responsible for doing the computing. People with jobs that required lots of calculations were called *computers*. Now, the word refers to the machine that is being operated by the person. Most people who haven't used a computer before know what one is, though they may overstate their lack of knowledge about the various computer parts and their purposes. I'm going to break down the individual parts and explain some handy metaphors for them. Please see the vocabulary section after this one, for more specific breakdowns of words that can be used to describe technology.

Parts Is Parts

One of the great first steps to teaching someone anything technology-wise is going through and labeling all the parts of their computer. This does not mean opening the thing up and saying "This is your RAM!" but going through their computer and talking about what the parts are and generally what they do. Novice users often complain about feeling inundated with terminology that they actually don't need and so I'd caution instructors to try to approach this step with some pragmatic thinking. For example, while it's good to know where a USB port is and what it's generally used for, knowing what the acronym *USB* actually stands for (Universal Serial Bus), doesn't actually help the novice learner actually do anything, so it's worth skipping.

I often tell students "This part of the computer does this thing. You're unlikely to need to know this, but it's in the manual if you need to know more." Doing an image search for a phrase like "computer parts" can get you some useful illustrations to hand out to students. Similarly, searching Wikimedia Commons is also a useful way to get many images of technological parts with use licenses that usually make them okay to use in at least an educational environment and often more.

Image illustrating proper hand/mouse placement.

So, sitting down and just spending ten minutes talking about computer parts is a great way to start, because it's a good way to determine your students' general knowledge level, share some basic vocabulary, and also to just give you and the user some time to get acquainted. In a public PC environment, having handouts or flash cards that have parts and labels can be very useful. I consider these sorts of handouts mandatory for a classroom setting.

Meet the Computer

For starters, just explaining some basic things like, "This is the monitor, it is not where the computer's brain is." can start people on the road to greater understanding. The trick from my perspective is to get people learning words that will help them as they use their computer and to talk to other people about it. Sometimes, this is difficult because it means passing up a completely accurate term like *CPU* (central processing unit) for a term that is more

Teach users to look for this symbol when they want to turn the computer on.

vague, but more useful such as *computer*. In a desktop environment, explaining the larger parts—monitor, screen, cables, computer, keyboard, mouse—is the first step.

This stage is also where it's good to disabuse people of some incorrect computer notions that they may have. I usually jostle the CPU around a little bit just to show people that while it's important to not drop the thing, a little bumping is unlikely to cause any major trouble. Usually, we'll step through how to turn it on and off, and how the monitor has its own power button and can be off when the computer is technically still on, and yet how if the computer is shut down properly, the monitor also turns off. I also show them how to open the CD drawer and how to close it by pressing on it, since the button can be hard to get to when the drawer is open. If things are hidden behind doors or flaps, this happens a lot with laptops, mention it but don't belabor it. When you're through pointing out the basic features, ask if they have questions.

There is very little symbology to the outside of a computer, but it's good to teach people how to locate the on/off switch. Technically, this icon means *standby* according to the International Electrotechnical Commission 60417 standard, but you can just tell people it's the on/off symbol. This is important for people to know because sometimes this button can be hard to find. On the Dell PCs that we use where I work, there is a large silverish circle that says DELL that looks much more like people's conception of a power button than the actual power button. You can show people that once they can recognize this symbol, they can find it on computers, monitors, laptops, and many other electrical devices.

On our PCs, again these buttons have lights in them that are either green when the computer is on, amber when it's in standby mode, and off when the computer is all the way off. It can be tough to see this light unless you are standing right in front of the computer staring straight at it, which is nearly impossible if the computer is on the floor beneath the desk, or if someone is visually impaired.

It's also good to point out to people that the computer can be on while the monitor is off, one of the easiest tech support problems to solve. People who have also not used a computer in years may also not know that all modern operating systems turn the monitor off when the computer is shut down. This did not used to be true and people may have habits based on older technology. I teach them to look for other signs of computer life such as a spinning hard drive (tough to hear for older ears, but people can feel for vibrations), lights on the keyboard, or the startup beep.

Show people the front and the back of the computer, how things like the mouse can be plugged in and unplugged while the computer is running. Modern computers are nice because you can basically tell a user "If the cable fits into the plug, it's okay to plug this in there." and that will work in 95% of computer configuration cases. I did once see that my landlady had plugged her printer's USB cable, the kind with the boxy end, into her ethernet port and then was wondering why she couldn't print. To be fair, she did give me a call once she realized something wasn't working. Along these lines, it's worth telling novice users that sometimes, for some reasons, things don't work as expected. This is true with our cars, our washing machines, and our computers. While an end user doesn't need to know how to fix every problem that comes up, they need to do the same sort of troubleshooting if this were any other oddly-behaving appliance. I will talk more about troubleshooting in the end of the next section.

Monitor/Screen/LCD

This is the part of the system that gets the most visual attention and yet once people realize that it's not where the thinking happens, they rarely learn about the other parts of it. This is mostly fine. It's worth understanding the short list of things that are good to know about monitors. Very little about the monitor is controlled at the monitor itself, as opposed to by software in the computer, but a few things are. This will vary from screen to screen. The major thing to know is that the monitor has its own power cord, and a cord that connects it to the computer, and an on/off switch. Most monitors will work with most computers. Large CRT (cathode ray tube) monitors are heavy and today most people buy flat screen monitors, which are now reasonably priced. The good news about this is also that old bulky monitors are more or less free, so if you are someone or know someone who is trying to put together a bare-bones system, this part of their assembly is often very low cost.

The rest of the monitor adjustments do things like adjust the height and width of the image, fix keystoning (when the image is wider at the top than at the bottom or vice versa), help the user center the image, and the mystery-meat function called "degaussing" which makes the image on the screen shake oddly, but is really about removing magnetic fields that may be affecting image quality. All of these things may be adjustable via buttons on the monitor, however most people rarely need to use any monitor buttons other than the on/off switch. It's useful to let people know that while you can explain what the buttons on the monitor do (just like some of the keyboard keys) they're unlikely to need to use them, though sometimes it's fun to press the Degauss button just to show them what happens.

Keyboard

Each part of a computer has a bunch of individual subcomponents that also need explaining. How much detail you go into depends on who you're talking to and how much time you have. Ask yourself, "What will give people a good foundation to move forward if they never come back for another computer class again?" The keyboard is probably the most important part of this entire system. This is the part users will be interacting with the most. While the mouse is certainly the most important piece to learn *first*, the keyboard is probably the most important hardware piece to learn *well*.

The keyboard controls the bulk of the user's interactive experience and can be very mysterious to people who have never used one.

And yes, it's possible that you'll have students who have never used any sort of keyboard. While my experience has mostly been that people have at some point in their lives used a typewriter, this is not always the case. So, certain things like typing a capital letter may need to be explained. Other things that are good to explain about keyboards include:

- How to type capital letters and the characters such as # that appear above the numbers
- Which keys repeat on both sides of the keyboard
- How to use the function keys. Note: on a laptop these keys may be activated by holding down the function key and tapping other keys in the keyboard; sometimes you can look for the blue characters on the keys
- The names for keys like ESC and CTRL; "This is the control key. This is the icon that you might see for it: ^"
- How to type key combinations like CTRL-ALT-DEL which is really more about holding down CTRL-ALT and tapping DEL than mashing them all down at once
- How to turn capslock and number lock on and off and where to look for lights that tell you they are on, on some keyboards
- What the arrow keys are generally good for
- What the page up/down keys do
- What the home/end keys do
- The difference between delete and backspace (backspace deletes characters in a leftwards direction, delete is the opposite)
- Special keys your keyboard may have that adjust the volume or keys that eject a CD or launch the Start menu
- How to pop a key off and put it back on, if appropriate

Keyboards are also one of the best situations for having a "These things may appear in different ways, but they have a lot of the same parts; let's look for similarities." discussion. Often novice users with high anxiety levels will get uncomfortable when confronted with a situation that isn't exactly like the situation they have at home or work. Maybe the return key is a rectangle and not an L-shape, or maybe the function keys look different. Try to be polite and compassionate about your response, while at the

Keyboards in 140 Chars.

I asked some people from Twitter what to be sure to mention about keyboards. These are some of the suggestions I received from them:

- Enter may be called return; the difference between delete and backspace, numlock and that the # keys are same in both places
- Keyboards can help explain how computers work. When plugged in they become a working part of the computer. Introduces components . . .
- I've found that people have problems navigating menus and managing windows so shortcuts like control-c, control-s, etc. save time.
- That the return and enter are different names for the same thing; delete versus backspace.
- Keyboards are one way you tell the computer what you want it to do and write the words you want to say to other people.
- Have them "find" Enter, backspace, delete and arrow keys. Explain basic navigation.
- How to use the tab key
- All the "locks" . . . caps, number, function. They are not only useful but easy to accidentally set and not know how to remove.
- Computers are at your beck and call but can't read minds; use this alphabet thing to give the stupid appliance orders.
- F-keys and media control keys, page up + page dow.
- They also need to know that Ctrl+ P, C, V, X, Z, and Y typically do the same thing everywhere.
- There are lots of keys you will never use and that's ok.
- They need to know *NOT* to touch the Function keys unless they know what they're used for.
- Capslock light will tell you whether caps lock is on!
- Function and modifier keys (ctrl, opt, open-apple, whatever), also whatever character map is available
- What the enter key does is a good starting point; also, backspace and how to turn numlock off and on.
- Modifier keys!! Corollary: how keyboard shortcuts are better for one's RSI than mousing over to menus for stuff like copy-paste, etc.
- I suppose it would also be good to show them how it connects to computers and the difference between USB and PS/2 connectors.
- Basic shortcuts, explain shift/ctrl; but it is worth mentioning when typing words wrap/no need for carriage return.
- Arrows, tabs, esc, diff bet cntrl & command, that other language layouts/keyboards exist and why, option, shift, 1 space not 2.

- I teach my pre-k class space, delete, enter, arrows, and spelling their names.
- Some keys (numbers and letters) result in that character appearing on the screen; others, like tab, page down, do things.
- The space between backspace and delete is like the cursor in shape and if you hit the backspace it goes to the left.
- Pressing shift is how you get the number keys to do the symbols—also the basic differences between Macs and other PCs.
- The various control/alt/option/command keys; return = enter in most cases; alt-tab to scroll thru open apps.
- Be sure to mention international caps lock day.

same time explaining that this approach to technology will not be helpful to them and in fact, it will get in the way of them being able to be a happy lifelong technology user.

One of the most common complaints I hear about technology from novices generally is "It changes all the time. I have to install updates and then it looks different!" Teaching users which things are likely to change and which are likely to stay the same is part of giving them an understanding of their entire technology system and enables them to be more in charge of their computing environment. So, in a keyboard situation, see if you can drag out a few other keyboards and show how the arrow keys may look different on different keyboards, but then explain how they do the same things. The same is true for Mac versus PC keyboards. Almost all the keys are the same, a few are different. Users with older computers may see a few weird keys like the Sys Rq or Scroll Lock keys and you can tell them that they may safely ignore them.

A word about keyboards and accessibility—while the standard layout of keyboards is more or less the same across the board, many keyboards can be configured with "hot keys" to perform frequently used tasks ("open internet browser" for example). And if a large-type keyboard isn't financially viable, keyboards can easily be enhanced with a lower-cost "skin" or overlay that has larger high contrast letters printed on them. This is a great temporary solution if you just have a few users who could use this feature and it has the added advantage of being easier to clean than a standard keyboard.

Mouse versus Touchpad versus Trackball and Others

The mouse is the device that most people will use for the bulk of their interaction with the computer. While the mouse seems fairly simple to people who have been using one for decades, the mechanisms involved in something like double-clicking—holding the mouse absolutely still, moving their one finger up and down quickly while not moving the mouse from where it is resting on the table—can be vexing to new users. This goes double for users with fine motor-skill or coordination problems. There are many different types of mice as well, and most are highly customizable. This can mean that picking up a random mouse in a random place can lead to a lot of unexpected results for a new user.

So, it's important to look at two aspects here: what you offer in the library, and what you tell users about the larger world of pointing devices. My advice for a library setting is two-fold, have a very simple mouse with basic features, and have assistive devices available for people for whom mouse use is challenging. It's incredibly simple to fit a PC with a trackball, even on the fly. There's no excuse for making a patron struggle with a mouse if they're having difficulty.

As I said above, the mouse is not the only way to interact with a computer, there are many other input devices available to users and many of them can be customized using software to provide an optimal experience to individual users, not just a generalized experience that is more one-size-fits-all. The major other types of devices are:

Trackball—where the base of the device stays put and users manipulate a ball to move the screen pointer

Touchpad—usually seen on laptops where users move their fingers across a touch-sensitive area, but also can be seen in accessories such as drawing tablets where people manipulate the screen pointer with a pen-like mechanism

Pointing stick—where a small joystick-like device is embedded in the keyboard and manipulated with a fingertip (sometimes called a nub or a nipple mouse)

There are also many devices that I consider "high-powered" mice or trackballs, which have multiple buttons that can be configured in a multitude of ways. By the time someone has come into the library, they may have seen some or all of these options. Or they may have only used one option and are unaware that there are

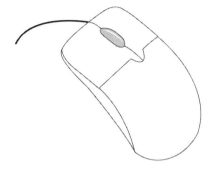

A generic-looking mouse.

others. So, it's a good idea to talk about the mouse in general terms and then move those on to the specifics.

A mouse is a pointing device with a primary button and a secondary button. Many mice nowadays also have some sort of rollerball device in the middle. Even though on most mice the two buttons are the same size, I always tell patrons that the lefthand mouse button is really what they'll be using 90% of the time. This is another good opportunity to explain the difference between "How this may work in this library" versus "How you can use this at home." My mother is left-handed and she often switches her mouse buttons around using software so that what we usually think of as "right-clicking" is actually performed using the lefthand button. Works great for her, but she has to mentally change gears when she uses someone else's computer, and I have to do the same when I use her computer.

Some libraries disable the right-click contextual menus, so it's worth letting people know that this may be another way that the library computers are different from "normal" computers. In fact, I'd suggest not disabling these menus, but we can't always make those decisions. Novice users often click the wrong mouse button and a quick "This is how you get rid of that weird floating menu" discussion (point to a blank area of the screen and click the normal button) is very helpful. Explain that "click" refers to the primary button and "right click" is the other button. There isn't really anything that people call "left click" unless they're trying to disambiguate it from a right click. "Double click" is always with the primary button. This system takes time to be understood. The simple phrase "Okay, now right click on the icon and then click the word Delete." almost always gets a "Right click or left click the word Delete?" response.

Contrasted with PCs, most Macs come with a mouse with one button, or what looks like no buttons. The two currently available mice sold by Apple have no discernible buttons. One comes with a small rollerball on top that scrolls vertically *and* horizontally and is clicked by pressing down on the front part of the mouse. The other has no obvious moving parts, a similar click mechanism, and allows the use of gestures so that a finger swipe across the top of the mouse's surface can cause on-screen scrolling, zooming, or page-advancement. While these are, in some ways, advanced mice, they are also the only ones that come with current Mac systems so you may see students who have them or who are used to them. The Apple Mouse, the one with the roller-ball, comes in wireless and wired versions, while the Magic Mouse is only available with Bluetooth. The Bluetooth mice also require batteries, usually included, which gives one more troubleshooting step to consider if you're having trouble getting them working.

Interacting with the mouse provides a good opportunity to talk about how the computer takes instruction from you. Tell students that their computer is basically a big dumb calculator, that it receives input from you and then does when you tell it. The general order of operations to doing most computer tasks is: Indicate, Select, then Act. That is, tell the computer what you want it to do something *to*, then tell it what action you want to perform. This is useful in word processing, web surfing, or playing Solitaire. The thing about this set of steps is that often people aren't clear about the difference between pointing to something, and selecting something. So, in this example . . .

Novice users often get confused between the location of the pointer—the I-bar between the words *when* and *I*—and the location of the cursor—the blinking line right before the word *go*. This is a critical point for them to understand. Until you've selected a

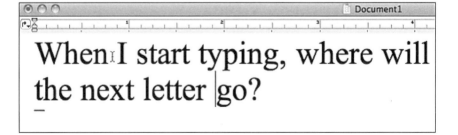

When I start typing, where will the next letter go?

location by clicking the mouse, you're just waving the pointer around on the screen.

Similarly, when text has been selected, whatever you do next happens to the selected text, unless you click someplace else to deselect it. So, in this example, starting to type will delete and replace the word *where*.

As far as an easy set of steps, make sure users know:

1. Indicate—point to the area
2. Select—click or double-click
3. Act—do the thing you want to do or tell the computer to do something

You can explain how this works when choosing an item on a menu, or pointing to and clicking a hyperlink on a web page, or typing inside a text box. It's also useful for people to know that there are other ways to move the cursor around on the screen such as the arrow keys on the keyboard. For people who really have a difficult time making the mouse work for them, I sometimes suggest using the arrow keys to move around as much as possible, and using the tab key to move between text boxes, and shift-tab for backwards movement.

Other pointing and indicating devices usually have many configuration options available via software. Some of these are pernicious and some are helpful. Usually they can be found somewhere in the Control Panel (for PCs) or the System Preferences (for Macs), but sometimes on a PC there is an entirely other piece of software somewhere on the machine controlling the input device. At some point a few years back, I started noticing that students who came to me with low-end laptops were having difficulty using their trackpads without accidentally clicking everywhere at the same time. These laptops had been configured to have the

> ## Click or Double-click?
>
> Students often ask "How do I know whether to click or double-click?" My general answer is "Only double-click when you are opening a file or running a program from the desktop."
>
> There are other situations where double-clicking may be useful, but none that I know of where it is mandatory. Additionally, they don't need to double-click anything online unless instructions specifically say to do that. Anyone who builds a double-click into an online tool is doing it wrong.
>
> Make sure when students are clicking that the computer does not think they are doing a click-drag and trying to move the item they are trying to open. This is a common error and easily fixed with practice.

"tap to click" option set to ON by default. For students who didn't even know what clicking really was, this was a confusing option for them. Turning this feature off, an option that many students did not know was possible, was a huge quality of life improvement for them.

Most of the other basic topics about computers are more appropriately referring to software or to people's interactions with the internet, and are addressed in the next few sections. Your patrons may not know the difference, but it is important that you do. You'll also find a few "myths" at the end of each section both to dispel common myths, but also just to get across that there is a lot of conventional wisdom about computers that is either outdated or just plain wrong. Keeping up with what is and is not true (for instance, screen savers are a totally different animal than back in the flying toaster days) is an important part of keeping current as a librarian generally.

A Few Common Myths about Computers

People who know about computers only through print media or movies and television will have a lot of shared misunderstandings about how computers in general work and specifically how the internet works. This is doubly true when they have friends who only "sort of" know about computers and have told them stories about them. By the time they are talking to you, you may be the last person at the end of a long game of telephone trying to figure out what people were originally talking about.

What follows is a list of a few common misconceptions—stories that I haven't heard just once, but multiple times in a variety of circumstances. I find that often people who don't know much about technology are somewhat innocent and trusting of other's opinions and perspectives. On the one hand, they believe what they hear; and on the other hand, they are looking for an expert to explain the way something really works. The combination of some decent knowledge and being able to speak as an authority on tech topics can be a stabilizing force to someone who is feeling adrift in a whole bunch of information and misinformation.

Additionally, I don't mean to be hand-wavey about this, but the literal truth about these myths is less important than the fact that they are gross oversimplifications of things that are actually somewhat complicated and worth explaining. So, I don't think you need to give users a treatise on the truth of these situations as much as explaining that the answers are complicated, though understandable, and that they should examine their facts closely before making decisions. You'll find a similar list to the end of the next chapter, "What Is the Internet?"

1. *Any computer slow-downs or difficulties are caused by viruses.*
   While viruses are a problem, they are not this ubiquitous and there are many things you can do to speed up a computer that is running slowly besides running virus scans. While viruses can negatively impact a computer's performance, so can low memory, an old operating system, an old computer, too many start-up items, or certain memory and CPU-intensive processes (graphics rendering, for example). People like to assume sometimes that computer problems are outside of their control and "computer viruses" become the boogeyman. It's also possible that a novice user doesn't have much of a sense of how quick a computer like theirs actually should be and may be comparing apples and oranges.

2. *Computers should always/should never be left running.*
   This is something else that comes to us from the days of older computers where this might matter more. While you should go easy on the power button just like you would any other mechanical part, turning a computer on and off if you do it in the approved way (i.e. don't just press the power button) is fine for a computer. Leaving

the computer on is also fine for a computer, though it uses more energy. Most modern computers have some sort of power saver mode that will turn the monitor off and power down the hard drive. These are generally a good thing. If power consumption is of the utmost importance, turn off your computer at the surge protector—you are using surge protectors, right?—but don't think that you have to do this to extend the life of your computer. Keeping your computer in a well-ventilated location, doing regular software updates, and keeping it free of pet hair and other ventilation killers will do more for your computer than any choices you make in an on/off direction.

3. *Pulling out a USB drive without using software to eject it can harm your computer.*
Similar to floppy disks of yore, USB drives should not be removed when the computer is reading or writing data to them. Look for a small LED on your USB drive that indicates that it's in use. While I am generally not enthusiastic about telling people to ignore error messages, this is one that I regularly ignore.

4. *Screen savers are necessary for avoiding "burn-in" on your monitor.*
For people who have been using computers since there have been personal computers, this is pervasive. It's also partly true and useful to understand. For older computers with CRT (cathode ray tube) monitors, this sort of thing was necessary to keep images from burning in to the screen. However, screen savers that had one non-moving or barely moving image would also cause this sort of burn-in. Modern monitors can sometimes display a sort of "image persistence," but this is not at all the same as permanent damage from screen burn. If people want to use screen savers because they are pretty, or good for security—some screen savers can be set to only be removed after a user enters a password—by all means don't dissuade them. Let them know that most modern computers have an energy-saver feature that will just blank the screen out which has the additional benefit of being power saving at the same time.

5. *Some variant of "If it's not broken, don't fix it."*
Just like automobiles and other complex machines, computers need maintenance. However, this maintenance

often comes in the form of software updates, not just hard-ware updates. People sometimes presume that if their computer is currently working properly, that they don't need to do any updating. They are suspicious of people trying to sell them things that they don't need. While it's true that a totally offline computer can continue to run its existing software so long as nothing physically breaks, any updating or upgrading to the system, such as a new printer or switching from dial-up to broadband, can cause a cascading effect where other things such as drivers or internet browsers need to be upgraded. Staying on top of regular maintenance means there is less likelihood that one small upgrade will result in a major software overhaul.

What Is an Operating System?

This is another question that is difficult to answer without relying on metaphor. While novice users don't have to think about the idea of operating systems too much, they're still a part of computer culture so it's a good idea to understand the basic outline of what one is. At the very least, when people ask you "Mac or PC?" you should know what they're referring to. Since the majority of the things people seem to do on our library computers are browser-based, any operating system with a browser is likely to be familiar enough to them. However, once they start working with files and programs such as Photoshop or Microsoft Office, there are likely to be differences that are important to understand.

Explain to students that an operating system is the set of instructions that the computer comes with "from the factory" that tells the computer how to take user directions and translate it into hardware instructions. More to the point, it draws all the pictures on the screen; it is the thing that is running the programs. This gets confusing because all operating systems also come with software programs. So, you can say that Solitaire is not part of the Windows operating systems, but you can also observe that all Windows computers have Solitaire on them. In fact, this was central to the *United States v. Microsoft* lawsuit[2] whether the browser could, in fact, be unbundled from Windows. It's no wonder patrons are confused!

But getting back to the operating system—there are three major flavors or brands of operating systems. I will speak in generalities, somewhat in the interests of getting to the point.

1. *Windows*, which includes Windows 95, Windows 98, Windows ME, Windows CE, Windows 2000, Windows XP, Windows Vista, and Windows 7. If you work in a public library, chances are that you are mostly dealing with the Windows operating system in some way. Most of the libraries in my neck of the woods are running Windows XP.
2. *Mac*, which includes numbered operating systems that started at 1 in 1986 with the current operating system called OS X for "Operating System Ten." I only know one library in my area that has a Mac and at that library, it is their only public computer.
3. *GNU/Linux*, which is really a bunch of flavors of one open source operating system. Ones you may have heard of include Red Hat, Ubuntu, Debian, and Fedora. I do not know any libraries near me who are running it, but several large library systems do run Ubuntu for their public access PCs.

Though I have had one novice user come in to drop-in time with her laptop which was running some flavor of Debian and start asking questions about how to get the sound card working, this is a very rare occurrence. Usually novice computer users are using a computer with some version of MacOS or Windows. While I am a proponent of open source operating systems generally and think that their easy distribution and low cost really can solve some problems for people, it's a bit of an esoteric angle for this particular task.

So, you have a student who is sitting at a computer and you want to explain what the operating system is. Where do you start? Wikimedia Commons has a nice illustration of the direction that communication happens in an operating system. This may or may not be a useful way to communicate it to your patrons, but I find it helpful to help categorize the different things we work with.

The user interacts with the application, which interacts with the operating system, which interacts with the hardware. The hardware responds, which affects the operating system, which affects the application, which displays a change to the user.

Capital and Small-W Windows

Both Macs and PCs use a windows metaphor. In some classes I teach, we don't even talk about the operating system much. This was a decision I arrived at with some dissatisfaction. However, for novice users, a skills-based approach to word processing, for

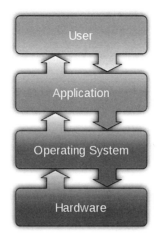

Image used for explaining where an operating system fits into the scheme of things.

example, wouldn't benefit from a lot of discussion about file systems if you only have a small amount of time. As a computer savvy person, this dismays me, but I also think it's practical. I do talk a little bit about moving around in a graphical user environment that uses the window metaphor so that students can use the program they have on their computers. So, whether you're using Word, Excel, or Firefox, some of the aspects of the environment are going to be the same. I don't talk about operating systems in a vacuum; I talk about how aspects of this one program that they are using will be replicated in other programs. This makes students happy. They like thinking that their skills are transferable, and feel that it's worthwhile learning skills that have multiple applications.

So, what are those things that make up the operating system generally, the transferable skills? Some of them are listed in the vocabulary list earlier in this chapter, but here's a brief rundown of a few general things worth knowing about. Most of these things are invisible to novice users, but understanding them can improve their technology experience markedly. Remember, even as you are teaching them to use a typing program or play Solitaire, or enter numbers into a spreadsheet, you are also teaching them small parts of a much larger system so the more solidly you lay the groundwork, the better foundation they will have for further learning and exploration.

What Is the Desktop?

For many users, the desktop is the thing they're spending all of their time staring at, but they have no idea it's an actual thing with customizable features and attributes. Depending on the operating system you're using, the desktop may be more- or less-central to the way you and/or your patrons use the computer. The desktop is what is seen on the monitor when the computer is turned on. Different environments have different features, which I briefly mention in the next section but there are two important points that should be mentioned here.

First, everything that can be done via the desktop can be done in some other way as well. This includes running a program, opening a file, and sending a file to the trash. Some people use the desktop for all of this, others barely touch the desktop. Second, what people will see on their desktop will vary a lot from computer to computer. It's easily the most customized part of the computer. On the desktop, people can change:

- the color, font face, and font size
- the size and placement of the icons
- the desktop background picture
- the screen saver
- whether there are files and folders and things that look like hard drives or iPods on the desktop

All of which contribute to computers looking very different from each other, even if they have almost the same functionality. From a public access computing perspective, this should be something to keep in mind. Strive to keep your computers looking similar not only to each other, but to themselves over time. This is discussed in more detail in the Troubleshooting and Supporting Your Systems section, but while it can be fun to allow people to change the desktop image to Wolverine and the font face to Comic Sans, this is giving other users a less than optimal experience. That said, a computer that is locked down so much that things like the Control Panel or System Preferences are not available, does not work very much like a regular computer so it's always important to strike a balance.

What Is a Window?

One of the things that an operating system allows you to do is juggle multiple programs that are running at the same time. The easiest example I have, that I sometimes show to students, is having a word processing document open at the same time as a web browser. Each program runs in its own window; each program does a very different thing. However, the frame around each program, the window, does exactly the same thing for each program. This is slightly different between a Mac and a PC, but not much.

Each program has a set of three buttons—loosely functioning as maximize, minimize, close—a title bar, a menu bar, a scroll bar on the right and sometimes one on the bottom. The status bar is also at the bottom. Many programs will also have a toolbar. The user manipulates a mouse to move a cursor across a screen to interact with icons (which may represent many different things), menus, and buttons. Windows OS has a task bar while Mac OS has the dock. Not all programs make use of all of these features, but nearly all of them do. Pointing out the things that are the same from program to program can give new users a sense of being able to make predictions about how to use their computers.

There are some differences which will throw off novice users, so if for some reason they are in a situation where they have to be able to work with multiple operating systems, it's worth pointing this sort of thing out.

Mac running OS X 10.6.

PC running Windows XP.

So . . . three circles or squares on the left or the right corner that have the functions quit, minimize, and maximize. Of course, the maximize button on the PC actually toggles between maximize and restore. And the quit button on the Mac actually just closes the window and does not quit the program. People who switch from PCs to Mac tend to leave a lot of programs running at all times because they assume that closing the window makes the program stop running as it would on a PC.

These windows can be moved and manipulated. You can pick up a window by clicking and holding its title bar. You can resize a window with the buttons or by dragging the edges or the corner of the window. I often try to layer the windows in such a way that a student can click back and forth between them without having to move them. For students who are new to computers, the idea of two programs running in two windows, and the idea of the "active window" can be a very difficult concept to grasp, so if you are discussing this, try to devote some time to it.

Multitasking: The Dock versus the Taskbar

Each operating system has a different way to show a user which programs are running, which files are open, and which other system activities have visible status. On a Mac, there is a feature called the *dock*, which has clickable icons for programs. The programs appear with a dot beside them when the program is running. The dock also shows icons for minimized windows. On a PC there is a *taskbar*, which is attached to the Start menu (and Start button) and which shows which programs are running, as well as showing minimized documents. The taskbar can also have shortcuts for functions such as "show desktop" and starting individual programs. In addition, the task bar contains a section called the "notification area" or "system tray" that contains icons for features that aren't otherwise visible on the desktop. This area is also where the volume and time indicators live. On a Mac, the volume and time settings along with other status icons, live in the upper-right corner of the menu bar and are sometimes called "menulets"— which I did not know until I looked up what that screen area is called.

Generally speaking, although these features may shift somewhat, it is useful to tell users where to look for information to see which programs are running and how to interact with certain adjustable features like volume control. The most useful tip that I give students is how to switch between currently running programs by using the keyboard: ALT + Tab on a PC and CMD + Tab on a Mac.

Basic Tasks

I find myself saying several times a day to patrons "This is another way the computer is better than a typewriter." or "Here's something you couldn't do on a calculator." Even though I think people are fairly clear that a computer isn't just a glorified typewriter or calculator (or calendar, or watch, or television), sometimes it's useful to highlight these differences and explain the ways in which most computers are similar to each other and yet unlike most any other tool they've used.

Click and Drag

As mentioned earlier, you can find Solitaire on pretty much any machine running Windows. This isn't because it's some sort of awesome game, a value-add to people buying a new computer. This is because Solitaire is a game that most people know or can understand the rules of and because it encourages people to practice one of the most basic computer skills: clicking and dragging. I can't remember the time before I could click and drag, but I'm certain there was one. Most of the people who I see coming in to use public computers with low technology skills don't know about clicking and dragging. They just leave the windows where they open on the screen and feel inconvenienced when one is directly on top of the other one.

Clicking and dragging—really clicking and holding and dragging—is possibly becoming even more ubiquitous as some websites are being built with "widgets" that can be dragged around on the screen and desktop software now allows for clicking and dragging of copied text, formerly just the domain of copy and paste. Clicking and dragging involves a fair amount of mouse control. A user has to be able to click the mouse button, hold the button, and move the cursor to someplace else and then release the button. It's a tough combination for people and can be made easier through use of a trackball or touchpad or other non-mouse device.

The clicking and dragging option can also be an impediment sometimes for double-clicking. If a person double clicks on a desktop icon but moves the mouse just a bit between clicks—a very common occurrence for novice users—the operating system will interpret this as the user trying to drag the icon. The icon will move slightly—you may see it, the user will probably not—and the computer will not behave as if the user has double clicked any-thing. The Mousercise program that is linked in the Webliography at the end of this book has some good double-clicking practice, which can be a starting point for users to understand why the computer is getting confused by their input. This is a worthwhile point—they're not doing anything wrong, strictly speaking, but the computer is a simple machine and their instructions to it are a little ambiguous.

Cut, Copy, and Paste

The good news is that the clicking and dragging mechanism is basically the same across operating systems. The same is true for copying and pasting. When I tell people why the computer is better than a calculator or a typewriter, a discussion that I still sometimes have with people, I usually tell them that it's because of two things—the computer does complicated math, and the computer can copy and paste. Again, this is something that many novice users have no idea a computer can do. They'll assiduously re-type something from a website into a word processing document or they'll print out an eight-page document so that they can copy a paragraph into an email.

Copying and pasting is slightly tricky because it doesn't work exactly like people expect it to. Here is how it actually works:

Cut—Removes highlighted editable text to clipboard area. Does not cut non-editable text.

Copy—Makes a copy of any highlighted text or other selected file type to clipboard area.

Paste—Inserts text or other file from clipboard area at the location of the cursor. Sometimes copies formatting, sometimes doesn't, depending on the program you are using.

I'll mention the problems I see people having with the whole idea of copying and pasting.

1. Using the copy command appears to do nothing. For peo-ple who are not sure if the computer "heard them," copy-ing can be intensely unsatisfying because there's no immediate visual confirmation that they did it correctly. They only know that nothing has been copied when they go to paste and the function isn't available to them.

2. Cutting only works when the text is editable. Once people get the general idea of cutting and pasting, they want to cut and paste everything. When they go and select text from a web page and try to cut it, they can get frustrated if it's not clear that what they need to be doing is copying.

3. Pasting is only available if something has already been copied or cut and—unless there are other clipboard programs installed—only can be done to the last item that is copied and/or cut.

The secret character in this whole drama is the clipboard, the invisible offscreen site where text or other copied/cut content resides. You might explain to students that there is a place called the clipboard, that it's a little tough to see what is on the clipboard, and that the clipboard can hold one item. You can put things on the clipboard by copying, or by cutting. The other skill that is useful to highlight when discussing copying and pasting is the idea of a greyed-out menu item. If a menu item is greyed-out it means that function is not available to the user. There is usually, perhaps always, a reason for this, but it's not often immediately obvious.

Here are some visual examples on the next page, from the menu of an HTML editor called Taco HTML Edit. When the program is first turned on, all menu items are greyed out if there is not pasteable content available from another program. This can be confusing: the state of the menus of one program can reflect things that a user has been doing in another program. If the user had copied test in a previous program, that would be available to this program. So, with no text selected and nothing in the clipboard, all menu items are greyed out.

Looking at these menu items is also a good opportunity to explain the funny characters off to the right, which also function at an operating system level. What the squiggle [⌘] next to the letter means, in English is "You can also perform this command by holding the command key and typing this letter." Note that the letter displayed is a capital letter but the user does not need to use the shift key. On a PC, this is only slightly different with the control key, often abbreviated CTRL, substituted for command. So, holding CTRL and typing the V key will perform the paste command. While some of the commands' letters make sense, CTRL-C for copy

1. When text has been text selected, copy and cut options are available, paste is greyed out.

Cut ⌘X
Copy ⌘C
Paste ⌘V

2. Once text has been copied to the clipboard, the paste option becomes available and cut and copy are greyed out.

Cut ⌘X
Copy ⌘C
Paste ⌘V

3. When text is highlighted and there is text in the clipboard, all three options are available to the user.

Cut ⌘X
Copy ⌘C
Paste ⌘V

or CTRL-A for select all, others are a little more cryptic such as CTRL-Z for undo. I have told many users that the reason CTRL-V is used for pasting is because CTRL-P was already in use for the Print command. Not super helpful, but each little bit of information helps users understand a somewhat mystifying whole.

Toolbars and Menus

This segues into a discussion of other graphical elements that are similar across operating systems, the idea of toolbars and menus. On a PC, the menu bar is attached to the window of the program. On a Mac, the menu bar runs across the top of the screen. When a Mac is not running any other programs, the menu shown at the top of the screen is for a program called Finder. It is the default program that is always running. This difference is a stark one to people who move between operating systems, but for most users it's just the normal operating procedure. Whichever window on the Mac is currently active is the one that will be represented in the menu bar at the top of the screen. On a Mac, the leftmost menu will always be the Apple menu, marked with an apple symbol. The rightmost menu is usually a Help menu, which includes program-specific help options. On a PC, the system options that would be under the Apple menu are accessed via a special menu in the lower left called the Start menu.

Many programs additionally have toolbars that run across the top of a program window. On the Mac and the PC windows, the operating system itself will have navigational buttons and other buttons depending on which specific operating system you're using. These can include things like a CD eject button, options for changing the folder view, or a search box. Toolbar buttons tend to follow the overall indicate-select-act model. The cursor or high-lighted text on the screen indicates what part of the document is going to be acted upon.

The specifics of these situations don't matter as much as the mechanisms themselves. Menus open with a click and items on menus are selected with a click. Sometimes menus have other nested menus which need to be slid into. These are often difficult for students with poor mouse control and need to be practiced. I also teach students how to look for "the little triangles" that various interfaces have. In this case, the triangle indicated a nested menu. In other cased it may indicate a collapsed list that could be expanded—frequently seen on the web—or possibly a toolbar button with multiple options—frequently seen in Photoshop.

In addition to having the key commands written on the menus, some menus also have little icons that indicate the toolbar button that is associated with this command. So, in Microsoft Word, the menu item for the print command will also have CTRL+P on it

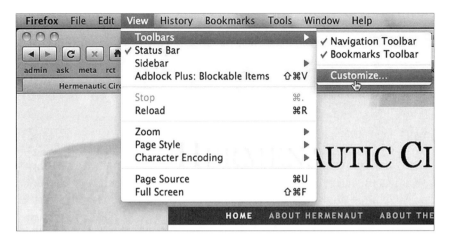

Firefox for the Mac showing nested menus.

plus a picture of a little printer. This is the same picture as the printer button on the toolbar. Show your students how to look out for cues like these that will make navigating around the computer easier.

Alerts and Dialogs

One of the quirky things about windowed systems generally is that once you think you've figured them out, there's a new type of window that requires your attention. Both major operating systems have methods of interacting with or alerting the user through windows that do not behave the way most windows behave. Specifically, they must be addressed before the underlying window is accessible. This happens usually in one of two ways, either when the user is customizing a setting and has some sort of dialog box open that requires some sort of choice—often OK or Cancel—or when the operating system is alerting or questioning the user and a response is needed.

These situations often throw novice users for a loop because they're not expecting to be put in a choice-making situation; they just know that they can't get to their browser or their document. Additionally, it's usually one of the first experiences a user has with buttons in the operating system sense of the word. Saying "Click the OK button" is somewhat confusing if a user doesn't know what a button is.

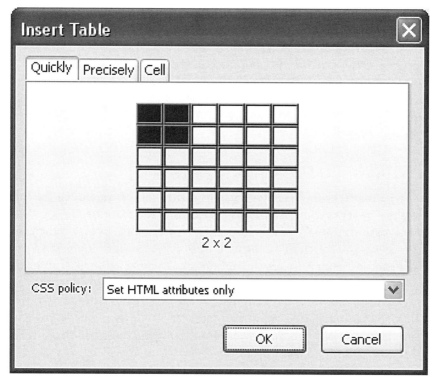

A dialog box for BlueGriffon, an HTML editing program.

Usually one of the options in the box is the default action, meaning it is the action the computer will take if the user hits the return key as opposed to making a selection from the two buttons. In the example shown, the OK option is the default and this can be intuited by the light outline around the OK box. Most novice users do not notice a difference between the two buttons. Some may not even notice that a box has popped up on the screen and may not realize they have to make a choice before returning to their document.

I often point out context-specific examples of this sort of thing, particularly ones that users are likely to see frequently such as the "Save changes before closing?" boxes commonplace in word processing software. I encourage users to read the boxes because there might be something important in them. I also tell them that some dialog boxes can be disabled—notably browser alerts that may be configured to pop up depending on browser security settings. This can be a confusing thing for some users because occasionally viruses that mimic normal dialog boxes may populate their screen and they're stuck reading and responding to them as if they were a normal part of the operating system. Teaching users the difference between normal and abnormal dialog boxes is a worthwhile though challenging exercise. The majority of dialog boxes will be straightforward, expected, and related to something the user is doing.

Files and Folders

All major operating systems use a file/folder metaphor for the file system. This metaphor is so ubiquitous it's now been included in the new iPhone OS. As I said previously, many people who use their computers primarily for web applications rarely even interact with this layer of the operating system. I often describe layered windows as being sort of like the files in a filing cabinet, where you can see the tabs peeking out from behind another window. Click that tab and the window "attains focus," or moves to the front. When people do need to interact with the file system, it's useful to know a few basic things.

1. *Where are my files?*
   Files live inside the My Documents folder on a PC and inside the home directory on a Mac. On a PC, the other folders for different media types (music, photos, movies) are inside the My Documents folder. On a Mac, there are separate directories for each of these media types that are at the same level as the Documents folder. If people do nothing and change no settings, the majority of software programs will default to saving files in these locations. Some PCs have a link to the My Documents folder on the desktop or you can find it on the Start menu. On a Mac, the Documents folder is usually on the Dock or you can get to it via the Go menu on the Finder. I have mixed feelings about public PCs and whether they should be saving files to the Desktop where they are visible, or the My Documents or Documents folder where they are predictably found.
2. *How do I move my files?*
   At the library, people often work on documents and then want to take them home with them. While we've been

good over the past few years at encouraging people to obtain USB drives for file storage, the steps required to save a file to a USB drive are still rather complex for novices. The simplest way to explain how to do this to someone working on a document is to have them use the "Save As" feature. That said, this is a path that often leads to unexpected results. Specifically, when you are working on one file and then use the Save As command, you are then returned to a program which is working on the new file. This is not obvious to many people. Exiting the program in order to click and drag the file onto the USB drive involves finding the file, finding the USB drive (and perhaps interacting with some helpful alert boxes asking you what you want to do with the USB drive), and then checking to make sure the file is copied correctly. For people who are new at file systems, the whole idea of multiple nearly-identical files is daunting at best. People know they need to be concerned about losing data, but they don't know the best way to go about that.

3. *How do I back up my files?*

   This is only sort of a file/folder issue, but there are basically two major ways to back up information on a personal computer—backing up just the personal files versus backing up the entire hard drive including the operating system and the software programs. For most people who aren't heavy software users and installers, keeping a backup of their personal files is usually sufficient, and is much simpler. Both major operating systems come with backup utilities that can be programmed to run at off hours when the computer is not being used, provided it is not turned off at night. External hard drives can be purchased cheaply and easily at most office or computer supply stores.

Looking and Feeling

The last point I want to make about operating systems is that there is an awful lot about how the computer looks and feels that is flexible, as in customizable or alterable. In fact, sometimes the operating system is so flexible that you can customize it to the point where it stops functioning effectively. (I'm thinking light yellow text on a white background, for example, which becomes basically

Some Things That Are Easy to Change

Colors—don't like the defaults, pick your own

Font Size—easier to read, more your style

Icons on the Desktop—make them bigger, change their names

Volume—easy to change, sometimes people's laptops wind up on mute by mistake

Screen Brightness—many people don't know that a laptop dims the screen when it's running on battery power

Folder View—view a list, view big icons or small icons

Mouse/Cursor—how fast it moves, how rapidly it accelerates

invisible.) New computer users should be made aware of customization that can help them out while at the same time, being given enough guidance into the sorts of things they really shouldn't change (your monitor's refresh rate, for example, or drivers for hardware that is functioning perfectly). Some of these are mentioned in the section about the Desktop, but there's much more to the operating system than just the Desktop. Offer a list of things that users might want to change with the assumption that having some degree of control over one's working environment can be an empowering thing. This is similar to what can get changed on the desktop, but includes things that aren't strictly visual.

These things are important for staff to know as well. Too often I've seen people struggling with a computer setup that doesn't work for them—bad colors, overly touchy mouse, dim screen—when their problem is solvable, if they only knew how to do it. Staff should be encouraged to modify their computing environment so that it works for them. If different staff members share a computer, they should be encouraged to have different logins so that they can maintain their own profile, My Documents folder, and customization settlings.

While there is a lot that goes into operating systems, they're often the most invisible thing to users who often only really understand them via metaphors and the small fraction of pieces of the operating system that they actually use. As much as I find operating systems interesting, most of the time my patrons just want them to function. Spending too much time giving patrons a background on operating systems is taking time away from teaching them actual skills. On the other hand, for staff who will need to interact with operating systems as well as potentially troubleshoot them, a deeper treatment may be needed.

6

What Is the Internet?

Libraries have long functioned to instruct people in information literacy skills. Now librarians need to have the technological proficiency to help our patrons navigate an increasingly digital society and to have the administrative support to offer lots of opportunities, either scheduled or on the fly, to work with our patrons to increase their digital information literacy skills.

—Becky Rudolph Karabatos, Reference Librarian,
New Jersey

There are few people who interact with a computer and are not curious about the internet, or wind up on it by mistake! The internet is a fairly ubiquitous presence in the lives of most Americans and when we're talking about the digital divide, it is the presence or absence of the internet in someone's life that we are mostly speaking of. At the same time, many of us don't really understand what the internet is or how it works. This is fine, most of the time. However, when we're explaining to someone who has really never interacted with the internet why they might care about it, it's good to have an elevator pitch. Keep in mind also that unless your patrons consume no media whatsoever, they probably have an idea of what the internet is that may or may not be accurate. When former Alaska Senator Ted Stevens referred to it as "a series of tubes,"[1] many of us knew that it *wasn't* that, but we may not have been entirely clear what it actually was.

The internet is also something that can be over-explained. If you're taking more than five minutes to talk about where it came from and why it's important before you actually show it to your patrons, you're likely giving them more information than they need or care about, at first. For many of us who were online before the web went graphical, we have more of an idea of the internet as a lot of different things you could do with a networked computer. You could send and receive email, you could browse information using Lynx or Gopher, you could search using WAIS (Wide Area Information Servers), and you could get to other computers via telnet. Now, most people use the terms *internet* and *world wide web* interchangeably. While this may not be technically correct, it also doesn't totally matter. You can explain to people that their email goes over the internet and so does all the content they view with their web browser. If they use Skype or listen to the radio, you can explain that the internet can be used as a delivery mechanism for audio, video, text, and all sorts of combinations of things. I have a short pitch I use to explain the internet, but I really believe in a "show, don't tell" approach to this sort of thing.

The internet is the worldwide network of computers used to transmit and receive information. The rest is details.

Most of your patrons will need a few basic facts explained:

- The internet is a set of computers that are all connected together that have files on them that other people can look at or otherwise interact with (watching a video, playing a game, etc.). Just because your computer can access the internet does not mean that people can access your personal files.
- Different companies (Internet Service Providers, or ISPs) can sell you access to the internet at home. Depending where you live this can be dial-up or broadband. Usually your phone and/or cable companies provide this. You do need electricity to have broadband internet.
- You can get temporary access to a computer with internet access at places like the library. Many have wireless access where you can bring your own computer and use that place's internet. This is sometimes free, like the library, and sometimes costs money, like at the airport (substitute your own examples here, of course).

For people who really are interested in the difference between the internet and what we call the "web," I like the metaphor as it's explained in this article by John Naughton in *The Observer*:[2]

A good way to understand this is via a railway analogy. Think of the internet as the tracks and signaling, the infrastructure on which everything runs. In a railway network, different kinds of traffic run on the infrastructure—high-speed express trains, slow stopping trains, commuter trains, freight trains and (sometimes) specialist maintenance and repair trains.

On the internet, web pages are only one of the many kinds of traffic that run on its virtual tracks. Other types of traffic include music files being exchanged via peer-to-peer networking, or from the iTunes store; movie files traveling via BitTorrent; software updates; email; instant messages; phone conversations via Skype and other VoIP (internet telephony) services; streaming video and audio; and other stuff too arcane to mention.

So the web is, loosely speaking, the internet that you interact with when you are using a web browser, but other applications also use the internet for their own purposes. It's a delivery mechanism, not a destination.

Internet Elevator Pitch

For more details on this delivery mechanism, this pull-quote from Wikipedia about the internet is hard to improve upon:

The origins of the Internet reach back to the 1960s when the United States funded research projects of its military agencies to build robust, fault-tolerant and distributed computer networks. This research and a period of civilian funding of a new U.S. backbone by the National Science Foundation spawned worldwide participation in the development of new networking technologies and led to the commercialization of an international network in the mid 1990s, and resulted in the following popularization of countless applications in virtually every aspect of modern human life. As of 2009, an estimated quarter of Earth's population uses the services of the Internet.[3]

In short, the internet was created in the sixties to be a large scale communications network that would still work even if parts of it failed to function. Remember the Cold War? We were really worried about nuclear strikes and how to manage them. The internet was used by many scientists to swap and transmit large scientific datasets and became owned mostly by commercial interests in the 1990s. To be on the internet, you have to be on a computer that is attached to the internet. Some people purchase internet access from an internet service provider and some people connect to it at work or school.

The work or school location is purchasing *their* internet service from an internet service provider, and up the ladder it goes. Every computer on the internet has a unique address, sort of like a telephone number for a computer, called an IP address. When you type a web address or URL into the address bar of your browser, the first thing the computer does if it's online, is change that word-based address into a series of numbers, an IP address, and then goes to find the computer at that numerical address. Every time you're looking at a web page, you're viewing a digital file that physically resides on a computer someplace, maybe in your building, maybe in another country.

The reason it's worth spelling all this out is because people are curious, and this is the sort of thing that you can explain. It's also useful when you're looking at things that don't work; sometimes it's worth knowing where things can break down. It's also useful to understand just how similar to the phone system the internet is at a basic level. People vaguely understand the phone system so sometimes anchoring the internet to a phone metaphor can be useful—especially since in many cases someone's internet service provider is also their phone company.

Internet Access

There are many ways people connect to the internet. For the most part, this does not have to be the library's concern except that people may have one sort of connection at home and have a bit of cognitive dissonance when interacting with the library's internet services. Here are some specific examples:

- The patron has dial-up at home and so their laptop is set up to "always dial a connection" even though the patron is trying to connect to the library's wifi.
- The patron sends and receives email using Outlook or Thunderbird and their computer won't send email if it's not connected to the same ISP as the one that hosts the mail server of their home ISP. They will need to contact their ISP for tech support, not the library.

- The patron's home page on their home computer is the ISP's home page; the patron doesn't know how to access their web-based email from another computer.

Or, you may just have a patron who shows up wanting to know how to get internet service at home. For the most part, this is something they have to discuss with their local ISPs but if you know other people in the area who have internet access, you may be in a good position to give them some advice. In my location, I know more or less where people can get broadband and where they can't and I know who offers low cost dial-up service and who does not.

Additionally, a quirky problem in some places is that ISPs that provide dial-up service may have connection numbers that are not technically local. I have seen this other places as well as in Vermont, but in Vermont it goes like this (using made up examples). I live in a town where the local exchange is 439. All calls to that exchange are free with my monthly service fee. A local ISP provides a dial-up number that has an exchange of 222. That number is also a local call, but there is a small charge associated with this sort of call (usually something like half a cent per minute). Total charges for these local calls are "capped" at $20/month. So, a month of dial-up using this local number would cost you an additional $20 in addition to the monthly phone fee and the monthly ISP fee. And a little ironically, many places in Vermont that have broadband available via the phone company, actually provide it at costs sometimes less than dial-up. My broadband connection at my last place was $17.95 a month when some ISPs are still trying to charge $20/month for dial-up!

For people who are unclear on any of these concepts, it may be worth at least trying to explain them. Or, you could go all out and have some fact sheets about local internet options in your library. I made a handout for my local library that included all the local libraries in the county offering public internet access, their hours and location, and whether or not they had wifi. For people in rural areas who are only using public internet access, a drive to the next town may be better than waiting several days to check their email. For information on how to actually *use* the internet, I'll talk much more in the Web section later in this chapter.

What Is *Our* Internet?

Most people really just want to know what sort of internet the library has, and how it affects them. While you don't necessarily have to go into bandwidth specifics, it's worth letting people know the sorts of things they can and can't do with the internet at your library. For example, is there any filtering or even traffic-shaping on the library's internet connection? Can people use it for Skype, or for uploading videos to YouTube, or for online gaming? If these things are prohibited, is the prohibition enforced through software and/or hardware, or just through a general "Be Cool" policy? Clear guidelines and examples will be helpful not just to novice users, but also to general envelope-pushers and people who may not agree with the current policy. These things more accurately come under the heading of "Computer and Internet Policy," but since nearly every computer in a library nowadays is an internet computer, to many patrons the two go hand-in-hand.

Here are few other things to think about that may disproportionately affect novice users:

- If you require that patrons use headphones, do you supply them, or must patrons bring their own? Can patrons obtain headphones at the library if they don't have them? Do you enforce the headphone policy if a patron is on their own computer?
- Similarly, if you allow patrons to save work to a USB drive, are those available for purchase? Do you show patrons how to use them? Can patrons save work to floppies? Burn work to CDs?

These are the sorts of things that should be in your Computer and/or Internet Use Policy (see the Our Toolbox section in Chapter 4) and available in some way so that patrons can access it. Keep in mind that as the internet evolves, your policy will likely evolve, but try to be mindful.

A Few Common Myths about the Internet

Here are some common misunderstandings that people have with the online world:

1. *Cookies and Javascript are pernicious and should be interacted with sparingly, if at all.*
   Cookies and Javascript are parts of how the modern web functions. Cookies are used to save personalization and login information and Javascript is part of most major websites. There are also less-savory ways that these tools

are used, mostly for advertising purposes. Privacy and security-conscious people should be aware of how these mechanisms operate and how and why companies use them, but dismissing them out of hand and setting your web browser to block them will cause more trouble than a reasoned approach where people can understand and evaluate how these things work and what they do. I have users who have set their browser to ask before accepting cookies, who get rattled when their browser asks them to accept four cookies to log in to the *New York Times* website. They may decide to not accept them and do without the personalization, certainly a valid option, but they should understand what they're doing, not just dismiss all cookies out of hand.

2. *You can/can't get rid of email spam by clicking the unsubscribe links in an email.*

   I lump my unsolicited commercial email into two categories: stuff I can sort of figure out where it came from, and totally random stuff. The stuff I sort of recognize maybe comes from a library vendor (thanks for selling my email address!) or someone who found my name on an old web page or mailing list. Usually, this is what I would consider "legit" spam meaning that the people work for a real business and just happened to have erroneously thought I might want to hear from them. If I get email from these companies, I click the "unsubscribe" link if there is one, otherwise I email them directly and politely ask to be taken off of their mailing address.

   The totally random stuff is porn, Viagra ads, emails that don't seem addressed to me, and other nonsense. In these cases, I don't bother looking for an unsubscribe link and I send it straight to my email's spam folder. Not only will this remove the email from my sight, it will train my email program (Gmail in this case) to move email like this automatically to my spam filter in the future. While I haven't been able to get rid of all email spam, I have certainly been able to cut down on it so that it does not interfere with my inbox for the most part.

3. *You can not shop or purchase services safely on the internet.*

   This is something that depends on people's general comfort level. There is really no such thing as total safety, and so for most people they are really talking about risk management.

Some people refuse to ride a bicycle without a helmet, others always wear their seatbelt and some people never use their credit card online. I think it is extremely important to point out to people that while there is specific research that points to much improved safety by using helmets and seat belts, the same is not true for shopping online. While people will always have anecdotes about how someone bought something online and their identity got stolen, there are many ways to reduce risk when shopping online—use known vendors, look for secure sites, keep close track of your financial statements, and don't give out personal information in response to odd-looking emails. People may still decide to not shop online because they prefer not to, but there are always small risks associated with making purchases and the online world is not fraught with peril for people who can follow basic safety rules.

The Web

The web is a big, broad topic and needs to be broken down into a few discrete areas or it can quickly become overwhelming. I've mentioned email in the previous section. The confusing thing about the email/web relationship is that for some people, their email is also on the web. For others, they access their email through a program that lives locally on their computer like Outlook or Thunderbird. So, some people will see a distinction between email and the web and others won't. The good news is that people who have webmail already have some experience using the internet, even if they're not totally aware of it. The bad news is that email is a pretty limited tool that sometimes operates differently than your average web page. So, let's look at some standard things people do on the web and how to explain what's going on to people who are trying to comprehend a lot of new metaphors all at once.

Web Browsing and Browsers

For most people this will be the main thing that they want to do online, surf the web. However, many people who don't have computers won't quite understand the difference between a computer that is online (i.e. most computers, in 2010) and a computer that is not online. There is a whole side discussion about how to get online that probably doesn't have a large place in this book, though it is mentioned in the previous "What Is the Internet?" section, but for the sake of this section, let's assume that the computer in question is online.

Okay, you are online. The computer is online. Now what do you do? For most people, they are attuned to "Click on the e," or "Click on the Firefox," or for old school users "Click on the 'connect to the Internet' picture." Whatever comes up next, the home page of the web browser, is often where they think the internet starts. Now, I do not in any way mean to mock people who have these misunderstandings, I just want to point out that these misunderstandings are so common in novice users that they need to be specifically addressed and not just dismissed as wacky misunderstandings. Here are the steps I take when I'm explaining to people the first steps of web browsing:

- Explain what a browser is, in simple terms. Note the different names for browsers. Explain that they are mostly the same but have some interface differences.
- Explain that when you double-click on the "e" (or whatever starts the browser) that you are starting a program called a web browser and you use the web browser to view material on the internet.
- The thing you see when you first open a web browser, assuming you are online, is the home page.
- You can change the home page on your own computer.
- The home page on the library computers is set to
  _____.
- You can get back to this page by clicking the Home button on your browser.
- If you are not online and you are expecting to be online, check the troubleshooting section.

At this point, I often have a few handouts that show the difference between situations in which the computer is not on the internet and situations where the specific page the patron is looking for can't be loaded—i.e., a broken link or a 404 page. These can be somewhat browser-specific, but it's pretty straightforward to have a few examples, even if they're not current. It's good for patrons to know that even if they can't get to a web address for some reason, the chances are very high that nothing is actually broken. There may be a typo, or there may be something that's not currently accessible, but this is very different from a problem that is not solvable.

Some people browse the web with Internet Explorer, some use Firefox, some use Chrome, or Opera, or Safari. For people who have a Mac, the one browser you know they have is Safari. For people with a PC, the one browser you know they have is Internet Explorer. Please note that there is no version of Internet Explorer for the Mac, and there hasn't been for over five years. All other browsers are available for Mac and Windows platforms. Some people browse on a desktop with a huge monitor; some people browse from their phones. For the most part, the web browsing experience is not radically different depending on what browser you're using. Again, I maintain that we need to teach people how the system works in general and not the exact steps to do tasks using one piece of software. No matter what browser they're using, it will change as they do upgrades over time.

What Is a Hyperlink?

Most people do not call links *hyperlinks* any more, but different computer manuals may or may not use this term. The big deal between the reality of a web page and that of a book page is that one page on the web may link to five, ten, or even a hundred other pages as opposed to the linear "Turn the page, now you're on the next page." progression that people are used to. And this difference is huge, and matters. Dealing with groupings of pages that expand out in a web-like fashion is much more complicated than just keeping a place in a book. The general progression for web surfing for novice users goes something like this:

- Open browser to home page.
- Search for website or type in URL (rarely are they clicking a link from our home page).
- Read page to see if it's what they're looking for.
- If "yes," print the page. If "no," start over with searching or typing a web address.

People often treat the web as if they're browsing books in a library, without much of an understanding of how they're all linked together. Similar to the issues reviewed in the previous chapter on email, people need to know that the spelling of a web address is important. In fact, they may need to know what a web address is. If they have only gone to websites by clicking away from their home page, or using a search box, they may not know how to go to *http://www.toyota.com* for example. Alternately, if they've only typed in URLs, they may not know how to search for something. In almost all cases, navigational tools such as book-marks/favorites or the back and home buttons are not in their tool-kit. The idea of idly surfing around the web is fun if you're killing time, but much less fun if you're goal-oriented. And most novice users are goal-oriented, so they don't find this new environment fun.

So, first we need to teach them what this tool IS and then we need to teach them how to use it to solve their own problems. Most of the classes I've given in a library setting are about subject-oriented ways to interact with the web such as Finding Medical Information Online or something similar. For totally novice users, we start with "What is online?" With any luck at all, we've been able to get them to Mousercise and they've practiced using the mouse to click on links and use a scroll bar and maybe click a but-ton. Now, we want to talk about how they can do something differ-ent. I have a handout that talks about the three different ways you can start exploring on the web:

1. Click links from the home page of your browser.
2. Type in a URL into the browser's address bar.
3. Search for a term using the browser's search box, or a search engine.

It's fairly straightforward to show examples of each one. The good news about showing people how the web works in a classroom setting is that you can use examples that students give you and do some of the work for them. The bad news is that the internet being the internet, sometimes you find things you don't expect. I always set Google's Safe Search to "on" before I start teaching a class, just in case. Here are some examples that I often use, with some "Did you notice . . . ?" follow-up questions for further discussion.

1. Starting from the library home page and clicking through to the history of our town on a different website.
   • Notice that the URL has changed?
   • How do we get back to the page we were on before?
   • How could we save this page for later?
2. Noting that most major companies use their company name as their web address, we'll type in the URL of a local business or university.

- Sometimes the simple URL will redirect to a longer more complicated one (I show this using the ala.org/bbooks web address) and I explain that mechanism.
- We'll click around the website a little and note how the address bar URL changes, but usually stays at the same top-level URL. So, it might go from http://uvm.edu to http://uvm.edu/education but the main part stays the same.
- We'll try to go to a typo of a URL and note that it will often go someplace else entirely. So, http://vt.edu goes to Virginia Tech, not the University of Vermont. Likewise, http://goggle.com directs you to a page where you may have already won an iPhone, just for mistyping google.com.

3.   Using the search bar built into the browser, I'll show students how to pick a search engine by using the drop-down menu. I'll also show them, building on the last lesson, how to open up http://www.google.com and type in a search term.

- There's more on this in the Google section, but teaching students both how to scan a results list and how to re-do a search if this one didn't get them what they wanted is a useful skill.
- Sometimes what students are looking for is pictures; show them how to click through to Google Images or even Google Books—my personal favorite with all those old *Life* Magazines.

At the point where students can reliably click on a link, click the back button, type in a URL and bookmark a website, they've nearly graduated from basic web class. This doesn't mean that they don't have questions, but that they'll be able to get places that they enjoy and you can spend your time talking about both troubleshooting and more broad-based ideas or looking at specific areas they are interested in. Just as with adult new readers, having a few sites with high ease-of-use and interest to suggest to people can be a good way to ease their transition into interacting with the web.

What Is on the Web?

Everyone uses the web for different things, but it's surprising how most people's web use centers around the same basic functions.

PAC Tip

What is the home page set to on the library computers? The library home page? A search box? Make sure it's something useful for the patrons.

Lately these functions, based on my totally non-scientific survey of the people I work with, seem to be:

- Interacting with people (e.g., on Facebook)
- Shopping
- Viewing media (e.g., on YouTube)
- Reading news or blog sites

Now, when I look at actual statistics of the most popular websites according to Alexa <http://www.alexa.com/topsites> or the DoubleClick Ad Planner <http://www.google.com/adplanner/static/top1000/>, this is more or less borne out with the addition of Wikipedia, search engines, and companies that offer software for download such as Adobe.com and Microsoft.com. So, it stands to reason that if you are helping someone use the web, you will likely be helping them use one of these sites. Which leads to the next important question: how much do we help people learn websites and how much do we teach people generalized web browsing skills and leave them to fend for themselves? With Facebook being simultaneously so popular and so confusing, we may have an opportunity to teach people how to untangle a complicated website, but one that they are actually motivated enough to continue to want to use.

I usually start with the basics as noted above, but there is a sort of second tier of basics for people who are new to the web which involves learning to use sites that they may spend a lot of time on, and learning to use those sites and their features specifically. We've had some luck at the place where I teach adult education classes having short sessions where people learn things like "How to Use Facebook for Promoting Your Business," or "How to Find a Good Book to Read," or "Making Sense of Health Information on the Web." Specialized classes that can be a bit of a tour through the mechanisms of one particular site or type of site can really help people who may have only one topic that is compelling them to be online in the first place.

Novice Behavior and Accessibility

Before I had even thought about writing this book, one thing I wanted to talk about was the quirky behavior that novice technology users exhibit that might be surprising to people who have been using technology for decades. Specifically: novice users read every word on a web page including the words on the ads. They generally don't know how to use font and color and placement cues to recognize what's important on a web page and what isn't. Most of us are good at scanning a page for the information or the feature we're looking for ("Oh, *there's* the submit button . . .") and have what some people call "banner blindness" where we no longer see most advertising. Novice users, on the other hand, are attracted to and distracted by the blinky, shiny thing at the top of the page and still need to have it explained to them that no, they have not won a new laptop. They can often not tell the difference between advertising and content. We were once in their position. I consider it a bit of an accessibility issue if patrons cannot use a web page because they can't figure out its purpose or can't understand its navigation.

Some of this behavior can be addressed either with education or with technological solutions. Using Firefox with AdBlock Plus stops advertisements from being distracting just as using Gmail for your email client hides long lists of email addresses if someone Cc'ed you and 75 other people on their picnic invitation. You'll have to decide how far you want to go in each direction, and some of this may depend on whether you're dealing with a user that will go home to their own computer, or someone who mostly uses the technology at the library.

Here are a few other context clues that you can teach people to keep an eye out for:

- Hidden menus—In an effort to put more information on a website and keep it from being overbusy, people often hide lists of clickable items in places a novice user would not think to look for them. I often counsel students to look for tiny triangles on sidebars to indicate that there may be a list of items hidden beneath it.
- Areas that "pop open" —Sometimes help files or FAQs will have a list of questions. Clicking on each individual question will cause the answer underneath it to expand like a window shade. This is a handy use of space if you're looking for it. Novice users are sometimes unclear that parts of a web page may shift while other parts remain static.

About ALA

> **Mission & History**

> **ALA & LIS Acronyms**

⌄ **ALA Governing & Strategic Documents**

> Constitution & Bylaws

> Council

> Officers & Executive Board

> Handbook of Organization

> Policy Manual

> Legal Guidelines

> Annual Report

> Financial Data

> ALA Election Information

> **Offices**

> **Contact Us**

ALA's nested lists in their sidebar navigation.

- Error messages—If people are filling out an online form, they may make a mistake that is caught before the form is fully submitted and the page may return an error. However, instead of a pop-up window or similar thing, there may just be a red mark or a notation beside a form element. Patrons may need to scan the page looking for an error message that may have not been there before.

The larger issue is that, unlike print publishing or even television broadcasting, there are no set standards for where to put information on a web page or how to move from one page to the next. Things you click—images, links, videos—can do various things—go to the next page, animate, play a song. There are emerging usability standards certainly and pages that are created by governments or academic institutions, for example, do tend to present similar information in similar ways. However, there will always be websites that are either using terribly out-of-date or terribly advanced web design and people new to the web may not understand why different web pages look so different. I'll address this in more detail in the bibliographic instruction section, but a quick tutorial in how "No One Owns the Web" can be useful, while at the same time explaining that generalize strategies can help with a lot of this. Once people get familiar with recurring patterns, they'll realize that they know a lot more about how to navigate a website than they thought they did.

It's also your responsibility as the person running the public access computers to make sure that actual difficulties with access, such as type that is too small or colors that are too similar, are a problem that you need to solve. All current browsers have a mechanism for enlarging type size and all current browsers have a method for changing web page colors. There are Firefox add-ons such as the Accessibar that make these changes even simpler for novice users to understand. Sometimes, it can be difficult to understand what is an access problem and what is a comprehension problem, but the end result is the same so we should come prepared with solutions to both types of scenarios.

Shopping

I would prefer to not get involved with my student's financial lives in any way. After all, my distaste for commerce is one of the things that landed me in the library in the first place. However, realistically, people want help making online purchases and I figure they'll have a better chance at doing an effective job with some moderate supervision. Teaching eBay classes is tough in this respect because I feel that I spend so much time explaining to people how to not get ripped off that we have very little time left for learning how to use eBay's incredible search features or browsing mechanisms. While many websites employ differing design features and navigation, moving through a shopping cart experience is often very standardized. Getting people comfortable enough so that they can find what they are looking for and decide to spend money on it is a fairly specialized activity. Without spending too much time on it, here are a few tips for helping students usefully shop online:

1. Often people need to make an account on the website in order to shop there. This includes having an email address and usually thinking up a username (which could be your email address) and a password. Come prepared with this and make sure to write this down once you've set it up. Often this step takes place after there is already an item in their shopping cart. You can assure students that their items will still be there once they have signed in.

2. Places that take credit cards online will often require that you have the credit card with you so that you can write down the security code number from the back of the card. They will also usually require that the shipping address of the item you are purchasing is the same as the billing address on your credit card. This can cause problems in rural areas where people may not get home mail delivery, but they DO get home package delivery. I've managed this by using a hybrid address with both my addresses—something like 123 Main Street/Box 345—which will make sense to mail delivery people and usually pass muster for getting my credit card accepted.

3. I have frequently been able to save money on online purchases by searching for coupons and discount codes. This may be a slightly advanced topic, but with the advent of sites like RetailMeNot.com and Priceline.com combined with community sites like BiddingforTravel.com, patrons should be aware that there are often ways to pay less for items by doing a quick search for possible discounts.

4. Purchasing items like tickets or hotel reservations may also include having to give a lot more information, such as who is flying or who will be staying in a hotel. Make sure you understand the terms of these agreements—i.e., Are you making a reservation or a purchase?—and print out copies of any pages that say "print this page."

People will need to work their way up to both deciding to do something like this and also feeling comfortable in an online shopping environment. I've been making purchases online for probably a decade and I still get tripped up occasionally when making purchases online. It's also worth letting patrons know that websites are occasionally fallible and following up with a phone call to confirm a reservation or a purchase that you are unsure about is a totally okay thing to do.

A Few Common Misunderstandings about the Web

For people who haven't interacted with the web much before, they may leap to conclusions or overgeneralize about things they've only seen a few examples of. It's worth taking a little time to make sure certain things are understood.

1. *All web addresses start with www.*
   I always tell people that the http:// before a web address is not necessary. This is true in all modern browsers; the browser will just add it for you and it's a blessing to my students to have seven fewer characters to type. I also let them know that while many web addresses start with www, they don't all start that way. So, if someone says "My web address is *libraran.net.*" that generally means you can type librarian.net into the address bar of a browser and be directed to the site. It also usually means you can enter www.librarian.net into the address bar and arrive at the same location. Many mail programs have a web address that is mail.yahoo.com or something similar. This will also usually work if you type in www.mail.yahoo.com, but why bother?
2. *The address bar and the search bar are interchangeable.*
   Many browsers now allow you to search by typing your search term either into the browser's address bar or into the search bar that is usually to the right of the address bar. Many novice users get to web sites by typing URLs

into a search bar or into a search engine like Google. While this will very often land them at the correct website, I feel that the ends don't justify the means. In my opinion, we should be teaching them, if possible, to use the tools properly so that they will work in the majority of situations, not just situations where the browser is configured the same way as the browser that they learned on. So, make sure you're showing people how to type an address into the address bar and how to search either from a search engine page or the search bar. Keep in mind that different browsers may have different default search engines, so show patrons how to tell which search engine they are about to use or have used.

3. *If I am not searching for pornography I will not find pornography.*

    This is, sadly, not at all true. Be sure to explain to students early on how they can use the filters that exist on most search engines and even on their computer at home if they are concerned with themselves or their families accidentally stumbling across websites they may find objectionable. That said, clicking the back button or closing the browser for the most part will solve most of these problems.

Google, The

This section could be about any major search engine, but it happens to be about Google. Google has become a verb, synonymous with searching, but most of us can remember back before it was the dominant search engine. Now, it's not only the biggest search engine, it's also getting into the email and word processing business. For a lot of people, the Google environment may be almost all that they need in order to interact with technology on a personal level. This changes, of course, when you're in a situation where serious privacy is concerned, but for people who just want to search, find, type, and explore, Google can be fairly helpful.

That said, it's important to understand what Google is doing at the same time as you explain to people how to use it. Add to this: why are most of the things Google gives away free? Google is another topic that could fill an entire book, but I'd like to focus on the main things it does and how they can be simplified for novice users.

Google's interface sets the standard for simple design.

Google is a gateway drug to the internet for many people. People who may be internet-skeptical can change their mind when they see a satellite view of their house, or can look up a local phone number, or find comparison pricing for toner ink cartridges. It's also a great example of how there are a lot of powerful tools on the computer, but they're only as "smart" as the syntax you use to talk to them. Google has been getting better at processing natural language queries such as "How do I find a book about bat populations?" but generally speaking, the more you learn Google's language, the better you'll be at finding the things that Google offers access to. They're also leading the way in user interfaces that people understand. Once you find the search box, most people can type into it and click "search" and they aren't waylaid with a lot of advertising-speak and other gewgaws. This is deceptively simple in some ways since there's a lot going on behind the scene, but for sheer novice-usability, Google is the company to watch.

What Google Knows

Wikipedia describes Google as "a multinational public cloud computing, internet search, and advertising technologies corporation." For many of us, the idea of Google as an ad agency doesn't really jibe with our perception of it, but it's important to realize that that's where the bulk of Google's income is coming from. While you do your searches, print your maps, and check your email, Google is analyzing what you type in the boxes and using your behavior to target advertising towards you. This is not necessarily a big conspiracy theory and I stop short of saying that they're spying on you (though some people say that), but it's useful to know as you move forward wondering why Google offers all this access for free. And for people who are new to the idea of the internet, this is all fairly inscrutable and perhaps, worth briefly explaining.

This is also where my practical approach may differ from that of other peoples'. While I do not think there's a conspiracy happening whereby Google and/or Facebook or whomever is lulling people into a false sense of security in order to get them to part with their personal information, I propose that we do our patrons a disservice when we present suggested websites with no real world context. It can be difficult, with novice users, to explain both how Google tracks what they do online, but also how most people in the world still use it. You can scare people off at this point, or corroborate their technology paranoia, so educate yourself first and have something appropriate prepared before you talk to your patrons.

We read in the paper a lot that the future of the library is in danger because "It's all on the internet!" This is not only not true, but sort of laughable. In the public library, we know it's not all online and *certainly* not online for free. I'm sure we all have our examples of things our patrons frequently want that we can't provide for them, but my favorite example is obituaries—not recent obituaries, but somewhat distant ones, like earlier in the last century, and not so old as to be published or referenced by something that's in the public domain. Genealogists love tracking down obituaries and it's a tough thing to do. Most local newspapers aren't digitized or if they are, they're poorly indexed or difficult to search. Even knowing the exact month someone died means you may have 30 some-odd days of microfilmed newspapers to dig through. So, while I certainly enjoy the utility of Google and other giant search engines, I also have a pragmatic approach to what they can and can't provide to me. For people who only know Google through reading about it in the newspaper, this may not be obvious to them.

What Is a Search Engine?

Google's main application is its search function. You can type into a box and Google will return a long list of results relatively quickly. The combination of speed and accuracy of results is the reason people keep coming back to it. Google has a gigantic index of web pages which are keyword indexed and searchable. It then has its own internal algorithms for determining which pages are most relevant for a particular search term. Companies devote their entire business strategy to trying to help other companies get their listings to the top of a page of Google results—who wouldn't want to be the first result when you search for a florist or a moving company?—and yet, this perpetual gamesmanship means that things are harder for our novice patrons when they're just trying to find a local realtor. This constant jockeying for Google positioning is also the source of a lot of the weird junky web sites out there: empty "landing pages" for parked non-active domains, splogs (or spam blogs) that contain lots of keywords but no actual content, and those sites that have a page for every town in your state with a link like "Find florists in RANDOLPH, VERMONT" and then you click and there are no florists nearby. Understanding this can help people understand the web, it's up to you how much explaining you want to do about it.

Google creates its internal page rankings that determine how high in the listings a page appears in a search for a particular term. They do this by not just determining how many times (or how prominently) a word appears on a page, but also by examining the inbound links to a page. It looks at those links and the pages they appear on and at *their* page rankings and what words they use to describe the page they are linking to. It's a sort of reputation-based ranking system. This can sometimes have amusing results when people decide to tamper with it. This technique is called *Google Bombing*, repeatedly linking to one page using search terms that aren't necessarily aligned with the content of a page. You can read about this by typing "miserable failure" into Google sometime.

So, when you're teaching people how to use a search engine, you're really teaching them how to talk to a computer using the computer's language. And it's worthwhile preparing them for the fact that other search engines, or really anything with a search box, may not use the same syntax. And while you can acknowledge that yes, that can be frustrating, it's also something that's possible to understand and that understanding it will help them not only use the internet more effectively, but find more things that are interesting to them. Google's help pages are good for explaining a lot of this. For novice users, here is a short list of things they may not know about searching. These can be made into a simple handout or even a laminated flash card or two and left by the public workstations. Explaining how these things work with examples (and good counterexamples or use cases) can help people see what's happening even if they have very little search experience.

- Searching for phrases by using quotation marks
- Using plus and minus, and AND and OR effectively
- Limiting results to a specific website or file type

So, a search string like "`George Clinton`"`-Bill filetype: pdf` would find pdf files about George Clinton that did not include the word *Bill*. A string like `free` "`excel tutorial`" `filetype: xls` would find Excel documents containing the phrase *excel tutorial* that also contained the word *free*.

If you use Google's advanced search page, you can actually watch the search string being created while you fill in the boxes telling Google what you're looking for. Google's help pages on these subjects are actually quite good, and can be linked to or copied for use in the library or in a class. A lot of this searching is second nature to anyone who has gone through library school, but may be all new to someone who has very little computer experience. If they've never used a computer, they've likely never used a search box, so just explaining the difference between the Search button and the I'm Feeling Lucky button is worthwhile information to pass on.

Fun Things Google Can Do

I also call this section "Stupid Google Tricks." Many people don't know what to do when confronted with a search box. They don't think of the world of information as a running river just there for dipping your ladle into. They see a blank box and they freeze. What to look up? Sometimes, I like to show people a few things that Google does do fairly well, things you might not think that you could do with a search engine:

- Math, including money and measurement conversions—type these straight in to the search box
- Weather—type in the word *weather* and a zip code and get a four-day forecast
- Find a phone number—type in a name with a city, state combination and get return phone numbers
- Track flight status—type in an airline name and a flight number
- Ego surfing—enter your own name in quotes to see what comes up when you click. I often combine this with showing them what comes up when Googling a celebrity, or even me, so that they can compare/contrast.

Keep in mind that where you see ONE search box, novice users may see two or even three.

Why would you use Google to do these things when you can do them perfectly well with the phone, print materials, or specialized web sites? Because you can do them all in one place and with one general strategy. Usually, new users aren't quite convinced of the usefulness of the "one-stop shopping" scenario that has been created for them, but sometimes change their mind when they learn to cut and paste from websites into their own documents or into an email.

Things Google Does Not Do Well

Sometimes, people feel better about technology when you tell them things that the technology can't do. This is not always my first choice, but I do like to remind people that while Google is the dominant search engine, there are some things that it doesn't do, or doesn't do particularly well. This may be useful to your patrons if they are trying to do one of these things, but also just in teaching us a lesson that the technology is only as smart or as flexible as the people who built it and the decisions that they initially made. Some of these things are, in fact, things that other search engines or database products or even the library catalog will do.

I asked my librarian brain trust via Twitter and this was a quick list of things they came up with that Google does not do well.

Things Google Does Not Do Well

- Sort results by date, or sort at all really
- Search for punctuation and other non-textual marks
- Do a Wildcard search, just the simple ability to use a * in my query
- Search for text that includes an asterisk doesn't work well, unsurprisingly
- Search within a set of results (e.g., results that cite X and also include keywords Y and Z in Google Scholar)
- Control things like clustering
- Subject facets, a la the old Clusty
- Not good at "that is not a thing"; there are always hits, even if your terms are wrong
- Doesn't allow filtering by author; can only do site which is sort of that, but more analogous to publisher
- Lacks case sensitivity
- Select which sources you are searching
- Provide recall; compare a search for Canadian metal bands in Google with the same in metal-archives.com
- Save in any kind of standard format for importing/exporting
- Very little "see also" capability (outside of Google Scholar), lack of controlled vocabulary

Many of these problems can be hacked up somewhat using other Google features such as the timeline or Google Custom Search, but many can't. And for the novice user who sits down and types something into the box and doesn't adjust any of the defaults, they will not be able to make use of any of this.

Results Are Not the End

I have not yet mentioned Roy Tennant's famous quotation "Librarians like to search, everyone else likes to find." when describing how librarians' approaches to searching generally are very different from that of patrons. However, I do want to mention that for people just getting used to the idea of a search engine, part of using a search engine should be, just like learning how to use a computer, learning how to talk to it. Accordingly, I often show people how to look at their search results not necessarily to see if the answer is in there, but to see if they're even asking the right question. Are they getting links to things that look like what they were looking for? If so, yay, let's start clicking. If not, let's figure

lsw	Search

About 1,930,000 results (0.27 seconds)   Advanced search

Welcome to LSW ☆
Offers single and flexible premium annuities for qualified and non-qualified markets.
Product line also includes universal and equity-indexed universal life ...
www.lifeofsouthwest.com/ - Cached - Similar

Contact Us	LSW & NL Group
Commonly Used Forms	Personal Finance
Teachers	Illustration
403(b) FAQs	IRA and Roth IRA FAQs

More results from lifeofsouthwest.com »

How to Contact LSW ☆
LSW Life Insurance 888-297-3990. For Assistance Accessing an On-line Account.
Toll-free Number: 877-654-3499. Plan Administrator. Toll-free Number: ...
www.lifeofsouthwest.com/Contactus.asp - Cached

Southwest High School - Home Page ☆
LSW is an exciting place to be! If you are a perspective student or staff member,
please take some time to get to know us better by navigating our website. ...
lsw.lps.org/ - Cached - Similar

LSW Podcast ☆
LSW PodCast #12 Feb 12th. Free speech in the news discussion: Cartoons,
Cartoons, ... LSW PodCast #11 Feb 09th. Google in the news discussion and Arts
and ...
lsw.lps.org/dhersh/podcast.html - Cached

LSW - Wikipedia, the free encyclopedia ☆
LSW may stand for: Contents. 1 Places; 2 Organizations; 3 Other; 4 Redlinks. [edit]
Places. Landessternwarte Heidelberg-Königstuhl, a historic astronomical ...
en.wikipedia.org/wiki/LSW - Cached - Similar

I am searching for Library Society of the World. Did I find it? What do I need to do differently?

---

out what we need to do differently. Again, you and your students should be able to do this just by looking at the search results.

Ways to Work with Google and Privacy

In many ways, Google is simplest when we let it do our work for us. If we use Gmail, we can have it import our attachments into Google Docs, play our music files for us, and even keep track of what we've searched for on the web. It's easier to stay logged in to our email than to log out, and yet staying logged in means that

Google's persistent cookies associate our other Google activity (searches, chats, RSS feed reading) with our main identity. Again, this is not necessarily problematic but people who are privacy conscious can counteract this somewhat. And it should be something that we understand if we're managing public access computers. While what I'm describing works for Google, it can also be used generally speaking with other websites that use persistent cookie-based tracking methods.

Firefox and Internet Explorer can be configured to automatically be started using a "private browsing session" which means that the computer will not in any way keep a record of which sites have been visited.[4] If we're serious about patron privacy, this is the sort of thing that we should have as the default setting on all staff and public access computers. Another option is the option to clear history when Firefox closes, which can be set to include cookies. This has the added benefit of also clearing out patrons' logins and passwords from popular webmail sites, in addition to making sure they are no longer logged in. For people who are extra-concerned about this sort of thing, there are browser plug-ins such as BetterPrivacy[5] that will delete long-lived cookies (including Flash cookies, which are not otherwise removed) on a user's hard drive.

For many people who are out there who do not understand what the big deal is about the internet generally, having access to and understanding what a search engine does can help them learn what on the internet is interesting *to them* specifically. This keeps them from just clicking through whatever Yahoo! News or the *New York Times* feels like pointing to. Google and other search engines make it their job to be usable and simple for novice users to understand. While there are definitely some caveats that power users should keep in mind, teaching people about search engines is one of the more immediately useful skill sets you can pass on.

7

Email Is Everything

[T]he first email message was something like "QWER-TYUIOP." It is equally likely to have been "TESTING 1 2 3 4" or any other equally insignificant message . . . this got turned into bald statements that "QWERTYUIOP" was the first email message. Probably the only true statements about that first email are the it was all upper case (shouted) and the content was insignificant and forgettable (hence the amnesia).

—Ray Tomlinson, inventor of network email

Email is both the simplest and the most complicated thing to teach people how to use. It's simple because it's designed to do one thing: send a message to someone who also uses email. It's complicated because there are many different email clients and many different ways people access their email and the precise combination of your email server, your email client, and your internet connection combine to determine your overall email environment. This means there are a lot of aspects people that might get hung up on.

The problem with email, also, is that it's fairly far removed from being library-oriented. It's not reference; it's not research. It's pretty much a personal communication tool. We don't help people learn to use their cell phones, why, then, is email different? For any librarian who has had a patron come to them with an email address on a scrap of paper and say "I need to send this person a message." and then admits that they don't have an email account of their own, we've asked ourselves this question. What has become a simple "I need to send a message." task has now morphed into an "I need an email account, and I need to learn how to use it." project.

My feeling about email is that it's one of the simpler tasks we can get involved with. That is, most of the programs are understandable to a non-novice technology user. Most of the things people are trying to do with email are "normal" (i.e., people seem to know what email does and does not do in a general sense) and you can get a lot of brownie points for helping someone through the most difficult tasks after which they are in more of a position to help themselves and potentially others. It's a high-return investment, to my mind. Additionally, people are going to ask for assistance whether we're on the record as helping with email or not, so my feeling is that we should be ready to help.

Break It Down—What Is Email Really?

The most important thing to do with email is demystify it. The second most important thing to do is be able to differentiate, for patrons or for yourself, what is a basic component of email generally and what is something that may come with a *specific* email program. The novice technology user can't differentiate between the specific and the general. So, if Yahoo! Mail does something, they are often not aware that other email programs don't do that same thing. And

Idle Thoughts

I have always thought that a killer application for a library to create and share would be locally administered email. People new to email could get a free email address/account through the library at the library's domain. The library could administer this using something simple and Open Source like SquirrelMail. People could come to the library to check their mail. The staff would know how to use the patrons' system and could answer questions. The system wouldn't redesign or change except as determined by the library. For patrons whose only interaction with email is at the public library, it seems sort of nutty for us to try to explain the ins and outs of Yahoo! Mail or Gmail when most of what we're telling novice users to do is "Ignore that ad." and "You don't need to know what all those features are." I'm aware of the problems this situation poses, but I still think it's a digital divide killer.

they believe that learning how to do that thing is "learning email" when, in fact, it's learning a specific email interface, and one that might change. Here we discuss the individual parts of email and offer ideas for how to approach and address these in an instructional environment. Generally speaking, effective instruction will focus on the generalities of email and encourage people to map the specifics to their own personal email program, with one caveat. Novice technology users like linear "step one ... step two ... " sorts of lessons, but wind up stranded every time their email provider changes a setting or changes their interface. If you want your patrons to understand how email actually works, you have to give them some background in what it is.

That said, this doesn't mean you can't have steps in a classroom environment for what things you decide to cover and the order in which you cover them. The most surprising thing to me about email classes that I taught at the library was how many people would sit through an entire class just to ask one question about their particular email circumstances. When I started teaching email, it was very important for me and my students to differentiate between web-based email programs and email software programs such as Outlook or Thunderbird. While this is still true to a small extent, I've found that in the past few years the preponderance of web-based email has meant that when I teach "email" nowadays, I'm most likely teaching webmail. People are also much less likely to be accessing software-based email on the public library computers. I'll include some notes about software-based email later in this chapter.

The metaphor that I use to explain webmail is "It's like your regular postal mailbox, except that it's on a computer far away and you have to manipulate it through robot arms from another computer on the internet." While this sounds clunky, I find it also very useful to get across a couple of key points:

PAC Tip

What happens when patrons in your library click on a "mailto" link on a web page on a library computer? Does Outlook launch? It shouldn't. Find a way to make sure that mailto links do not cause a bad user experience for library patrons.

- Your mail stays in this "mailbox" even when you are not online and you can receive email when you are not online.
- You *do* need to be online in order to interact with your email.
- Your email is safe and secure on the other computer, and unless you actively delete something, it will stay there no matter what happens on the computer that you are accessing it from.

For people who have never used email before, it's often unclear to them where the messages are or what happens to them when they are not online and looking at their mail. Here are a few more points that are worth getting across to people who are completely new at email:

- Web-based email is free, but advertiser-supported.
- Having an email address does not give you an obligation to check it (or check it on a regular basis), though most people in this day and age will expect you to.
- If you used to use email years ago and didn't like it, you might want to give it another shot, as much has changed.

I am omitting, for the time being, service-based "software suite" systems such as AOL and, formerly, Compuserve where email access is wrapped into a larger internet access system sometimes called the "walled garden" approach. People using such systems should know that they can often access their email via a standard webmail client in addition to being able to access it from home. In fact, many people who use a software client like Outlook or Thunderbird may also have a web-based email option, which can be useful if they are trying to access their email from the library.

So, email can be considered to be a tool for sending and receiving messages and digital files to other people on the internet with access to email. Here is a short list of things that I feel generally come along with email. I only outline them because they're good things your students might not know, and they might work well on a handout. Email programs have the ability to:

- send a message with a date, subject, and a reply-to address
- cc and bcc multiple people
- maintain an address book
- reply to email and forward email to others

- file and store messages
- save draft messages
- search your email
- filter your email messages automatically into folders
- send and receive multiple attachments
- send email to multiple people at once, usually through a group mail feature
- discard messages or mark messages as spam
- learn more about the email program via help files
- customize some aspects of the email program via a settings file

Many, in fact probably most, email programs also allow the ability to:

- send large attachments, though most have a file size limit
- send HTML email with formatting in the message itself
- set a vacation or "away" message
- view images sent as attachments
- receive error messages if a message delivery fails (These can be suppressed by the email provider; they are a normal part of any email system.)

Some email programs also allow:

- storage or archiving of email in a variety of format
- encryption of email messages
- return receipt where you can verify that a message was open or read

So, when I start to explain email to people, I let them know the things that email is designed to do, and the things email is not really designed for. This both frames the topics that will be appearing in classes, and also lets people know how to set their own expectations about what email is supposed to do. As we all know, email *can* do a lot of things that it's not necessarily designed to do, but it's important to understand which of these things are an integral part of email and which are extra services. If Gmail was the only email program you had ever used, you might think that chat was a part of email services generally and this is not true. Similarly, the fact that you can send attachments via email does not mean that any size or any type of attachment will be allowed to be sent.

What Is Your Email?

The first thing you need to know from a patron who is trying to access their email is which email service they use. Novice technology users may not be aware that their email address represents a brand or a company, and one that they are responsible for keeping track of. You can ask people "What is your email address?" or "How do you get your email?" in an attempt to figure this sort of thing out. Or, you can just ask people how they get on the internet at home, and the answer to that question will help you determine what they use for email. It's useful to tell people a few things about email:

- They are not required to use the email that comes with their home internet access, though they are welcome to use it.
- If they do use that email address, the address will generally no longer be available to them when they switch internet service providers.
- A free webmail option will remain available to them even if their service provider changes.
- Advanced options like domain hosting can also provide consistency of email addresses.

Once you understand what a patron's email address is, you can tell them some things about email addresses generally. I enjoy this, because it's one of the things that makes sense, even to brand new technology users. A common error that novice users make is when someone tells them "Contact me through my website www.example.com." and they try typing this address into the To: line of an email message. This does not work. Maybe the website has a contact form on it, or a mailto link, but it's also clear that not everyone understands the difference between an email address and a web address. When I teach my "no computer needed" email

One of the things found with the research on Millennials is that despite the punditry claiming that "email is for old people," Millennials use email about the same amount as their older counterparts (more so if they've been to college) up until we hit what Pew Research calls the "Silent Generation," who use email significantly less than anyone else.[1] Millennials also communicate in a lot of other ways. So, let's not discount email as a dead technology just yet.

class, I spend some time focusing on web and email addresses. I explain the difference something like this:

An email address is like a phone number. It contains specific information about how to get to you, encoded in such a way as to make sense to computers. So, when you call someone, their phone number is not just ten random digits, it contains human-readable information also.

If you look at a phone number, you can see the area code. That gives you general location information such as state (for small-population states like Vermont and Wyoming), or at least regional information such as approximate state or city location. In Vermont for example, if you know someone's area code and extension, you know what town they live in. This is becoming less true as people get cell phones, but is very true for landlines.

To break it down ... My work phone number 802-728-9595 gives this information:

802—This person is in Vermont.
728—This person is in Randolph.
9595—This is the specific location in Randolph.

For an email example, you can look at something like this. My usual email address, jessamyn@gmail.com, gives people this information:

jessamyn is my username
@ means this is an email address not a web address
gmail is the company who receives email for me
.com is a suffix usually, though not always, used to designate a company

Usually, I'll talk to people about their own addresses and what they are saying. Sometimes, you'll know people's internet service providers, where they work, whether they attend or work at a school, and whether they are from another country. None of this is secret per se, but it is maybe not immediately obvious. Here are other things I tell people about email:

- There are never any spaces in an email address. An email address that looks like it has a space probably has an underscore, as in jessamyn_west@yahoo.com
- There is never more than one @ sign in an email address.

- Spelling is important. Sending email to jessamyn @gmail.cmo will not work. Even though a human could tell who the intended email recipient is, a computer cannot.
- Email addresses are not case-sensitive. Jessamyn @Gmail.Com is the same address as jessamyn@gmail.com

It's a fun exercise to go through the various email addresses and say what you know or don't know about the address. I sometimes give students a handout with some "broken" email addresses and ask them how to fix them. Check the Webliography at the end of this book if you are curious about the rules for special characters in email. It's generally outside of what novice technology users need to care about, but it can be useful for an instructor to know both just what's not allowed but *why* it's not allowed.

So, You Need Email?

More often, we see someone in the library who is email-curious, but does not yet have an email account. Often, they need to get an email account because they are applying for a job, or they need to communicate with someone far away. (We see this with parents whose children are going off to school or to the military.) I actually have a handout prepared for this sort of thing, so that not only can I explain a few of the things involved in email, but I can give people a sheet to take home with their relevant information on it. It looks like this, with big friendly letters, on one sheet of paper.

Patrons will not only have this sheet with them when they go home, they can show it to someone else if they are having trouble

---

Your email address is _____

The web address to get to your email is _____

Your username/login is _____

Your password is _____

Your secret question/answer are _____

with any of the steps and that person will be able to help them access their email.

I know as librarians we're supposed to give people access to resources and then let them make their own decisions. Generally speaking, I agree with this approach. However, in choosing technology, most people feel that they don't even understand the resources that they are being given to help them solve this problem. When patrons ask a question like "Which camera should I purchase?" or "What computer should I buy?," my personal experience has found that 25% would like to go read *Consumer Reports* or other rating and ranking publications, and 75% just want you to give them a name and a reputable low-cost place to purchase it. In fact, the big difference between my technology instruction that happens outside of a library and informal instruction that happens inside a library, is that in my non-library classes I actually feel okay telling people "I think you should buy this one." because I feel that's part of my job.

Accordingly, when people ask which email provider they should use, I first ask them what email service their friends use. My general rule of thumb for almost all novice technology adoption is that if you have a friend who uses something, whether it's a camera, webmail, or a laptop, having something that your friends are already using will make your path to learning that thing much easier. We've all seen people who do price and feature comparisons, trying to pick the perfect back-up hard drive for months. All that time they could have picked one that is good enough and been backing up their data. I'm aware that this is a personal preference, but I also think that one reason people who are offline may continue to be offline is they overthink the steps and investments required and never make the first step at all. Computers and their accessories used to be big expensive purchases that required a lot of deliberation. Now, a computer costs less than a year of cable TV.

So, in my library we used to set patrons up with a Yahoo! Mail account, but now we're leaning towards Gmail for the few reasons below:

1. Text-based ads are less confusing than the blinky graphics Yahoo uses.
2. Gmail drops you directly into your inbox when you log in, this is not true for Yahoo! Mail.

3. We suggest Google for searches; it's easy to give newer technology users fewer choices.
4. Gmail is what I use.

Of course, I can direct people to "how to choose an email address" resources, but this is usually more than they need. Additionally, while I am aware that many people have privacy concerns with webmail generally and Gmail specifically, I feel that's beyond the scope of basic instruction. I do let people know that there are general privacy issues with having your email stored on a machine that you do not control. I also explain that the ads they see are actually based on the words in their emails, but beyond that I can give them resources if they want to read up more on email and internet privacy on their own.

If you are a librarian, you likely have more than one email account. I got my first email account in 1985, but I could only use it to email other people at my high school. I've had email basically since I could drive. If you've never signed up for an account, you may have forgotten what is required to sign up for an account. Or, if you just breeze through the sign-up process, you may be surprised at what novice users find as sticking points. Let's look at the email sign up process. I have clicked "create an account" at gmail.com to start a process that Google calls "free and easy." In fact, if you have a Google account for other reasons, you may already have a Gmail account. Let's look at what someone needs to know how to do, and what information they need to give.

All the Required Steps

1. First Name and Last Name—while these can actually be anything you want, most people put their real names in the boxes. You can give them reasons why they might want to do this or not do this.
2. Desired Login Name—explain to users that the login will be what their email address becomes. Explain to them that Gmail has literally millions of users and that if they have a common name, any variant of that is taken. I entered Mary Smith as a first/last name combo and was given marysmith185 and mary.msmith.smith039 as options. Users can either choose the optional usernames that Gmail suggests, or they can choose a username of their

own devising. I often suggest geographical designations, words from other languages, meaningful numbers, or other options. For most novice users, this will be the most complicated part of the sign-up process.

3. Choose a Password—this needs to be eight characters long. While I am aware that it goes against conventional wisdom, I strongly suggest encouraging something memorable and writing it down for them on the handout. Words that you can find in a dictionary are bad choices. Most other words that are not a pet or family member's name or a birthday are fine. Google called my password "weak" when it was the same as my username, but the program still let me use it.

4. Stay Signed in/Enable Web History—these are Google specific and maddening in that they should be *UN*checked when in a public computing environment. The default setting is checked.

5. Security Question—here you will need to explain the idea of a security question, and be clear that the question's answer is NOT the user's password. The default questions are often not great for novice user—asking for a frequent flyer number, first teacher's name, first phone number, or library card number—but having a student write their own question involves a lot more steps. Use your best judgment. Remember that we are going to write down the question and answer on the handout the student will take home with them.

6. Recovery Email—you will leave this blank. Explain the process of password recovery briefly if you feel that he student is interested.

7. Location—this defaults to the United States, and should be okay for most purposes.

8. Birthday—let students know that the reason this is required is so that Google has some personal information to ask for to verify their identity should they require a reset password.

9. Word Verification—this is commonly known as a CAPCHA. You can let students know that this process is so that Google knows they are a human being and not a robot submitting the form automatically. This part of the process can be vexing to novice users because the text can be hard to read.

Additionally, for the Gmail sign-up process, these letters are not case sensitive. In some cases elsewhere on the web, they ARE cases sensitive.

10. Terms of Service—this involves reading through Google's Terms of Service, Program Policy and Privacy Policy, which is roughly 7,000 words. The box that displays the Terms of Service displays about 100 words at a time. This is a tough situation. People want to stay informed and yet almost none of these documents contain relevant information to them and do contain a lot of words they won't know, as well as the usual ALL CAPS boilerplate text. I offer to print these documents for people (for free!) if they want them, but I also try to summarize them—don't do anything illegal with your email account, don't use it to harass other people, don't assume your email is 100% private—and encourage moving forward. You can personally decide how to go with this. I'm aware that this is a complicated issue.

Some Optional Steps

If you've gotten through all ten steps then congrats you can click the "I accept. Create my account." button. At this point, your user will be whisked to an inbox already full of "helpful" mail from Gmail. I believe there is still one more necessary step for getting them ready to actually use and enjoy a Gmail account—and similar things are true for Yahoo, so feel free to extrapolate—and that's what I call the Reality Check step. It's also another good opportunity to have a talk about default settings. Gmail's default settings are geared towards things that are better for Gmail and not necessarily better for your patrons. This includes things like:

- Chat is set to "on" by default.
- Google Buzz is set to "on" be default.
- "Web Clips" including text ads are set to "on" by default.

When asked, patrons generally want all of these to be off and did not know they were on in the first place. Step them through how to do these things and ask them some other preference questions. Would they like to change the colors of their email environment? Would they like to change to a 24-hour clock? Would they like to change their date format? Some of these may not be at all appealing, but it's good to sort of talk over the idea of preferences and what sorts of things exist within the realm of the changeable.

Make sure the patrons send at least one email message once they've set up the account. It's not really that helpful to set someone up with an account and then say "Okay, see ya!" I have them send a test message, often to me, but if they have someone else's email address, that works too. If you feel that they're up to it, have them Cc: themselves so that they can get an idea both how to do that, but also how their inbox looks when they've gotten another message.

Email Parts

When I teach my most basic email classes, we don't even get online. We spend time learning to identify the different parts of an email program or an email message by looking at different email program screenshots. I maintain a lot of web-based email accounts that I barely use, primarily so that I can use them for screenshots or live examples in classroom settings without worrying that people are going to be staring at all of my email. So, I'll give students black and white handouts of a MSN email inbox, a Yahoo! Mail inbox, a Gmail inbox, and a SquirrelMail inbox. I'll ask students to circle the locations of the address book, the "compose a new message" button, the ads, the trash, the spam folder, and other things. I find that helping people generalize really helps them understand the mechanisms and not just learn the paths through their own system.

The same is true for whatever the Compose screen looks like. I'll make copies of three or four compose screens and have people identify the different parts of a message as an introduction to discussing what those things do. Usually, we'll do this in the form of question and answers as shown below:

- "Okay, I am addressing this email to my friend, where do I put his address?"
- "I want to send a copy of this message to my mom, where do I type her address?"
- "If I also want to send a secret copy of this message to my lawyer, where do I type her address?"
- "I'd like to attach a photo to this image, what do I click?"

Sometimes, the Cc: or Bcc: fields will be hidden from normal view. If so, show students what they need to click to access them.

Topics like forwarding or replying to a message can be addressed using examples. Novice users don't really understand why a message they're forwarding is editable while the same message before they've forwarded is not editable. And many people do not understand the "proper" use of the Subject line. I try to explain early on in an email class, the idea of Netiquette and how the online world has some social conventions of its own, most notably:

- ALL CAPS IS PERCEIVED AS SHOUTING.
- Forwarding chain letters or joke emails is not everyone's idea of a good time.
- Similarly Cc'ing your email to 100 people can make email headers unwieldy; use Bcc instead.
- Do not send as an attachment what you can include in the body of a message.
- Do not reply to all unless requested to.
- Do not forward other people's emails; at the same time do not send things over email that absolutely must be 100% private.

There are more tips you can share and everyone has their favorites, but it's a good idea to at least get across the idea that there is such a thing as email etiquette and, like all etiquette, some people follow conventions more than others. Keep in mind that we're not just showing our patrons how to use technology, we're helping them get adjusted into a technology culture. Therefore, it's appropriate and even possibly necessary to make sure that they understand the customs at the same time as they learn the tools.

Email Attachments

Email attachments are the bane of most technology instructors' existence. Every email program deals with them somewhat differently, and teaching someone about attachments usually involves giving users a crash course in learning about file systems. That is, a user needs to be able to navigate to the file they want to attach, which may be the first time they've seen a file-selection dialog box. They're transported outside of their email program and outside of the look and feel of the email program and they are often confused. While I don't want to go into the mechanics of attachments too much, I do want to mention common hurdles people come up against. I explain attachments to people in this way:

You can send your email along with other digital files. The digital file needs to be adhered to the email message that you are sending. This takes a few steps. You can send most digital files as attachments, but there may be a limit to how large your attachment can be. In order to read an attachment from someone else, you must have a copy of the program they used to create it, or a similar program.

This glosses over a lot of challenges people have. They are trying to send an attachment that is over the limit of their email program. They miss the last step of actually attaching the digital file they've chosen to the email they're writing. They get an attachment that they can't read and are not sure why. So, there's teaching people what the Attachment Experience is all about and there's realistically dealing with this issue in the library so that users have the most decent experience that they can. Here is a short list of things that can go wrong on public access PCs when people are dealing with attachments:

- The PC is not set up to automatically open the most common types of attachments—image files, Microsoft Office files including docx files, PDFs—and patrons get stuck having to choose a program to open the attachment with.
- The downloaded files go to some random location on the computer where the patron can't find them after they've been downloaded. (My suggestion is to set the browser to download all files to the desktop where they are immediately visible.)
- The patrons download a zip file which either can not be opened because of the lack of an unzip utility or unzips the file to a random location the patron can't find.
- A patron wants to attach a file they've brought in on a USB drive, but the computer doesn't show the USB drive in an obvious location.

Remember the section about library patrons in Chapter 1? Think of use cases that patrons using email are going to have. Supplement this with other things you've seen patrons try to do and have the public PCs act in ways that they expect and that enable them to do the tasks that they want to do.

Advanced Email—Tips to Improve the Experience

Email can quickly become overwhelming for users who are not used to it. Often they get an email account, sign up for mailing lists, and then check their mail a few days later and are surprised to see their inbox filling up with new messages. There are a few things you can tell them about in general terms that should help them manage their new communications.

1. Now, later, or never? This is what I tell people to ask about when they'll need to see this message again. Does it need a fairly quick response? Do you want to keep it for later, but not need to do anything with it now? Or, can you just delete it? Teaching students to file messages to get them out of the inbox can reduce what we sometimes call "inbox apnea," that shortness of breath you get when you see an inbox full of unread messages. Similarly, if you're done with a message, toss it! People who are good with organization skills will find email another good place to exercise them; people who are not very organized will find that their email will quickly get as disorganized as the rest of their life.

2. Pre-filtering! All major webmail programs will let you filter messages even before they get to your inbox. You can send mailing list email to its own folder or even send mail from some addresses straight to the trash! Check your email's help files for instructions specific to your program.

3. Get rid of spam. Junk mail is a part of life with web-based email, or any email really. The good news is that major webmail companies have fairly advanced spam-fighting techniques that actually learn as you use them. Encourage students to not just delete junk mail, but actually mark it as spam. This way they are helping the spam filters learn what is and is not acceptable email and the spam still winds up out of their inbox.

4. Unsubscribe. It's fairly straightforward to unsubscribe from any legitimate mailing list. Show students how to click the unsubscribe link in an email message for a list they no longer want to be on, or a list they got on to by mistake. Encourage them to not report mailing lists as spam.

5. Sort and Search. Their inbox is not just browsable, it's searchable and sortable. Usually by clicking on the header

of any column, you can sort by that column. Looking for email from a certain person? Sort your inbox by name? Need to find an email about a certain topic? Use the search box and let the computer do the work for you.

6. Who? If they do not recognize the email address or the name of the person sending the attachment, do not open the attachment.
7. Why? If they get the email bounced back to them it is likely that the email they get back, amidst all the code and technical terminology, has told them why it was returned. Nine times out of ten this is because they spelled the person's email address wrong.

Non–Web-Based Email

For the most part, patrons accessing email at our libraries will be using some form of web-based email. However, if people are used to getting their email at home using Outlook, or Thunderbird, or an internet service like AOL, they may still be able to get their email at the library. The usual steps I take to see if this is the case are:

1. Ask them their email address. If they do not know their email address, this pretty much needs to stop here.
2. If they know their email address, make a URL out of their domain. So, if their email address is *ruby@slippers.com*, go to www.slippers.com and see if there is a "Check email" link somewhere on the page.
3. If so, help the student log in to their email account providing that they know or can recover their password.

Students may be confused by the webmail interface if they are used to the one they use at home. Be sure to tell them that this doesn't change the way they can access their email at home, it just provides them an alternative for checking their email when they are not home. Students may also bring their laptops into the library and find that they have problems sending email using the library's internet. In almost all cases, this is because the users' internet service provider has restrictions on how people send email through their email servers. If users can receive but not send email when connected to the library's wireless network, direct them to contact their ISP (or you can check yourself on the ISPs website) to determine how to properly configure their email program for sending mail while away from home.

Bad People and Email

There are ways that people try to scam or swindle people using email. While I do not think that it is the library's job to keep people safe from every unforeseen circumstance, as people who have been around the block a few times email-wise, we can take a few minutes out of our class time to explain some well-known scams and how to not fall for them. I have a short list of them here, but you can add your own:

1. No one who wins the lottery gets notified by email. Have you played the lottery lately? No? Then you did not win the lottery.
2. The same goes for people requesting assistance. Do you know them? Do they know you? Then you should feel okay about not assisting them with their international banking transfers.
3. Any time you click a link in an email that asks you to log in someplace, check the web address to make sure you are actually going to the right website. If you are not sure, navigate directly to the website and log in there. If you are getting email from a bank that is not your bank, ignore it or send it to your spam folder. If you are unsure, you can always call your bank to ask if the email is legitimate.
4. In fact, I rarely click links in email that is sent from someone I do not know. I also keep images turned off in my email and on a case-by-case basis, turn them on. This is a feature that Gmail and Yahoo! Mail have that is very useful.

Let patrons or students know about the term *phishing* and give them broad outlines of the 419 Scams and other similar types of fraud. I try very hard to get the message across to students that these problems, while they may not go away, are manageable by using a combination of common sense and a cautious approach. If I feel that students are interested and won't be put off by some racy language, I show them what's in my spam folder and how you can tell that a certain email that may seem legitimate really isn't. This is more of an advanced approach to email, but for people who are new to email, there are a lot of milestones they need to reach and pass before they're going to be fully competent in all the differing aspects of email use.

There's really not much else to say about spam. It exists and is noxious and pervasive, but all web-based email programs now have tools for managing and dealing with it. We do ourselves and our patrons a disservice when we focus on all the downsides of a technology as powerful and problem-solving as email. More attention to spam will not solve the spam problem and will not be a good use of our limited time and attention.

8

Office Software, Databases, and Social Software

The world has arrived at an age of cheap complex devices of great reliability; and something is bound to come of it.[1]

—Vannevar Bush, *As We May Think*

Office software generally means Word and Excel, but it could be expanded to include PowerPoint and other software that people would be likely to use on the job. Maybe Quicken or QuickBooks? Lotus Notes? But not things like Photoshop or iMovie. Usually, it's "whatever comes in Microsoft Office," which can alternately include MS Access or possibly Publisher. Most of the time when I'm talking about office software, I mean MS Word and MS Excel and this is mostly what is covered in this chapter. When people use computers for work, sometimes all they know how to do is open these programs and do stuff with them, entirely within the universe of that piece of software. They don't know anything about file systems and they don't know any troubleshooting, although they may understand fairly sophisticated aspects of these programs such as how to make a pivot table in Excel, or how to use Word Art in MS Word.

My discussion here centers on specific brands of software here with some caveats. We're a little behind the times here in Central Vermont, so the bulk of my experience is the "pre-ribbon" versions of Word and Excel, before their recent user interface redesign.

OpenOffice, a free open source office suite of tools, is also in the pre-ribbon phase. The Mac version of Microsoft Office is developed independently from the Windows version and so has a ribbon, but it's slightly different. While I'm certain that the digital divide will be with us for years to come, the most dated aspect of this entire book may be that it covers the older versions of Microsoft software.

Libraries that have Gates Foundation computers and have not paid or gotten grants to upgrade their software will have older versions of Microsoft Office. All of the libraries in my region have Office 2003. At the school where I work, we maintain multiple copies of Office software on each computer so that we have newer versions for students who may be entering workplaces with updated software, as well as legacy versions for adult education students who need to use what they have on their computers at home. It's a bit of a pickle, and while I know it's not Microsoft's job to make sure that their software is predictable and regular—and know many people who swear that the ribbon interface is a huge improvement—the new user interface has been a big setback for people for whom even the *idea* of a user interface is somewhat sophisticated.

This chapter covers Microsoft Office software basics and also discusses how to organize a class around these topics. Handouts that I've used in my classes that are available for examination, use, and reuse can be found at: http://librarian.net/digitaldivide.

Do You Know Word?

Similar to how we call our planet's moon *Moon*, we call our main word processor *Word*. This is confusing to people. In fact, the idea of "word processing" can sometimes be a little challenging. I explain it like this to my students:

> *When I was in school, I typed all my papers out on a typewriter. While this was an easy system to use, it meant that I had to do a lot more work to make changes or even to move things around. A word processor is like a fancy typewriter that allows you to do a lot of things with formatting as well as move type around without resorting to scissors. We'll learn to do basic formatting, copying and pasting, and show you how to move*

documents around so that you can use them on whichever computer you want.

In the basic Word classes that we teach in adult education, we literally start from scratch. If we're lucky, people know how to click and double click, but many of them don't know what a menu is and they don't know how to select text. We focus on the basics, and on small project-based lessons. The downside to project-based lessons is that sometimes students can't extrapolate from one set of instructions ("Here's how to type a bulleted list.") to a very similar set of instructions ("Here's how to type a numbered list.") and so, I try frequently to draw similarities between one task and other related tasks that a student might want to do.

Getting Started

Not everyone has the ability to customize their work environment, especially if they often use public computers. Word and Excel both have a lot of customization options that can make people's experience with the software go more easily. So before you get started, explain the most useful thing for novice students to know: the idea of defaults and how there are things they can change and things they can't change.

Start with the software in its default state. If students have questions about how the interface works, tell them that something is either changeable (and show them how to change it), or not changeable. Here are a few quick examples of things that are changeable and not changeable in Word:

Changeable

> the default font face and size
> which toolbars are visible when you start the program and
> their locations

PAC Tip

Some default settings such as personalized menus on Word are confusing to patrons. Spend a little time configuring Word's default settings to be as straightforward as possible. Do not allow defaults to be changeable by patrons.

whether you start the program with a blank document or with
the template gallery
turning the spell checker and grammar checker on or off

Not Changeable

the colors of the interface (It's changeable at a Windows level,
not from within the program.)
changing what fonts appear on the font list (again, changeable
outside of Word)

Changeable But Complicated

the look of the toolbar buttons
the contents of the menus
the key commands associated with an action

The next thing I tell people is that Word does about 1,000 things
(I made this number up, but it's a big number.), and we're going to
learn to do maybe 15 to 20 of them. One of the daunting things for
novice users is that they often feel that people who understand computers know what all the buttons and menu items do. This seems
like a lot of work, possibly too much work, to many people. A lot
of what I teach is how to ignore or look past the features they will
not be using to find the features they do want to use. Some of this
can happen through customization if they are using their own computer. Some of it is just practice and muscle memory, learning how
to do the motions that create the actions. It's a little counterintuitive
to say that a lot of my instruction is about how to ignore things, but
there's a lot of that in teaching people how to use MS Office tools.

Many of the basic topics covered in the previous chapter apply
to these programs and if people already know what a menu is, say or
a toolbar, they'll be a little ahead. Make sure that the computers are
already configured to open up to a blank document. The first thing
to show students is how to click the little "X" to make the right hand
menu disappear which will increase their screen space and not give
them a contextually changing, blinky thing on the right-hand side.
We'll also go through a few other setup routines which are good
practice if they'll be using public computers. Have students examine
their environment and ask a few questions:

- Are the toolbars I need visible?
- Am I looking at this document in the view that I am comfortable with (normal versus page layout)?

- Are spelling and grammar checking turned on/off, the way you'd prefer?

While You're in Process

The biggest and best things you can teach students learning office software in general is about permanence—what is permanent and what is not, what is problematic and what is not. Turning on Auto-Save means that problems like power failures—still a big deal in my neck of the woods—won't undo hours of work. Let's look at some of the other permanent and impermanent things about office software:

- Accidental deletions? Don't worry, you can use CTRL-Z and undo them. There are two things that I always teach students the key commands for: F1 for help and CTRL-Z for undo. In fact, I'll often go around the room and randomly say "What if your cat jumped on the keyboard right when you were going to move that paragraph you highlighted? It's okay! You can type CTRL-Z and get it back!"
- Made a giant mistake that you can't undo? Close the document and don't save it. Your last version will still be saved. For things that are what I call "mission critical," I often encourage students to save a few copies of the document—keeping track of which is which—so that they have a backup even if something catastrophic happens. For people who aren't quite at the USB-drive phase, sometimes we'll end the class by having students email the documents to themselves.
- Formatting snafu? Easy to change. Maybe you can't remember what you did, but there's certainly a way to either CTRL-Z your way back to how it used to be or get someone who can explain how to get to that point.
- Can't find your document? If you are sure that it's on the hard drive (and sometimes students aren't), then you can track down the file as long as you know a few words that were in the document, or better yet, approximately when you last worked on it. Search tools are more powerful than many people expect, items are rarely truly lost.

You can look at the sample handouts linked in the Appendix to get a feel for how classes go. In a two-hour class—not something you'd likely have at the library but fairly standard for adult education—the timing would break down something like this:

0:00–0:15	review of last week's materials, asking for questions
0:15–0:45	new information, demonstrations
0:45–1:00	practicing new information on their own
1:00–1:10	break
1:10–1:40	guided exercises working with new information
1:40–1:50	questions
1:50–2:00	review and preview of next class

The most crucial part, to me, is that there's repetition, time for watching, time for doing, and a lot of review. I don't think it's as important that students type the examples themselves, as it is that they get practice working with the tools on their own to see some of the odd ways the software can behave, and how to work with it. Often with novice users there is a lot of "WHY does it do this?" questions when confronted with something that is counterintuitive to their idea of how a program should work. Having a reasonable response to this sort of thing that acknowledges that yes, it's weird but also yes, they will have to learn it, is a good approach moving forward.

Bibliographic Instruction—Teaching Our Tools

It's another pervasive myth that if our tools, really mostly our web interfaces, were simple enough, people would automatically know how to use them and we could dispense with bibliographic instruction altogether. While that's a nice fantasy goal, the truth is that people using even the simplest interface like Google can benefit from some tips or pointers. In fact, often the interfaces that look the simplest can be the most complicated to use because people miss out on advanced features and don't know how to use them in any way other than the obvious one: type what you're looking for into the box and click the nearest button.

I went to library school in the Dialog era and someplace I still have handouts explaining how to create advanced queries in databases that charged users by the access minute, or by the query, or by how many records you had to "print." These are charming antiquated handouts. That said, I think that initial approach to searching—aiming for elegance of the query and high relevance of the result—was a good way to learn about how to really do effective searching. *Relevance* and *recall* aren't terms you hear as much in the age of Google, but I think they're still key in learning to do nice searches.

That said, we're talking about novice users here and mostly they're trying to find a book in the catalog or an article in a database. I treat this as if it were some sort of a board game. Our job is to help them find what they're looking for before they give up in disgust or frustration. The clock is ticking. Let's go!

Databases—What Are They?

Novice users do not know what a database is. They may even use databases and not really know what one is. This is one of those terms that we should probably get rid of. The term makes so much sense to librarians and information workers generally, but sadly it's not very evocative for our patrons. If you say something like "You can get *Smithsonian Magazine* via the computer!" their ears perk up, but if you say "We have many periodical databases." you wind up greeted with the thousand-yard stare. Often, as discussed in Chapter 1, libraries have access to different types of content databases because we buy these products or access to these products from database vendors.

This is all pretty much inside baseball at libraries. Most people, even librarians, don't know what these databases cost or what sort of usage and access statistics they have. Often the offerings change without notice, as with the recent exclusive deals that EBSCO launched with many popular magazine publishers. When explaining or showing off library databases to patrons, it's often good to not get too technical at first—just dive right into doing something that shows results that are interesting. Saying "Hey, there is interesting stuff here." and then showing what that stuff is gets you further than explaining that you have a "keyword indexed database with full text retrieval and blah, blah, blah. ... " Use words and phrases people know, "You can search the *New York Times* back to 1980." and "You can search for people in any U.S. Census up through 1900."

In fact, I'd go one step further and find a way to surface these sorts of things as regular offerings in whatever manner you normally communicate with patrons. Many libraries have concerns about what uses they might possibly have for social software. What would they talk about? To me, this is a prime opportunity to point out things in the collection that you think will have high value to people, but that they might not even know you have. *Consumer Reports,* for example, is a much loved and trusted magazine. If people can access back issues of it from home, they'd like to know how. Mention it on Twitter or Facebook, or put it on a handout or the library's website in a rotating "highlights from our collection" box. I know that a lot of libraries have a New Books section, but how often do you announce (or are even aware of) new offerings in your databases? I'm not even sure how I'd know if the offerings in the Vermont Online Library changed if we didn't get announcements from the state's Department of Libraries.

Just Play the Hits, Man

Some people may be learning the whole concept of online searching by interacting with your library catalog. While at some level this is too bad—OPACs are notorious for having difficult interfaces—this does mean that you should probably make sure that patrons know some of the standard things that you learned in library school about doing an effective search. Again, I am handout-crazy, but having a few examples of things that work and things that look like they would work but don't work, can help. Here are some examples and terms that I like to make sure are clarified:

- *She's Not There* by Jennifer Boylan—Searching for this book by title fails in some OPACs if you don't search for it as a bound phrase, meaning putting the title in quotes. Why? The "not" in the title is taken literally.
- *Time* Magazine—How do you find this? Do users have to select "periodicals" specifically? Do they know what a periodical is? When people search for periodical titles in your OPAC, will they find references to that periodical in your online databases if you have them?
- Keyword versus subject—Do users know the difference between these terms? Do they need to in order to effectively search the library catalog?
- Gin AND tonic versus gin OR tonic—There are many simple examples that people can remember about what using AND and/or OR will do to their search results.

- Finding movies—We had an OPAC once where you needed to type the word VIDEORECORDING if you wanted to limit the search to movies. I could not explain that to a patron with a straight face.
- Time limits generally—As noted previously, you may need to examine what some of these searches look like from a patron's perspective to see if it's possible to make them more user-friendly. We had a setting in an OPAC I once used where it would list items chronologically starting from newest first. This was terrific except that the newest items in our OPAC were the ones that were "on order" and hence, not actually available.

Other features of database searching that patrons may not understand include setting limits on retrieval sets, sorting results and marking results, an option which many OPACs have. An odd wrinkle that we have encountered in our rural libraries is that most patrons weren't even aware they had a library card number until they started needing it for database logins. Usually you just tell the librarian your name and she'll check the book out to you. We don't have fines; we're a pretty loose bunch. The hurdles and limits that are commonplace in the world of access to copyrighted content are new for many people and need to be introduced in a "Here's why you might care about this." sort of way. Unlike general internet and mouse skills, I think people can live their entire lives without using an online database, but they just might find worthwhile reasons to use one if they just knew what one was.

Federated Searching—One-Stop Shopping

The holy grail of continuing database improvements has been some sort of one-stop shopping situation where all the materials that an institution has legal access to can be searched using one standard search box. We see this sort of thing on the open internet where people can put a search box on their website that just searches their website, or searches other websites, or searches most anything online that they choose using Google's Custom Search (or other options) and the search results come out quickly, and in a standard format.

This is generally not true with the databases that we have available in our libraries, for the most part. If we're lucky, the databases are at least grouped by vendor so that we can do some simultaneous searching of multiple databases but for the most part, bigger libraries have a long list of separate databases or groups of databases that people can search. If people are really lucky, there will be some sort of a proxy server so that they don't have to log in to each database each time they want to do a new search.

I'm a generalist and I work mostly in public libraries, so I'm usually not searching for any one specific crucial research thing; but even so, I'm often wondering how this could be made simpler, and I'm hoping that's the sort of thing that content providers are working towards. In July 2010, Open Library announced that they're facilitating the lending of ebooks via their (nice-looking) interface for anyone who belongs to a library system that uses OverDrive. I've mentioned how I feel about OverDrive earlier in the book, but I think I'd be more partial to their services if I wasn't also stuck using their website to access those services.

Remember, many people just see the back of a monitor when they ask us to look things up for them; and they often think there is some mystical information trove that we get secret access to when we get out of library school, and we know the magic words to conjure the information out of it. The truth is much more prosaic. We know generalized search approaches, can figure out which ones work, and have a good idea of which sources to start looking into first. Also, we type quickly. Many of these things can be learned, and taught, though I'm also happy to just look something up for someone and have it seem like a vaguely enchanted experience.

Social Software and Syndicated Sites

Even though social software isn't really a "Tech 101" sort of topic, more and more people are finding their way to the web because of either Facebook or other social networking sites. I say "other sites" but really 99 times out of 100 what I really mean is Facebook. The other one time I probably mean Twitter. Occasionally, there's another site that people are curious about. And by the time this is in print, there will probably be some new site that no one could have even predicted at the time I was writing this.

People read about these sites in the newspaper or get pressure from other friends to connect. This is especially pernicious among novice users, mainly because Facebook is geared towards sharing. It's easier to invite your entire address book to be your Facebook

friends than it is not to. So, people who are new to technology wind up sending invitations to other people who are new to technology and sometimes people have joined before they even quite know what's happened.

Lest anyone think I'm being overly dramatic, let me assure you that I see this sort of thing weekly. This is not me making up an invisible clueless user who can't find the "any key"; this is me watching how people behave when confronted with a page like this one after their first login to Facebook.

It is unclear from looking at this box that the next step is to sign in to Google and add the people from your address book who are already Facebook members. The next step is to invite the rest of them who aren't yet members to join Facebook. Now, if you read all the text, you know what's going on, but people don't always read all the text. And then, whammo, all your student's friends have gotten email inviting them to Facebook, and the cycle continues.

Novice users are often surprised by how many choices they have in the online world compared to, for example, at the post office or with the hone system. Novice users are also concerned about the things they don't understand, and worry that sharing information online will lead to some sort of identity theft at some later point. The FCC's 2010 broadband survey addresses this somewhat obliquely saying that "non-adopters are almost 50 percent more likely than broadband users to say they believe it is too easy for personal information to be stolen online." Their surveys indicated that over half the non-adopters strongly agreed that it's easy for personal information to be stolen.

This is another digital divide issue. I also think it's too easy for personal information to be stolen online, but that's because I *know* how that sort of thing happens—phishing emails, fraudulent websites, and insecure credit card transactions. I don't think it's easy for MY personal information to get stolen, because I am a savvy web user. That said, even I've had trouble with fraudulent charges on my credit cards, but I'd prefer one small headache with my bank every few years to never purchasing anything online. For people who are unfamiliar with internet mechanisms generally, the whole social software system seems fraught with pitfalls along these lines.

That said, for many people, Facebook and other social software sites allow people to keep in touch with other people and institutions with possibly the lowest amount of effort. This may not be great news for the social fabric, but for people who are looking for a reason to get or stay online, it's worth at least understanding what's going on. As a librarian, I get asked to speak about Facebook more than possibly any other Web 2.0 tool. It's mysterious and inscrutable to people and yet, unlike a lot of other technology, people feel that they want or need to participate.

The first thing I tell people is that no, they do not need to participate. I'm active on Facebook, but my sister who is tech savvy and otherwise online, isn't. My mom uses Facebook, my dad doesn't. Sure, there's a sense that if all your friends are there, deciding to not be there might be problematic, but I don't think that's what we're looking at for novice users. So with that out of the way—yes, joining Facebook is entirely optional—here is some more guidance for novice users dipping their toes in social software.

Social?

The first thing is to understand what the term *social* means in this context. Loosely speaking, a website is social if it allows you to make a profile and make links with other users. Some sites have a main purpose and are also social, like LibraryThing for example, and some sites have the social aspect as their main function. I think Facebook doesn't even call itself social software, preferring the term "social utility." As another example, you can interact with Twitter mainly as a reader, as a writer, or as someone who interacts with friends on Twitter. So, for some people Twitter is a very social tool and for others, not so much. For people who are mainly used to real-life interactions, the idea that you could have 1000 "friends" that you've never met, or that you could be "friends" with Toyota or that you might not be "friends" with your Mom (Note: I am friends with my mom on all social networks.) can be confusing.

It's also worth pointing out that:

1. There are ways to use social software without thinking of it as a social tool.
2. Often newer and more popular tools have better interfaces.
3. The idea of social software is more of a marketing than a descriptive term.

Except for being able to make a profile and link to other users, social software does not necessarily share a lot of other attributes. And I always add this extra caveat: *no matter how you use technology, there will be someone around who will tell you that you are doing it wrong, so it's worth learning how to just ignore that some of the time.*

So, oddly even though social software can be complex in its functionality, it may be one of the easier tools for people to interact with at first. I am surprised that I have students coming to drop-in time who are Facebook users, but who don't know how to type a document or use email.

Privacy and Utility

When people drop in and ask about using Facebook, I always ask them "Well, what do you want to use it for?" and then we can move on from there. Also, similarly to how I help students set up email the way I think they'll like it—with a minimum of intrusive advertising and "push" notifications—I also help people get Facebook set up so that the level of information they're sharing is the level of information they want to be sharing. For the most part, adults who are not in the dating scene are usually okay sharing pretty much nothing at all outside of their friends, family, and professional contacts. This is a bit of an overgeneralization, but not much of one.

There are a few Facebook privacy analyzers that can let you know how much information you're sharing and gives you simple instructions on how to adjust the settings if they're not to your liking. I'd outline the specifics, but they've been changing even since I've been writing this book; so I have no doubt they'll be different by the time you're reading this. My routine for helping people get set up on most social sites is the same:

1. Sign up with username and password that you WRITE DOWN.
2. Check the preferences of the site to make sure you're only sharing what you want to share. Turn off extra features you don't want such as built-in chat and/or geolocation.
3. Set up a profile with a decent photo and the personal information that you want to add.
4. Check the profile to see how it looks to other people.
5. Add a friend or two, not your whole address book! If anyone wants to know why I have so many Facebook friends, this is why. I wish there was a metric to show how many people's first friend I was.
6. Click around a little and see what looks interesting on the site. Maybe add a comment or two. Learn about the internal messaging system.
7. Advanced step: if you are on your own laptop, we can check out Greasemonkey and see if there are any scripts that might help tamp down the advertising and other parts of Facebook you don't like. I use a script called Facebook Autocolorizer; and it makes the website take on the colors of whatever photos are prominent on the page. I sort of like it.

There are enough people bumbling around on social software nowadays that you really don't need to feel that you're doing it wrong. Many other people are learning at the same time. I may be a little overly optimistic, but I've actually been heartened at seeing all the tech novices using online tools because they want to and not because they had to. Social software may turn into many people's "genuine option" so let's be ready for them when they ask us how it all works.

RSS: Really Simple Syndication

Let me start off by saying that calling anything "simple" in front of novice computer users is asking for trouble, but if you have to tell them what RSS stands for, you will have to tell them that it stands for Really Simple Syndication. This is not much of an explanation, so you can follow-up by saying that web pages with rotating content such as blogs, newspapers, and weather reports, almost always have the content available in a computer-readable way so that you can read the content without having to go to the specific website that it's on. This is a bit of an advanced topic for novice users, but it's worthwhile to generally understand because using RSS can solve a problem for people. And they don't have to use new software to do it.

The really basic way that I explain this is "What if you could subscribe to a website's content the same way you'd subscribe to a magazine and it would just arrive in your mailbox?" To many people this would be appealing. Fewer URLs to remember, one interface to interact with, an easy metaphor to keep in mind. For people who interact with the web much like they would another media source like television or print media, this can allow them a simpler way to view content in one interface. The simplest way to do this is via one of the customized portal pages that comes along with free webmail such as My Yahoo! or iGoogle. There are also standalone websites that do this such as Netvibes.

More importantly, popular social software websites such as Twitter and Facebook offer RSS feeds for their content, so if someone is Twitter-curious but really has a hard time clicking around the website, they can subscribe to a Twitter account such as, for example, the State of Vermont's feed, which has just a few daily updates. For a lot of people, getting this sort of information in your inbox or on a website that you frequently visit, can highlight what's nice about the web without including all the daunting parts.

RSS in Your Inbox

For people who are already using webmail, this process is fairly straightforward. Gmail calls this feature "web clips." Yahoo! Mail has been trying lately to nudge users to interact with RSS feeds using the My Yahoo! page, which is only slightly more difficult. Again, it's better to talk in generalities than tell people a step-by-step path they need to take to accomplish the result. The path may change, but if they know how to find the path, they'll be set in future iterations. That said, they often want the steps.

If you use the web clips feature of Gmail, for example, you'll see headlines from whatever feed you subscribe to along the top of your mailbox. Of course, you'll also see sponsored ads. I subscribed to the State of Vermont's updates just by typing Vermont in the search box. However, I could also go to their Twitter feed or their website and look for the address for the feed. A URL for an

This is the bright orange icon that says "RSS feed available" You can teach students how to look for it, often in the address bar of their web browser.

RSS feed looks like a regular web address but with one or two small differences:

> The URL for my website is http://www.librarian.net/.
> The URL for my website's RSS feed is feed://http//www .librarian.net/feed/ (note the missing colon after http)
> This URL will also work http://www.librarian.net/feed/
> Some URLs end with a file with an XML file extension.

Patrons and librarians alike should know that you can right-click on a link to an RSS feed and use the Copy command to copy the URL of the RSS feed address. Then, you can go to a super-simple website like FeedMyInbox.com, paste the URL into the top box, type your email address into the bottom box, and then you'll get updates in your email inbox when the website updates. Feed-MyInbox is a good tool to get started with, but you can only use it for a few feeds (five) before they'd like you to pay for the service. So, once you've figured out what RSS is good for, you can move on to using an RSS reader to get the same functionality—updates sent to you when a site updates—in your email program of choice or all delivered to one website. Websites like Bloglines or portal pages like the ones I've mentioned above are great for reading updates. More adventuresome people might want to try an in-browser solution like the Sage RSS reader <http://sagerss.com/> for Firefox.

People feel better when they can get the information that they want in a format that works for them. RSS feeds are the great equalizer because they allow the content to be accessed independently from the design of the website where it originally appeared. Not only is this a boon to control freaks like myself, but it's useful for accessibility purposes because the RSS reader can be customized with the font face, size, and colors that are easiest for the user to read. I know the idea of something like RSS feels like it's really technical, but once people know how to copy and paste, it's probably one of the simpler things to do that I've mentioned in this chapter—and one of the most rewarding.

9

When Things Go Wrong, or Right

Damage to information is inflicted almost entirely by human actions and rarely by equipment failures.[1]

—Paul A. Strassmann, *Knowledge Management* column

The largest gap that persists between people who understand technology and those who do not, is the ability to troubleshoot a problem. Generally speaking, troubleshooting just involves attacking a problem and attempting to diagnose why something isn't working the way it's supposed to be working. For someone who is skilled with technology this is a methodical, though dull, process where possible causes for the problem are systematically eliminated until the cause is, hopefully, found. Sometimes, this requires calling in experts, or swapping out parts, but it's a process with a direction and one with an eventual resolution.

Many people do troubleshooting differently, but many other people don't do it at all. People who are not familiar with computers don't know the difference between a small problem and a large one, between the "blue screen of death" and something requiring a simple reboot. I often hear about someone's computer at home that does "something unexpected" which rattles the user so much that they turn off the computer, put it away, and don't turn it on again until they have someone with them to look at it. Of course, since nine times out of ten a reboot will solve most simple problems, the computer is miraculously cured by the time it's turned on again. While this is somewhat nice—Hey, the computer works!—it also doesn't teach the user anything about how to manage computer problems on their own.

At the school where I work, tech support is expensive. We contract with an IT company who fixes our problems at the rate of about $100/hour. I get paid to fix problems at a rate of considerably less. Obviously, if someone can fix their own problem, then no one has to get paid any extra at all. You might think I have some sort of self-interest in keeping people in the dark as far as how to fix their computers, but really, I'd love for them to better understand their systems. Because once the simple problems are taken care of, I get to work on the really complicated problems, which are, actually, a lot more fun.

Troubleshooting and Supporting Your Systems

So, I've taken some steps in my workplace to try to help people learn to solve their own problems, and I've given some talks about how to deal with what Rachel Singer Gordon calls the Accidental Systems Librarian problem: you're not trained in systems librarianship, you just know more than the other librarians about technology, so you're the new systems librarian! In many small libraries, there is one librarian who is the de facto systems librarian since they're the "everything" librarian. It can be tough to have the free time to untangle a complicated tech support issue and some libraries may find that it's actually a smarter use of resources to pay someone to fix computer problems. That said, many small problems can and should be dealt with by the people encountering them, and here are some guidelines.

Serious Problems

First, I find it helpful to outline what sorts of problems are fairly commonplace and what sorts of problems are not. This can be tricky because some problems that indicate bad things happening— the hard drive suddenly stops functioning—can resemble less-problematic occurrences like a screen freezing up. One of the things that I assure staff who are not totally confident in their tech skills, is that doing basic troubleshooting steps will not make bad problems worse (in nearly every case), but it can solve a lot of simple problems.

Here are some lists from a handout I devised for the teachers at the school where I work. The goal of this two-sided handout was to give people some basic troubleshooting steps and some resources to look things up. We figured we could maybe save a few tech support calls and also get them to funnel medium-sized problems to me before filling out a trouble ticket. I made a friendly handout with a cartoon computer on it and tossed one of these into everyone's mailbox. You can get print examples of a variation of these handouts at *www.librarian.net/digitaldivide*.

Ninety percent of all repairable tech support problems can be solved by a "do over." This means . . .

- seeing what the last thing was that you did before the problem started
- looking to see if the computer is asking you a question, and answering it
- restarting the program you are working on (You may lose your unsaved work.)
- making sure everything is still plugged in
- turning the computer on and off again (Don't forget the ten-second power button trick.)

The idea here is to get people into the mode of seeing most computer problems as uncomplicated, i.e., not requiring a lot of mucking about to fix, and also thinking about basic causes, the same way you would if the computer were a toaster. Is it plugged in? Did you do something to it right before this happened?

The ten-second power button trick is one of those things that provides a real "Aha!" moment for many people. Their computer freezes. They try to restart it with CTRL-ALT-DEL and that doesn't work. Then, they try to hit the power button and *that* didn't work. To them, this indicates a serious problem. This is a totally reasonable conclusion, but it turns out that in order to force a reboot on a frozen computer, sometimes you have to hold the power button in for ten seconds (on a PC or a Mac incidentally). Ten seconds or until it reboots, really. For many people at my school, this was the item that had been missing from their toolkit and it solved a lot of problems. Once the frozen computer was forcibly restarted, it was often just fine.

The other 10% of all repairable tech support problems are usually a combination of

- hardware problems
- software conflicts
- incorrect or problematic system or software settings
- gremlins (actually, no)

Even though there are some things that can't get quickly fixed, people like to know why stuff happens. I think it's important to let people know that basically their computer is a giant calculator; it's not going to just fail randomly for no reason all the time. We may not always know the reasons, but there are reasons.

Occasionally, something really breaks:

- Computers should NOT smell like anything.
- They should not make clicking or clunking noises.
- They do not like spilled coffee, sudden movements, or lots of dust or cat hair
- If *everyone* seems to be off the network, you don't have to trouble-shoot your own network problems.

You want people to call you when there is a serious problem like a clunking sound, a smell, or a spill. It's worth letting people know that even if they pour coffee into the keyboard, it's not going to break the rest of the computer. Unless that computer is a laptop in which case all bets are off. Also, learn about specific problems versus general problems: Is it just you? Is it the whole office? Is it the whole school? Learn to ask these questions so problems can be approached with more information that might be useful.

What you should make note of if you do need to ask for help:

- Are you the only person having this problem, or is it affecting every-one?
- What were you doing before the problem happened?
- What happened, or what didn't happen?

- What were you expecting to happen?
- What is the text of the error message you got, if any?
- What steps did you take to try to fix the problem, and what happened?
- What computer were you using and what, if any, login were you using?

Self-Tech Support

People need to feel not only deputized, but encouraged to investigate their own problems and to try out what they've found. One of the most incorrect assumptions about me and the work I do is that I've seen it all and know it all. Patrons assume this is true about my knowledge of computers, or even about library reference. I get emails from random people sometimes asking me reference questions because of the URL of my blog, librarian.net. I tell them that I do reference work for a job, that I am not working at a library at the moment, and that as a result, I'd just be Googling, the same way they would, though possibly faster. Similarly, people think that when something goes wrong with a computer, I've seen it before and can identify and fix the problem. In point of fact, I'm usually looking up error messages in the same way as they are, only faster. So, I like to tell people how to do some of the same things that I do. One of the things I do frequently is read the help files and another is Googling error messages.

This is not "cheating," these are actually approved problem-solving methods. In fact, I had an amusing experience just today. I was trying to solve a problem with my laptop and part of the troubleshooting steps involved a thing you do on the Mac called Repair Permissions. After running this process, I noticed an unusual message in the logfile generated by the program.

Warning: SUID file "System/Library/CoreServices/RemoteManagement/ARDAgent.app/Contents/MacOS/ARDAgent" has been modified and will not be repaired.

Sounds scary, right? I dropped the entire phrase into the Google search box and the first result was an Apple Support document entitled: *Mac OS X: Disk Utility's Repair Disk Permissions messages that you can safely ignore.*[2] So, problem solved, or at least safely ignored, thanks to some good troubleshooting!

Most of the major tech companies have decent websites with support documentation, as well as user forums where people discuss the problems they are having, all of it keyword searchable. If you can't find a support document outlining your problem, maybe someone else has had a similar problem and asked the community about it. As librarians, we're used to the idea of searching, but you may want to remind your patrons about effective ways to search these spaces.

Doing an Effective Support Search:

- Think of a few keywords to describe your problem. (You may want to help them with the vocabulary.)
- Think of a few other words describing these topics.
- Do a search on the site, making sure you are cognizant of the site's search syntax. Not all sites search like Google, though many do.
- Scan the first few results and see if you're on the right track. If not, try changing the scope of your question to make it more broad if you're getting too few, answers or more narrow if you're getting too few.

Here are some popular support websites:

- http://support.microsoft.com
- http://apple.com/support
- http://www.annoyances.org
- http://forums.macrumors.com
- or just Google it! Use the help files to make sure you're using the correct terminology.

It's hard to explain to people that free phone support is not really part of the support model for most computers or software nowadays, and neither are printed manuals. Many computers come with digital manuals, either as PDFs or online, but this does little to no good if you can't navigate the processes needed to access them. Brand-new computers often come with some amount of free support, which can range from terrific to terrible depending on the problem you are having and the level of support you need. It's important to let individual folks (as opposed to people working in offices with IT staff) know that computers do come with warranties, and so if something seems really broken, their first step should be to call the dealer or the manufacturer. However, again, novice users may not know what "really broken" means and may have a hard time untangling that idea.

So, to the above self-tech support tips, I add the *Reality Check* module. This means bouncing ideas off of other people, not necessarily experts, in your area to get an idea if what you're seeing your computer do is normal, abnormal, or broken. It will help them get a ballpark idea of what the next step is, from "Suck it up and deal with it." to "Call the IT guy." to "Call Dell." This includes talking to other people, but also having a general idea if what you are expecting out of the technology is, in fact, possible. Maybe, you can't make the printer print double-sided handouts because the printer doesn't actually print double-sided. Maybe, you can't print the images from the online slide show because they're specifically designed to make printing difficult, if not impossible. Maybe, you're trying to do something using MS Word that you really should be doing using MS Excel.

Reality Check-In

Talk to your colleagues:

- Have they dealt with the same problems?
- How did they handle it?
- Did it work?

Know what's possible, and how:

- A printer should be able to. . . .
- A website should be able to. . . .
- MS Word should be able to. . . .
- MS Excel should be able to. . . .

And last, users need to be able to see the tech system for what it is: a system. There are parts that all combine to form one functioning unit and if one part is a little off-kilter, it may affect other parts in ways that seem unusual. Make sure you can isolate the different parts and understand what some of the structural limitations are for it, so that you can set them aside as you're digging through the possible causes of your problem. This is a follow-up to the "know what's possible" section above, except that the "what's possible" section can be addressed by talking to people who aren't necessarily familiar with your personal system's configuration, whereas the "what's prevented" section is likely to be much more contextually specific.

For example, I work in a high school. We use content filters and each person has a login to the system which allows them certain kinds of access depending on where in the building they are (staff offices or classrooms). If I am having trouble accessing a particular website, it may be because there is an issue with my login, with the filters, or with where in the school the computer thinks I am. If other people are also having trouble accessing the website, there may be issues with the school's internet connection at a larger level and asking a few questions would help determine that. If no one can get on the internet at the school, it's likely not a filtering problem.

Know what's prevented, and why:

- What does the filtering software filter? And how?
- Is there a wireless network that I can use? Does it require a password?
- Don't trust people who say the computer has "issues." Ask for an explanation in English.
- Tech support problems are not magic. Repeatable problems should also be explainable.

Have a system:

- Troubleshooting involves testing each part of the equation in turn to try to isolate what is causing the problem. Keep a list.
- Keep a log of whether these problems happen at similar times or under similar circumstances.
- Ask for a timeline for when larger problems will be fixed.

If you are providing this sort of support in a public computer situation, you must balance the needs of patrons with the ability of the library to respond to tech problems in a timely and effective way. Sometimes, you can't fix everything right away, but good handling of the problem means at least responding to the "Hey, this is broken!" request in some sort of useful way.

I used to shop at the co-op in town, when there *was* a co-op in town, and they had a suggestion book where people would write down what they'd like the co-op to buy. The best part about this book was that it was open for everyone's perusal, and that co-op members would actually reply to suggestions with a "Sure, we'll buy that, but it might take a while." or "We haven't found a good source for that item, so it's not on our list of things to buy for the next order." I liked the transparency of this sort of system; people could check on the status of their requests on their own and get a decent answer, even if it wasn't the one they may have wanted. I may be alone in this assessment, but I think that most people would prefer a polite "no" to no answer at all. Accordingly, letting people know what's going on with a computer that is not functioning is a polite thing to do. People who are waiting in line to use a public computer who see one or two machines with "out of order" signs on them would probably like to know:

- What is wrong with those machines?
- Has a repair person been called?
- When are they likely to be fixed?

In some cases, they'll adjust their opinions about the library according to their answers they feel that they get from these questions. It's tough to be in the position of wanting to use a small slice of a finite resource and feeling that your needs are not a priority of the larger institution. So, let's go back to our mantra of people who are offline being offline *for a reason*, and let's see if we can calm these concerns some.

We took two steps when working with our PACs. First, we made small signs for our public access PCs that indicated that the computer was not working, the date the problem was reported, and that a technician (or whatever word you prefer) had been notified. This was a good indicator for staff and patrons that there was an outstanding problem, and was also a good visual reminder for our technician about which computers needed attention.

Then, we had a behind-the-desk log book of problems we were having, large and small. This could include things like the printer jamming or being out of paper, or a set of headphones not working, a browser not being able to display a certain website, or a computer needing the latest copy of Flash installed. These were all listed with a date when they were noticed and a date when they were resolved. The goal, obviously, was to have these dates be the same. This allowed us to track recurring problems, notice maintenance issues that may have gone by the wayside, and make front-line staff more responsible for being part of the troubleshooting system. In this library, we did have part-time IT staff, but reference staff were encouraged to try to work out small issues on their own, thus saving our library money on the technician and also giving us a better chance of having more PCs working more of the time.

Top Ten Tech Support Requests

This is just a list from ten years of my general tech support duties, in case it helps to commiserate and realize that the problems your patrons are having are the same troubles people everywhere have been having since there was tech that needed supporting.

1. My Yahoo (or MSN, or Google, or whatever) is broken. (aka internet access issues of unspecified etiology)
2. I can't turn my computer off.
3. I turned my computer on, but the screen is blank.
4. My laptop can't connect to the wireless.
5. I am getting email spam.
6. My computer has a virus.
7. My computer is slow.
8. My home page has changed to some other site.
9. I was typing and all my text disappeared.
10. I tried to send this, but the other person didn't receive it.

If you don't have a handy routine that you can use to respond to these, or similar concerns, you may want to create one.

Feedback and Assessment

Now that you've looked at some approaches to technology in the library, you might want to try some of them. Or maybe you've tried some of these things, but they didn't work and you're not sure why. This is where assessment and feedback come in. At its most basic, this is just gathering feedback from people either verbally, with a web survey or index cards. What worked? What didn't work? What could we do better? However, that's really just the beginning. Ideally, feedback goes both ways and is a cycle, not a process with a fixed beginning and end. People give you feedback, you make adjustments, you try something else, you get more feedback, you make more adjustments, and you keep going.

Many people are under the misapprehension that there's some nirvanic point in the technology cycle where once and for all, everything is working the way it's supposed to and everyone's happy and then you can just rest. Or die. This is not the case. First of all, our patrons don't get to this point since they always have new questions, and in many cases we have new patrons. The tech world also doesn't stay the same. So, even if everything is working fine, things will need upgrades, new purchases will need to be made and integrated with the existing systems, and older equipment will need to be de-accessioned or supplanted. And even if things *are* working well, you can always decide to improve them. Is your website as clear as it could be? Is your library signage up to date and accurate? Are your patrons suffering from "note blindness" where there are so many notes affixed to library machines that they tend to ignore all of them?

Ideally, feedback doesn't all go into a black hole where it's never heard from again. Just as we have a process for processing books and managing other workflows, dealing with feedback, both giving and receiving, should be a process built into our technology systems. People should be able to see the results of the feedback they've given. This can be challenging because sometimes the actual result is "We've heard you, but we're not going to implement your suggestions." However, in my opinion this is a more genuine interaction than not responding because you don't want to tell some people "No."

In this next section, you'll find ways to give and receive feedback with patrons, but also to give feedback to vendors and other people you do business with. As previously mentioned in Chapter One, in many cases the people who build the systems we use don't seem to hear us when we tell them that they could use improvement. I'd like to make sure we're giving people constructive and useful evaluations so that they can in turn help make things better for us.

Getting Feedback from Patrons

At its most basic, as humans we want to get feedback that someone has understood us. I always dreaded reference transactions as a librarian where it was clear that I hadn't answered the patron's question, but also equally clear that they were sort of done with the interaction for whatever reason. I see this a lot in technology settings where I'll give people a few steps to follow to solve a problem, and then walk away, and notice that they seem stuck on step two. Worse yet, when working with a few people at drop-in time I sometimes need to float between them; and I've had some students, rarely, who literally stop interacting with the computer until I am back in their area. I am never sure what they are experiencing because it is so far outside of my range of experience it doesn't make sense to me. I ask them "Did you try the thing I suggested?" and they'd say "No, I decided to wait for you to get back."

There are a few different ways to get feedback from patrons, and a few different topics to get feedback about. Many libraries have the traditional suggestion box or some functional equivalent, but these only get the free-range "Oh, I just thought of something." types of feedback, usually spur of the moment, and quite frequently relating some negative incident that just happened. Instead, let's look more in a technological direction and talk about the patron as a tech user, and think about the usability of the technology that they interact with. Here are some situations that are rich for not just obtaining feedback, but for channeling the feedback you get into improvements or adjustments. When I'm thinking about a change in the library, I'm thinking about something like a new website design, or a readjustment of the public PC arrangement, or a change to a new printing system, or possibly, a new fee structure. Change management means getting feedback on the process as it's happening, not just before and after. So, you'd collect people's feedback in a few ways:

> *User survey*—You're just talking to people in the library. What are they using on the computers and how would they like them to work? Anything they want that they're not getting? Anything that they really like?
>
> *Prior to a change*—You're making some changes. Are you giving people some advanced notice? What are their concerns? How will this affect them? What might you not have thought of that might be an unintended consequence? Can you give some users a preview and do some actual user testing?
>
> *During a change*—What is happening? This is an opportunity for informing people and getting their feedback at the same time. Maybe, you upgraded the PCs or changed the website. How do people get where they usually go? How is the library handling the transition?
>
> *After a change*—How does the change feel now that it's in place? Are you able to do what you need to do? Have your concerns been addressed? Is this system better or worse than the old one? Why?

Keep in mind that people aren't always the best reporters even about their own situations. In cases where you want to see what patrons are doing and not just what they're reporting, consider doing some usability studies. There are a few links in the Webliography of this book to sites where people discuss doing low-cost usability testing. The general idea is to sit people down with your website—or other online content, I've always wondered about doing this with some of our databases and then giving the results to the database vendors—and give them a set of tasks and observe what they do. This is different from just asking questions such as "Can you find the library catalog?" to which they'll often say "Yes." even if they're not sure. So, ask them to find it and see what they do. And if they don't do what you expect, try to figure out why and what you can do to address that issue.

You can't redesign the website to suit every patron, obviously; but you should make an effort to make sure that it can perform the basic functions for the majority of the patrons who will be interacting with it. There's a whole industry built up around usability testing and it's a large topic, but at a small scale observing users doing tasks online may be able to give you more insight into their actual habits than asking questions alone would do.

Feedback to/from Staff

Often, we spend so much time interacting with our patrons that we ignore the staff, the people who have to use the library technology much more than the majority of our patrons. There is sometimes a balancing act that has to occur between making the technology we use easy for patrons to use versus being easy for staff to maintain. At the school where I work, we have to deal with mandatory filtering which occasionally filters web content that teachers need to access. This is what I consider to be a normal small-scale hassle trying to balance multiple-user needs. However, there is no easy way to actually let the IT team know that a page needs to be unblocked, except for sending out an email to a support address that may not result in a return email and/or the website being unblocked. People need to feel that the feedback loop that they are investing time into is functional and achieves results.

Staff meetings are sometimes a good time for this sort of thing to come up ("Hey, how is the new system working for everyone?"), but that really depends on people's willingness to speak up in front of a group or even recognize issues that they may be having with a system. I've seen some libraries try to have intranet-style blogs for announcements and comments. They work well if the staff is tech savvy enough to interact in a blog environment in the first place. While we want to do a little better than just having the black-hole comment box, we do want to make sure that we can offer a place for people to give constructive feedback that is listened and responded to. As mentioned in the third section of this chapter, staff can feel a large amount of technostress if they are placed in situations where they feel that they are getting pressure to do things, such as instruction or technology assistance, that they do not feel competent or capable at. Make sure there is some sort of way for staff to express concerns or doubts about technology in a supportive environment where they can be responded to and, if necessary, given professional development options to increase their confidence and lower their tech anxiety. Sometimes what staff need more than anything else is time to explore new tools before feeling like they are being pushed out onto the front lines as the "experts." See if there is a way to gauge what it is that they really need when they are giving you feedback on the library's technology directions or offerings.

Giving Feedback to Vendors

This is a topic that I sometimes harp on, but if the technology tools that we are using and offering for patrons to use are not working for us, it's our responsibility to let our vendors know about it. This is not to say that they will always hop up and immediately do something about it, but if they don't know what our issues and concerns are, we can not expect them to magically read our minds. While there is a certain amount we can do in-house to make our software tools more usable, we can also start demanding more usability "out of the box" when we're working with major vendors who are designing custom products for us. This is the ideal situation in the Open Source community, where the people who are using the tools are also the same people who are building them, so that the feedback loop is much smaller, and problems and even idle feature requests get attended to much more quickly than with standard software release schedules.

Some larger-scale commercial software products such as big ILSes actually have user groups where people share tips and ideas and troubleshooting ideas. All the major operating systems have user forums online, which are good for getting quick tech support assistance and also good for reporting problems that you might have to see if anyone else has had the same problem. Recently, there have been cases where I've been grappling with some odd peccadillo with my laptop, and I was temporarily assuaged by learning that the same problem affected many laptop users with similar set-ups to my own. This doesn't necessarily solve the problem, but it can help you feel less alone in wrestling with the problem.

And of course, talk to people at library conferences. I've made a list before going to ALA in the past of vendors who I wanted to speak to and specific questions I've had to ask. Depending on which vendors you need to speak with, you may get someone who mostly knows the products from a marketing perspective or you may be talking to the programmer who built the tool himself. Obviously, cater your message to the person you are speaking with, but be sure to tell them that you use their product, that it's mostly okay (assuming it is), but that you have a few problems with it that you'd like them to address. I've had conversations like these from topics ranging for Netscape support for iBistro (back in the day) to Mac support for OverDrive (more recently). The good news about the social web is that you can both have these personal conversations with vendors and at the same time, share what you know about their products on the larger internet, again to answer the "Is it just me?" question. The difference between a tool that doesn't work for just you and a tool that doesn't work for many people is substantial and worth getting a vendor to pay attention to.

10

Things That Work—Examples from the Field

If the Library is to fulfill its purpose in the future, librarians must commit to a culture of continuous operational change, accept risk and uncertainty as key properties of the profession, and uphold service to the user as our most valuable directive.[1]

—The Darien Statements on the Library
and Librarians

This is my favorite topic and I've saved it for last. There are library systems that are doing great things with very little, all over the United States. In nearly all cases, these library systems had very little in the way of resources, a problem they were trying to solve, and were able to roll out a professional-looking program using more ingenuity and elbow grease than cash and infrastructure.

In many cases, there were one or maybe two staff people responsible for creating and maintaining these programs, many of which have grown beyond their original scope. One of the things that is great not to do in technology is re-invent the wheel. While it's compelling sometimes to make our own course outlines, our own PAC policies, or our own "how to use email" handouts because we can use the font we like and get the margins just so, often people smarter and better (or just luckier) than us may have already been there, and done that.

The library profession, even in just the United States, is huge and fractured and the people who are most in need of technological know-how are often not able to travel to professional development opportunities like conferences and in-service trainings. While the few examples I've highlighted here are ones that I have personal experience with, there are many other libraries doing many other things. I get a lot of my brainstorming ideas from clicking about in the Library Success Wiki[2] and reading a few superterrific blogs that focus on how-to things, <http://www.libsuccess.org/> which I'll mention in the Appendix.

Obviously, everyone's communities are different and one-size-fits-all approaches are often not quite right, but getting that spark of inspiration or seeing someone really jazzed from a successful program, workshop, or exercise can really be a jumping off point to finding a way to make breakthroughs in your own community. I hope this section gives you some good ideas.

Informal Consortia in the Green Mountains and Elsewhere

I have a bit of a skewed view on some of this stuff because my state is a little unusual. We have no consortia and we have no state funding for libraries. Our state Department of Libraries (DOL) does some statewide programs and many other things, but they do not manage funding for libraries or operate a statewide catalog the way the state of Georgia does. They may soon. In the meantime, however, the state is full of a lot of teeny tiny libraries that make their technological way largely isolated from one another except as they interact on mailing lists, in person informally, or once a year at the annual conference. Economies of scale that are regularly available to larger library systems for purchasing and similar processes were often unavailable to us.

In late 2007, a group of small libraries that were interested in downloadable audiobooks got together to see if they could combine forces and use the combined purchasing power of all of their service areas to strike a deal with a digital audiobook company. What they wound up with was a reasonably priced contract with OverDrive, a statewide program called ListenUp! Vermont, and the beginnings of the Green Mountain Library Consortium. <http://gmlc.wordpress.com/>. The GMLC now has 140 members from all sorts of libraries, with a service population of over 400,000 as of this writing. They have other projects that they've worked on under the umbrella banner of the GMLC, including the thirty libraries working on customizing and installing a Koha OPAC and the eighteen libraries using Mango Languages. The original Listen Up! program has grown to include eighty public and school libraries; and as I mentioned in Chapter Three, the "Leading versus Following" section, this project has actually gotten many Vermonters to invest in their own MP3 players and learn a little bit about digital content. While the organization is still quite young—they had their first official meeting in May of 2008—they've been able to get a lot done thanks to a few people who are tenacious and motivated and very encouraging of other people getting involved.

Along the same lines of informal support organizations, Library Society of the World <http://thelsw.org/> deserves mention. It's a small group of librarians and others who interact primarily online for the purposes of "promoting libraries and free information, building friendships and alliances, and fostering communication and collaboration." They're part serious and part not, but overall are a great group of people who create a positive space online for others to interact with libraries and technology using actual technological tools. Their commitment to sharing good ideas in a collaborative environment means it's easy to find tech information and examples of "stuff that works" on their multiple websites (a blog, a wiki, a FriendFeed room). They've even been instrumental in putting on a conference called Library Camp of the West. If you're tech-friendly and possibly in a workplace that is not, I'd encourage you to try to find ways to interact with some of the LSW folks to help you stay sane and stay focused.

I could say similar things about Radical Reference, the Desk Set, and/or various computer user groups. These solutions may not work for you for whatever reason, but it's worth stressing that if you're not getting what you want from your existing organizations, it may be time to seek out some new ones. There are many types of formal and informal library and non-library organizations that are always looking for new members and new ideas.

MyKLOW—Consortial Blogging

MyKLOW stands for My Kansas Library on the Web. <http://www.mykansaslibrary.org>. It is a program run by the Kansas

Regional Library Systems and the State Library of Kansas. It allows any public library in the state of Kansas to get a website up and running with an absolute minimum of technical know-how via a centrally installed and managed version of the content management system WordPress.

The librarians in Kansas realized that just telling smaller libraries "Hey, you can make a free website using WordPress!" was actually not solving the problem of getting those libraries online. Their solution involved creating a single install of WordPress MU (the multi-user version) on a centrally-maintained server administered by the Northeast Kansas Library System (NEKLS). Any public library in the state of Kansas can request an account on the server which they can use to create a website or blog with all of the functions of a WordPress-run website.

NEKLS maintains the server, installs plug-ins and themes for users, and is responsible for software upgrades, training, and tech support. In their own words:

> *The My Kansas Library on the Web project is an attempt to allow small public libraries across the state have access to high end web-based tools to facilitate easy web development.*
>
> *Translation: It's a way to make your library's website all that it can be and more by giving you easy to use tools that are accessible from ANYWHERE there is an Internet connection.*

As of the beginning of 2010, there were 159 Kansas libraries whose web presence was facilitated by the MyKLOW project. This is nearly half the public libraries in the state of Kansas. This is a BIG deal. Other things that make this project really effective include the centralized support and maintenance, as well as the intentionally limited scope of the project. The understanding is that if libraries are sophisticated or staffed well enough to run and maintain their own WordPress install, it will be easy for them to move to their own system at this point. Libraries who do not feel that they are at this stage can work within the structured environment maintained by MyKLOW and learn the ropes in that way.

Goals and Accomplishments

While the obvious goal of this project was to get libraries set up with websites, there are a number of tangential goals that were involved with this project:

- Getting libraries comfortable with the idea of a content management system.
- Getting libraries working knowledge of an open source tool.
- Giving libraries an option to add their own content or start a blog using a tool they were familiar with and could get training on.
- Allowing small libraries some autonomy over their own website, site design, and content.
- Giving NEKLS an opportunity to roll out a high visibility and highly effective repeatable program.
- Getting grants to run a highly effective statewide program with high buy in.
- Showcasing the Kansas State Library and NEKLS as leaders in consortia-based small library solutions.

There are many more details of this program on their website, but I wanted to outline just how straightforward running this program can be. The central piece of this system was a server that was running a copy of the free, open source content management system WordPress which has a multi-user version allowing one central piece of software, but with the ability to run many individual sites simultaneously. The install is administered by NEKLS staff who also oversees installing themes and plugins, setting up the sites initially and giving people logins, and making a few widgets and generally answering questions and giving people training and help. The program has been running for several years and has been, by all accounts, tremendously successful.

Technology Petting Zoo—Up Close and Personal

For many people, technology doesn't become real until they've seen it, touched it, and maybe played with it a little. Part of the success of my drop-in time is that people can touch a computer and get used to it without worrying about breaking their own expensive machine. The more positive experiences they have with technology, the less risky it feels and the more they feel "Hey, this is something I could actually find a use for someday." At many library conferences or in-service days that I've attended, people have put together some sort of show-and-tell time slot, basically an informal time for people to bring their gadgets and let other people take a look at them and ask questions. The gadgets can range from cheap library-branded USB hubs to new smartphones and iPads. People can take a look at them and, more importantly, ask questions of someone who has experience with the item and who isn't trying to sell them something.

Remember, people affected by the digital divide often don't even know anyone with a computer; and this is also true for other technological gadgets. I made it a point whenever I went to drop-in time to bring my other tech tools—laptop, camera, iPhone, USB key, EVDO dongle, smart card reader—and have them out and available. I used to feel a little odd and ostentatious having all this tech gadgetry with me all the time. However, I found that being willing to share and explain what things are and, most importantly, to let people interact with the tools themselves was a great leveler. At various "petting zoo" events, I learned about smartphones, USB hubs, and flip cameras. They're a great icebreaker at library events, and they require little to no planning time or start-up costs.

23 Things

23 Things,[2] also known as Learning 2.0, is a project that tries to get library staff involved in using Web 2.0 and social tools in a fun low-hassle environment. It was started by Helene Blowers when she worked for the Public Library of Charlotte & Mecklenburg County (PLCMC). The basic problem she was finding was that staff often didn't have time to experiment or use social tools before being asked to implement them at work. Often staff did not use these sites or tools at home, so they felt a little pressured to keep up with social software at work, without being given training or time to experiment and play. The object of the program was to get people some hands-on time, at work, where they could try out many different tools in a fairly structured environment. And there were incentives, prizes of some sort, to keep people plugging away even if they were feeling a little unmotivated.

The project blossomed into an excellent training tool that has spread worldwide to libraries and other environments where this sort of learning project—small parts, working with colleagues, keeping the fun level high—has a good chance for success. There are no centralized rules and nothing to buy; you learn by doing. We've been doing the program in Vermont for several years now <http://vermontlibrarieslearn.wordpress.com/> and participating librarians get professional development credits or credits towards state library certification for participating. The project happens over time, the Vermont program takes place over 11 weeks, and is intended to take up no more than a few minutes per day. In the words of the About page from the Vermont website, the program is designed to:

> . . . *encourage all of us to learn more about emerging technologies on the web that are changing the way people, libraries, and society access information and communicate with each other. The program aims to show you and your colleagues 23 Things—new (or newish) web tools and trends that are increasingly popular in libraries and increasingly popular with our patrons.*

The great thing about this project is that it uses the tools that it talks about; the map is actually the territory. The weeks' assignments, small tasks such as "Learn about tagging and discover Delicious.com" are posted on a blog that is the central location for participants' interactions. So step one, learn about blogging, is taken care of when participants start with the program.

There is one central person who helps guide the explorations; in our case, it was someone working at the Department of Libraries, but the project is otherwise self-directed with the exception of the cross-pollination that happens when you get a lot of people with like interests in a similar social space online. Each week has a few grouped tasks that involve exploring new online spaces or ideas. People learn about RSS, wikis, and social networks generally.

By the end of the project, people have dipped their toes in many different 2.0 technologies in a low-risk sort of way—people are allowed to post using pseudonyms if they really don't want to mix work/play—and can get an idea if any of them might help solve a problem for the library. Since all of the tools are free, there's no pressure to buy anything, and equally no pressure to sell anything. Rhonda Murphy, a librarian who lives in my area, participated in the program. I asked her if she could send me a few sentences about how she was feeling about the project well after completing it. She writes:

> *I did indeed participate in the 23 Things project and thought it was fantastic. There are things I learned that I continue to use just about everyday, such as the RSS feed. I am in the process*

*of converting our website to run on Wordpress in a blog for-
mat. There are other things from the project that I don't necessarily use consistently, but at least I feel like I know what they
are and how others use or might use them. When people have
questions in the library I feel much more prepared to help them.
The self-paced nature of the course was very helpful.
I also made friends with some of the other participants online
and made sure to meet them in person at subsequent library
events. I would heartily recommend the 23 Things Project!*

Five Weeks to a Social Library—
Collaborative Learning

Another group project created around social tools is Meredith
Farkas' Five Weeks to a Social Library program <http://
www.sociallibraries.com/course/> (FWSL hereafter), which is
available for reuse thanks to a Creative Commons license. Similar in
some respects to the 23 Things project, the intent is to get librarians
comfortable with social tools and familiar with some of the ways
these tools can be used in a library setting. Through a combination
of podcasts, screencasts, and webcasts that are all available online,
the creators of the course content interact with a selected set of library
professionals. The program was targeted specifically at underserved
librarians; the forty people who were selected to participate in the
program created participant blogs and interacted with the six organ-
izers using online tools over the course of five weeks. All of their
interactions have been archived online.

The project mostly took place in 2007, so some of the archived
discussions may be talking about tools that are not currently "hot,"
but at the same time, many of the general topics such as looking at
your library's website or using social software in special collections
are broad-based enough that they are still applicable today. More to
the point, this model of online instruction—collaborative and using
freely available tools—is easy to replicate for whatever your training topic is. Obviously this sort of thing will not work well for novice users, but for people who are trying to find communities of
practice or like-minded people in the profession to learn alongside,
this sort of content delivery model is straightforward and available.

Meredith Farkas explains the goals of the program:

We created a learning model that worked well for people new to technology because everything they learned was re-emphasized in so many ways. They read about a specific technology, then they used it in a practical exercise, then they reflected on the experience, then they discussed their learning synchronously as a group. This sort of experiential, reflective and social learning makes knowledge so much more sticky and appeals to a wider variety of learning styles.

11

Why This Matters and What to Do

We must not confuse the thrill of acquiring or distributing information quickly with the more daunting task of converting it into knowledge and wisdom.

—the Technorealists

Again, my apologies for being long on philosophy and short on specifics. Every question I answer seems to lead to ten related questions. I feel that the problem we've been saddled with over the years is that there's been no shortage of manuals, handouts, and help files, and yet we've observed all of this information not actually solving the problem of helping novice users get over the tech hurdle and achieve technological competency. It's a little odd to see this sort of thing happen under our roof in the library and think "We're problem solvers, why are we not handling this?" and have a hard time figuring out what to do next.

That said, intractable problems like the digital divide are similar to other entrenched social issues like poverty and homelessness. Giving someone money or a place to sleep doesn't actually solve their poverty or homelessness problems (though it may mitigate them temporarily), because at the root of it, there's a lot more going on. Many different things combine to form institutionalized poverty, in the same way that the digital divide is made up of much more than people who haven't learned to use computers yet.

And while we try to address the issues that can be tackled within our walls, by having classes, by being a welcoming and encouraging environment, by not spreading fear uncertainty and doubt, we also have work to do in the larger world. We have to advocate for our patrons in other areas where they may be underrepresented, areas where we may have some leeway, some clout. We should push for more usable software, more sensible news reporting, more results and less lip service to serving the underserved. We should send letters to the editor from the library, petitions to software manufacturers from our consortia, and letting our money, what little we have, talk for us by making more sensible purchasing decisions. Because there is no one point, no for-profit, non-profit, or government institution, that is more at the center of this than we are as librarians. And so even though we have a lot to do, this challenge falls on our doorstep.

And we need to work together. This is my particular Achilles heel because I live in a rural area and I'm often on my own trajectory doing my own thing, but we get more done together than we do apart. Large consortia have more pull with software manufacturers than individual library systems do; and statewide systems have even more pull than consortia. Some of the most effective programs I've seen have been rolled out competently and effectively on a shoe-string by just a few people working for a statewide system. But before we start pushing, we need to be confident that we're pushing for the right things.

People don't often enter librarianship because they're looking forward to a job filled with conflicts and struggles. We're frequently the peacemakers. This has a downside, however. We can sometimes lack confidence in our own perceptions. It's okay to tell a vendor that it's nonsense if they can't build an accessible website in 2010, and it's totally okay to stop paying for it. But it's not an easy conversation to have and the alternative products may not be looking any better.

And it's not just dealing with complicated software. There are complicated websites, complicated machinery, and complicated staffing issues that also need to be carefully negotiated. I'd be fibbing if I said it was going to be easy, or even uncomplicated. But I think it can be done—partly through setting good expectations and good examples, and partly through politely and respectfully not taking no for an answer.

This is the same attitude we should be encouraging in our patrons—You CAN do this, you CAN learn this, you can master these tools, yes you. I think attitude may have more to do with solving this problem than any one other variable. Enthusiasm and competence is infectious; being able to solve problems and learn things is infectious. And when things are looking a little less rosy, I crib a (slightly edited) line from Eleanor Roosevelt: "No one, and no thing, can make you feel inferior without your consent." Technology is a tool, and you CAN make it work for you.

Appendix and Bibliography

There are some resources that I've felt would be useful to have included in this book. Some of them are copyrighted and I don't have permission to reproduce them here, notably Phil Agre's *How to help someone use a computer*, which could almost be a three-page pamphlet replacement for this entire book. That document and other resources are linked in the Webliography which is also available on the website for this book http://librarian.net/digitaldivide

Other resources are public domain and/or homemade so I can put them here.

A. Aspects of Computer Literacy (slightly edited)

What is a computer
- what are its limitations
- what is a program (not necessarily how to program)
- what a computer cannot do
- some seemingly simple problems are not so simple
- all computers have the same computing ability, just differences in memory capacity and speed
- performance depends on more than CPU clock speed

Understanding the concept of stored data

What are the real causes of "computer errors"

The implications of incorrect (buggy) programs

The implications of using a program incorrectly (garbage in, garbage out)

Issues rising from distributed computing

Computer security

- trojan horse (computing), computer virus, email spoofing, URL spoofing, phishing, etc. . . .
- what to do when a security certificate is questioned
- password creation (how to avoid bad ones)

Social implications/aspects of computing

- Netiquette (or at least E-mail Etiquette)
- identifying urban legends (and not forwarding them)
- critical assessment of internet sources
- criminal access to financial databases

Keyboarding, mousing (using input devices)

Plugging in and turning the computer on

Using/understanding user-interface elements (e.g., windows, menus, icons, buttons, etc.)

Composing, editing, and printing documents

The ability to communicate with others using computers through electronic mail (email) or instant messaging services

Managing and editing pictures (from cell phones, digital cameras, or even scans)

Opening files and recognizing different file types

Multimedia literacy, including, but not limited to:

- making movies
- making sound files
- interactivity
- Creating web pages

A higher order of computer literacy involves a user being able to adapt and learn new procedures through various means while using a computer. Reprinted from Wikipedia's Computer Literacy article.

Accessed June 10, 2010 http://en.wikipedia.org/wiki/Computer_literacy

B. Usability.gov's Research-based Web Design and Usability Guidelines

This is a nearly 300-page book, a free download. It was created, in the authors' own words "to provide quantified, peer-reviewed Web site design guidelines." All the guidelines are presented with scores for "relative importance" (i.e. how important the issue is related to other usability issues, with the awareness that often tough choices much be made) and "strength of evidence" which is how supported by research the guidelines are. Since the document is a government publication, it is in the public domain. I am reprinting two small parts from the book's appendix, though I encourage people to download and read the entire publication or just keep it handy.

In the appendix, the authors rank all the usability guidelines they provide with two scores. I am reprinting the things that attain a five out of five rating in either category. The items are listed with their chapter and guideline number to simplify location in the actual book.

Guidelines Ranked by Relative Importance

Chapter:	Relative Guideline
1:1	Provide Useful Content
1:2	Establish User Requirements
2:1	Do Not Display Unsolicited Windows or Graphics
3:1	Comply with Section 08
3:2	Design Forms for Users Using Assistive Technology
3:3	Do Not Use Color Alone to Convey Information
5:1	Enable Access to the Homepage
5:2	Show All Major Options on the Homepage
5:3	Create a Positive First Impression of Your Site
6:1	Avoid Cluttered Displays
6:2	Place Important Items Consistently
6:3	Place Important Items at Top Center
8:1	Eliminate Horizontal Scrolling
9:1	Use Clear Category Labels
10:1	Use Meaningful Link Labels
13:1	Distinguish Required and Optional Data Entry Fields
13:2	Label Pushbuttons Clearly
15:1	Make Action Sequences Clear
16:1	Organize Information Clearly
16:2	Facilitate Scanning
16:3	Ensure that Necessary Information is Displayed
17:1	Ensure Usable Search Results
17:2	Design Search Engines to Search the Entire Site

Guidelines Ranked by Strength of Evidence

Chapter:	Relative Guideline
1:1	Provide Useful Content
2:3	Standardize Task Sequences
2:5	Design for Working Memory Limitations
6:7	Align Items on a Page
9:3	Use Descriptive Headings Liberally
11:1	Use Black Text on Plain, High-Contrast Backgrounds
11:6	Use Attention-Attracting Features when Appropriate
11:7	Use Familiar Fonts
11:10	Emphasize Importance
12:1	Order Elements to Maximize User Performance
13:22	Use Data Entry Fields to Speed Performance
14:1	Use Simple Background Images
14:4	Use Video, Animation, and Audio Meaningfully
14:15	Use Images to Facilitate Learning
15:6	Use Mixed Case with Prose
16:4	Group Related Elements
16:9	Use Color for Grouping
18:1	Use an Iterative Design Approach

C. Trust-Inducing Features of Graphic Design

Also on Usability.gov is an article by Susanne Furman, a usability engineer with the U.S. Department of Health & Human Services about how to design web content to induce trust. This is of large concern to DHHS and it should also be something that we as librarians think about. Furman cites an article in *Computers and Human Behavior* by Y. D. Yang and H. H. Emurian where they outline a framework for what they call "trust-inducing features." I think these are important considerations to keep in mind when designing digital content for libraries. Read these and think of your library's website, or think about the websites of vendors who you do business with. How trust-inducing is the digital content?

Graphic Design: graphic design factor—first impressions

- Three-dimensional, dynamic, and half-screen size clipart
- Symmetric use of moderate pastel color of low brightness and cool tone
- Use of well-chosen, good-shot photographs

Structure Design: Overall organization and accessibility of information

- Easy-to-use navigation (consistent)
- Use of accessible information (e.g., no broken links)
- Use of navigation reinforcements (e.g., tutorials)
- Page design techniques (e.g., white space, visual density)

Content Design: Informational components, either textual or graphical

- Display of brand-promoting information (e.g., prominent display of company logo)
- Up-front disclosure of all aspects of the customer relationship (e.g., company security, privacy, financial, or legal concerns)
- Display of seals of approval or third-party certificate
- Use of comprehensive, correct, and current product information
- Use of a relevant domain name

Social-cue design: Embedded social cues, such as face-to-face interaction and social presence

- Including of representative photograph or video clip
- Use of synchronous communication media (e.g., IM, chat lines)

D. Credits

In addition to the screenshots I've used which I assert qualify as fair use, I've also used several images from Wikimedia Commons in this book. The URLs to the originals and credits appear here:

- Index card:
  http://commons.wikimedia.org/wiki/File:Notecard.jpg
  (CC 3.0, original image by E.m.fields)
- Headshot:
  http://commons.wikimedia.org/wiki/File: Devonejones.jpg
  (CC 3.0, original image by Devonejones)
- User icon:
  http://commons.wikimedia.org/wiki/File:Im-msn.svg
  (GPLv.3)

- Mouse:
  http://commons.wikimedia.org/wiki/File:Souris_schema_svg.svg
  (public domain)
- Standby icon:
  http://commons.wikimedia.org/wiki/File:IEC5009_Standby_Symbol.svg
  (public domain)
- Operating system diagram:
  http://en.wikipedia.org/wiki/File:Operating_system_placement.svg
  (CC 3.0, original image by Golftheman)
- RSS feed icon:
  http://commons.wikimedia.org/wiki/File:Feed-icon.svg
  (GPLv.3)
- Dialog box:
  http://commons.wikimedia.org/wiki/File:PolicyAttributes.png
  (public domain)

Webliography

Here is a list of things that are online that are worthwhile. This list is not intended to be comprehensive and by the time this book is in print, it may not even be accurate. However, it's a carefully curated list of things that I think will be helpful to you, most of which I use regularly in my work.

Clickable links to these are available at http://librarian.net/digitaldivide.

Local Links: The Small Libraries I Worked with in Vermont

Chelsea
http://www.chelseavt.org/

Randolph
http://kimballlibrary.org

Roxbury
http://roxburyfreelibrary.wordpress.com/

Sharon
http://www.sharonvt.net/

Tunbridge
http://tunbridgelibrary.org

Washington
http://www.librarian.net/calef/

Williamstown
http://ainsworthpubliclibrary.wordpress.com/

Files I've Used for Teaching

RTCC home page and blog
http://www.randolphtech.org/
http://randolphtech.wordpress.com/

Rutland Free Library class websites (2006)
Heritage Quest
http://librarian.net/digitaldivide/classes/heritage.html

Email
http://librarian.net/digitaldivide/classes/email.html

What can't be in an email address?
http://www.remote.org/jochen/mail/info/chars.html

Reports

IRS Advancing E-file Study
http://www.irs.gov/efile/article/0,,id=188314,00.html

Falling Through the Net: Toward Digital Inclusion: A Report on Americans' Access to Technology Tools (2000)
http://search.ntia.doc.gov/pdf/fttn00.pdf

Libraries Connect Communities: Public Library Funding and Technology Access Study (2008–2009)
http://ala.org/plinternetfunding

Broadband in the Mississippi Delta: A 21st Century Racial Justice Issue by the Center for Social Inclusion (2010)
http://j.mp/MS-broadband

FCC Broadband Study (2009)
http://hraunfoss.fcc.gov/edocs_public/attachmatch/DOC-296442A1.pdf

Pew Internet Life Home Broadband Survey (2009, 2008, and 2005)
http://www.pewinternet.org/Reports/2009/10-Home-Broadband-Adoption-2009.aspx

http://www.pewinternet.org/Reports/2008/Home-Broadband-2008.aspx

http://www.pewinternet.org/Reports/2005/Digital-Divisions.aspx

U.S. IMPACT Public Library Study
http://cis.washington.edu/usimpact/projects/us-public-library-study/

Connecting America: The National Broadband Plan (2010)
http://www.broadband.gov/download-plan/

Scaling the Digital Divide: Home Computer Technology and Student Achievements
http://sites.google.com/site/jacobvigdor/digdivide072908.pdf

IMLS Report—Public Libraries in the United States (2007)
http://harvester.census.gov/imls/pubs/pls/pub_detail.asp?id=122

New York City Broadband Landscape and Recommendations (2008)
http://www.nyc.gov/html/doitt/downloads/pdf/bac_presentation_7_30_2008.pdf

Closing the Broadband Divide (2007)
http://www.pewinternet.org/Reports/2007/Closing-the-Broadband-Divide.aspx

The Millennials: Confident. Connected. Open to Change.
http://pewsocialtrends.org/assets/pdf/millennials-confident-connected-open-to-change.pdf

State of America's Libraries Report (2009 and 2010)
http://www.ala.org/ala/newspresscenter/mediapresscenter/americaslibraries/index.cfm

http://www.ala.org/ala/newspresscenter/mediapresscenter/presskits/ 2009stateofamericaslibraries/2009statehome.cfm

Accessibility

Introduction to Web Accessibility
http://www.webaim.org/intro/

Designing More Usable Web Sites
http://trace.wisc.edu/world/web/

The Center on Human Policy
http://thechp.syr.edu/

Universal Access: Making Library Resources Accessible to People with Disabilities
http://www.washington.edu/doit/UA/PRESENT/libres.html

ASCLA "Library Accessibility—What You Need to Know" tipsheets
http://bit.ly/asclatips

Check your site for accessibility
http://www.accesskeys.org/

Accessibility at Microsoft
http://www.microsoft.com/ENABLE/

Accessibility at Apple
http://www.apple.com/accessibility/

Ubuntu Accessibility
https://wiki.ubuntu.com/Accessibility

AbilityHub
http://www.abilityhub.com/index.html

Usability.gov's Research-Based Web Design and Usability Guidelines Manual
http://usability.gov/guidelines/guidelines_book.pdf

Web Content Accessibility Guidelines
http://www.w3.org/TR/WCAG10/

Keyboard shortcuts for Windows
http://support.microsoft.com/kb/126449

Mac OS X keyboard shortcuts
http://support.apple.com/kb/ht1343

Advocacy

Internet for Everyone
http://www.internetforeveryone.org/

ALA's Poor People's Policy
http://j.mp/ALA-poorpeople

Greening Your Library
http://greeningyourlibrary.wordpress.com/

Design and Usability

Quick & Dirty User Testing
http://www.alistapart.com/articles/quick-and-dirty-remote-user-testing/

Library Usability Testing on the Cheap
http://www.newrambler.net/lisdom/188

UseIt.com—Jakob Nielsen on Usability and Web Design
http://www.useit.com/

Instruction

How to help someone use a computer
http://polaris.gseis.ucla.edu/pagre/how-to-help.html

Tips for Teaching Older Adults to Use Computers
http://skyways.lib.ks.us/tricon/2005/handouts/tips_for_teaching.pdf

ACRL Multilingual Instruction Glossary
http://j.mp/ACRL-multilingual

Online Dictionary for Library and Information Science
http://lu.com/odlis/

Wikimedia Commons
http://commons.wikimedia.org/

Library Success Wiki
http://www.libsuccess.org/

How to use the web for topic search tutorials
http://www.intute.ac.uk/

Internet and Browser

I want a Firefox extension to . . .
http://www.econsultant.com/i-want-firefox-extension/

Firefox Help
http://support.mozilla.com/

Google Chrome Help
http://www.google.com/support/chrome/

Internet Explorer Help
http://www.microsoft.com/windows/internet-explorer/support/help.aspx

Safari Help
http://www.apple.com/support/safari/

Open Source

SquirrelMail
http://squirrelmail.org/

Open Source Alternatives
http://www.osalt.com/

Free and Open Source Software Directory
http://www.webi.org/

Free Software Foundation
http://www.fsf.org/

Open Source Initiative
http://www.opensource.org/

Policies

Library Social Software Policies
http://www.web2learning.net/archives/1250

Academic Library Privacy Statements
http://libraries.universityofcalifornia.edu/privacy/otherlinks.html

Viruses/Updates/Safety

Malwarebytes
http://www.malwarebytes.org/

AVG
http://www.avg.com/

Browser Security Comparison
http://www.webdevout.net/browser-security

HijackThis
http://free.antivirus.com/hijackthis/

HijackThis logfile analyzer
http://www.hijackthis.de/

Snopes Rumor Debunking
http://www.snopes.com/computer/computer.asp

Wired Safety
http://www.wiredsafety.org/

Bibliography

Getting Started with Technology

Here is a short annotated list of books you can buy for your library and publishers that you should consider.

The Senior's Guide to PC Basics by Gateway Press (2003)
> Large print and sensible, I liked this one. Slightly out of date, but fine for basic vocabulary and concepts.

Easy iMac: See It Done, Do It Yourself by Lisa Lee, Prentice Hall (1999)
> Another older book with good pictures and general Mac concepts. A good part of a larger tech collection.

Teach Yourself Visually Computers by Paul McFedries, Visual (2007)
> More nuts and bolts than most people want, but very picture-oriented with a lot of good explanations about what things are doing. Some people love/require this, some don't.

How computers work by Ron White, Que (2007)
> Same deal, a very picture-oriented book with good explanations.

Is This Thing On? by Abby Stokes, Workman Publishing Company (2008)
> Comes recommended with delightful companion website.

The First Week with My New iMac by Pam Lessing, Capital Books (2000)
> This book is very friendly and chatty and I keep hoping there will be an updated version published. Contains a good overview, there is one for PCs as well.

Dummies guides http://www.dummies.com/ for the low-tech approach

O'Reilly books http://oreilly.com/ for the higher-tech approach

Visual Steps books http://www.visualsteps.com/ very popular in libraries

Professional Development

No amount of reading material will be useful to staff if they do not pick it up and actually read it. There is, I believe, a surplus of writing on library and technology. While most of it is good, care should be taken to have a decent, but manageable professional development collection that is engaging to read and does not simply duplicate online information. Here are some suggestions of books that I have actually read.

Accidental Systems Librarian by Rachel Singer Gordon, Information Today, Inc. (2003)

Adaptive Technologies for Learning and Work Environments by Joseph J. Lazzaro, American Library Association (2001)

Designing the Digital Experience by David Lee King, CyberAge Books (2008)

Library 2.0: A Guide to Participatory Library Service by Michael E. Casey and Laura C. Savastinuk, Information Today, Inc. (2007)

Reflective Teaching, Effective Learning: Instructional Literacy for Library Educators by Char Booth, American Library Association (2010)

Social Software in Libraries by Meredith G Farkas, Information Today, Inc. (2007)

Teaching Web Search Skills: Techniques and Strategies of Top Trainers by Greg R. Notess, Information Today, Inc. (2006)

Technology Training in Libraries by Sarah Houghton-Jan, Neal-Schuman (2010)

"Technophobia, Technostress, and Technorealism" in *Information Tomorrow* by Rachel Singer Gordon, Information Today, Inc. (2007)

Time Management for System Administrators by Tom Limoncelli, O'Reilly Media (2005)

Other Titles

It can be tough to find good books about design philosophy that aren't also just architecture porn. Designing with access in mind can still result in functional and attractive outcomes. Here are a few suggested titles that approach their topics with dignity.

Access by Design by George Covington, Van Nostrand Reinhold (1996)

Beautiful Barrier Free by Cynthia Leibrock, John Wiley & Sons Inc. (1992)

Design for Dignity: Studies in Accessibility by William Lebovich. John Wiley & Sons (1993)

Don't Make Me Think by Steve Krug, New Riders Press (2005)

In the Beginning Was the Command Line by Neal Stephenson, Harper Perennial (1999)

Pedagogy of the Oppressed by Paulo Friere, Continuum (1999)

The Measure of Man & Woman: Human Factors in Design by Alvin R. Tilley, Wiley (2001)

Why Things Break: Understanding the World by the Way It Comes Apart by Mark Eberhart, Harmony (2003)

Notes

Preface

1. Eastlake, Donald & Panitz, Aliza. "RFC 2606 Reserved Top Level DNS Names." The Internet Society. http://www.rfc-editor.org/rfc/rfc2606.txt

Introduction

1. Bickner, Carrie. "Down By Law." *A List Apart Magazine.* http://www.alistapart.com/articles/downbylaw/
2. Seattle Public Library. "Notices by U.S. Mail Stop July 1." http://www.spl.org/pdfs/paper_notice_change.pdf
3. Horrigan, John. "Closing the Broadband Divide." *Pew Internet & American Life Report.* http://www.pewinternet.org/Reports/2007/Closing-the-Broadband-Divide.aspx
4. Murray. Teresa Dixon. "As e-filing turns 20, IRS trying to win over remaining third of taxpayers from paper returns." *Cleveland Plain Dealer*, February 21, 2010. http://www.cleveland.com/business/index.ssf/2010/02/as_e-filing_turns_20_irs_tryin.html

Chapter 1

1. Kupersmith, John. "Technostress and the Reference Librarian." http://www.jkup.net/tstr_ref.html
2. James, William. "The Will to Believe and Other Essays in Popular Philosophy." Project Gutenberg EBook #26659. http://www.gutenberg.org/files/26659/26659-h/26659-h.htm

Chapter 2

1. Apple Corporation. "User Experience." Apple Developer Guidelines. http://developer.apple.com/ue/
2. Colbow, Brad. "Why DRM Doesn't Work." The Brads, March 1, 2010. http://bradcolbow.com/archive/view/the_brads_why_drm_doesnt_work/
3. Listen Up! Vermont. "Help - Basics - General." Green Mountain Library Consortium. http://www.listenupvermont.org/10/434/en/Help-FAQ-General.htm
4. Moos, Katja. "NetLibrary Contract." Federal Library & Information Center Committee Contracting/Vendor Products & Services website. August 26, 2010. http://www.loc.gov/flicc/contracts/Vendor/netlibrary_NE.html
5. Obama, Barack. "Speech to the Democratic National Convention." July 27, 2004. http://librarian.net/dnc/speeches/obama.txt
6. West, Jessamyn. "Sarah Palin, VP Nominee." librarian.net. September 2, 2008. http://www.librarian.net/stax/2366/

Chapter 3

1. Matis, Michael. "It's 2004: Do You Know Where Your Patron Data Is?" SUNYergy, April, 2004. http://olis.sysadm.suny.edu/sunyergy/22patrondata.htm
2. West, Jessamyn. "How the Other Half Lives, Touring the Digital Divide." Presentation given at SXSW March 16, 2010. http://www.librarian.net/talks/sxsw10/
3. "Opportunity for All: How the American Public Benefits from Internet Access at U.S. Libraries." April 2010. http://cis.washington.edu/usimpact/projects/us-public-library-study/
4. American Library Association. "State of America's Libraries Report." April 2008. http://www.ala.org/ala/newspresscenter/media presscenter/presskits/2009stateofamericaslibraries/2009statehome.cfm

Chapter 4

1. International Ergonomics Association. "What s Ergonomics?" http://iea.cc/01_what/What%20is%20Ergonomics.html

Chapter 5

1. Google Operating System Blog. "A Browser Is a Search Engine." June 17, 2009. http://googlesystem.blogspot.com/2009/06/browser-is-search-engine.html

2. Wikipedia. "United States v. Microsoft." http://en.wikipedia.org/wiki/United_States_v._Microsoft

Chapter 6

1. Stevens, Ted. Untitled audio of a speech before Congress concerning net neutrality. June 28, 2006. http://media.publicknowledge.org/stevens-on-nn.mp3
2. Naughton, John. "The Internet: Everything You Ever Need to Know." *The Observer.* June 20, 2010. http://www.guardian.co.uk/technology/2010/jun/20/internet-everything-need-to-know
3. Wikipedia. "The Internet." http://en.wikipedia.org/wiki/Internet
4. Mozilla Project. "Private Browsing." Firefox Support Knowledge Base Article. http://support.mozilla.com/en-us/kb/private+browsing
5. Mozilla Project. "Better Privacy." Add-ons for Firefox. https://addons.mozilla.org/firefox/addon/6623/

Chapter 7

1. Pew Research Center. "Millennials: Confident. Connected. Open to Change." http://pewsocialtrends.org/pubs/751/

Chapter 8

1. http://www.theatlantic.com/magazine/print/1969/12/as-we-may-think/3881/

Chapter 9

1. http://www.strassmann.com/pubs/km/2001-2.php
2. "Mac OS X: Disk Utility's Repair Disk Permissions Messages that You Can Safely Ignore." Apple Tech Support Article TS1448. December 16, 2009. http://support.apple.com/kb/ts1448

Chapter 10

1. Blyberg, John, et. al. "The Darien Statements on the Library and Librarians." Blyberg.net blog post. April 3, 2009. http://www.blyberg.net/2009/04/03/the-darien-statements-on-the-library-and-librarians/
2. Blowers, Helene. "Learning 2.0." Public Library of Charlotte & Mecklenburg County. January 12, 2007. http://plcmclearning.blogspot.com/

Index

About the Author

 JESSAMYN WEST is a librarian, technologist, and writer who lives in Central Vermont. She received her MLib. from the University of Washington and has been doing bibliographic and technology instruction since 1993. She runs the long-running library weblog librarian.net and her own website at jessamyn.com. She teaches basic computer skills to adults at a vocational high school and speaks to librarians locally, nationally, and internationally about technology topics including the digital divide, social software, and technology policy. She sleeps three feet away from the complete OED.

West co-edited the book *Revolting Librarians Redux: Radical Librarians Speak Out* and edited *Digital Versus Non-Digital Reference: Ask a Librarian Online and Offline.* This is the first book she has written.

Personal website: jessamyn.com
Professional website: jessamyn.info
Blog: librarian.net

<http://librarian.net/digitaldivide>